Puzzle Play

Authors
Dave Youngs
Michelle Pauls

Illustrator
Dave Schlotterback

Technical Illustrator
Michelle Pauls

Editor
Michelle Pauls
Betty Cordel

Desktop Publishing
Tanya Adams

This book contains materials developed by the AIMS Education Foundation. **AIMS** (**A**ctivities **I**ntegrating **M**athematics and **S**cience) began in 1981 with a grant from the National Science Foundation. The non-profit AIMS Education Foundation publishes hands-on instructional materials (books and the monthly magazine) that integrate curricular disciplines such as mathematics, science, language arts, and social studies. The Foundation sponsors a national program of professional development through which educators may gain both an understanding of the AIMS philosophy and expertise in teaching by integrated, hands-on methods.

ISBN **1-881-431-95-9**

Printed in the United States of America

I Hear and I Forget,

I See and I Remember,

I Do and I Understand

—Chinese Proverb

Puzzle Play

Table of Contents

Introduction

Puzzle Play is a collection of over 70 mathematical puzzles, problems, and paradoxes for students in grades four through eight. This book has three goals that are directly related to mathematics instruction. The first, and perhaps most important one, is to help students develop a positive attitude toward mathematics. Math educator Marilyn Burns notes in her 1998 book, *MATH: Facing an American Phobia* that: "More than two-thirds of American adults fear and loathe mathematics. Math is right up there with snakes, public speaking, and heights." If Burns is correct, then one of the major tasks teachers face is to keep their students from developing this unhealthy phobia. One of the ways to do this is incorporating puzzles into the mathematics curriculum. By their very nature, puzzles foster positive feelings toward mathematics according to teachers who have used them with students. This is not surprising, since archeological evidence dating back thousands of years shows a long-standing human fascination with puzzles.

A second goal of this book is to help students build persistence. Developing this key trait is critical if students are to succeed in mathematics, yet our modern society with its fast foods, video games, and culture of instant gratification tends to foster impatience rather than persistence. When students work on puzzles they learn to persist, since few solutions come quickly. As they succeed with easy puzzles, they build the persistence necessary to solve harder ones.

Puzzle Play's third goal is to help students develop and practice problem-solving skills. Puzzles are a great vehicle for this since many of them require divergent and creative thinking to solve. This book includes a broad range of puzzles that will give students practice in a wide variety of problem-solving strategies.

An additional benefit of using puzzles is the effect they often have on underachieving students. Teachers frequently find that these students are good puzzle solvers. Success with puzzles helps build the self-esteem of these students and this success sometimes spills over into other academic areas.

It is my sincere hope that this book and its puzzles will help you and your students embark on a wonderful mathematical journey. As you travel together you can explore the power and beauty of mathematics while simultaneously experiencing doing math just for the fun of it. Bon voyage!

Dave Youngs

Some Suggestions for Using Puzzles in Your Classroom

- **Be enthusiastic and show that you enjoy the puzzles**
  If you want students to develop positive attitudes toward mathematics and puzzles, it is critical that you model these same attitudes. If you become excited when students solve a puzzle, they will see that you value and enjoy puzzles as an important part of mathematics.

- **Build persistence**
  One of the most important characteristics of a good puzzle and/or problem solver is persistence. Students who give up too quickly will never become puzzle or problem solvers. Encourage them to keep trying if they don't find an immediate solution.

- **Do the puzzles yourself**
  You can't teach problem solving effectively unless you become a problem solver. Trying to solve each puzzle yourself before assigning it to students not only gives you the chance to apply your own problem-solving strategies, it also gives you a clear idea of what your students will face. So, please resist the temptation to read the solutions before you've tried the puzzles.

- **Don't give away answers**
  A cardinal rule when working with puzzles is not to give away the solutions. Students need to be reminded that when they tell or show others how to solve a puzzle, they are robbed of the opportunity to solve it.

- **Emphasize the process as well as the product**
  Students often have the mistaken idea that the only important thing in math is to get the right answer. Help dispel this notion by valuing the process of working on the puzzle as much as getting the solution(s).

- **Encourage multiple methods of solution and divergent thinking**
  Many of the puzzles in this book can—and should—be solved in multiple ways. Unlike computation, where a single method is often stressed, good problem solving is divergent and open-ended. There is no single "right way" to approach these puzzles.

- **Create a classroom puzzle-solving strategies chart**
  As students gain experience in solving puzzles, they begin to use strategies other than trial and error. After your students have gained some experience in solving puzzles, have them work together to create a classroom *Puzzle-Solving Strategies Chart* that lists these strategies. Add to this chart whenever students discover new strategies. Your chart may include such things as using patterns, drawing pictures or diagrams, organizing information in tables and charts, working backwards, doing similar simpler problems, and asking insightful questions.

- **Explore the puzzles in-depth**
  Many of the puzzles in this book lend themselves to in-depth exploration. This type of exploration requires an investment of time, but this investment should prove valuable.

- **Facilitate—don't tell**
  It may be difficult to do, but try to get students to discover the richness of each puzzle through their own explorations, not your explanations. This takes practice, but is well worth the effort. For example, a question like, "How might you organize this information to help you solve the puzzle?" might push students to come up with their own organizational scheme, while saying, "Put the numbers in a table according to the following rules ..." solves the problem for students and robs them of the chance to find an organizational scheme for themselves.

- **Let students make the puzzle "theirs" by extending it**
  Many of the puzzles presented here can be extended quite easily. While some of the puzzles include suggested extensions, it is always best if the ideas for extensions come from the students. When students think of interesting questions to explore, they make the problem their own. This is exactly what mathematicians do when they explore new problems.

Toothpick Puzzles
Introduction

The puzzles in this section come out of a rich historical tradition which dates back to the nineteenth century when matches were first manufactured. Invented in 1827 by the British chemist, John Walker, matches soon replaced the tinder boxes which people had formerly used to light fires. As matches grew in popularity and became ubiquitous later in the century, they spawned a new form of entertainment—matchstick puzzles—which became quite popular when several match companies printed these puzzles on their boxes. Capitalizing on this interest, publishers began to print books of matchstick puzzles. By the turn of the century, many people had developed a personal repertoire of these puzzles which they used to challenge friends and acquaintances. The toothpick puzzles in this book are modeled after the classical matchstick puzzles. For safety reasons, these puzzles use flat toothpicks instead of matches.

Most of the toothpick puzzles presented here will require patience and persistence to solve. However, they tend to be a bit easier for students who have well-developed spatial-relationship skills. Often, these students are not the highest achievers, and their ability to solve these puzzles faster than their peers is a great esteem builder. Conversely, this type of puzzle often frustrates those students who usually do well at traditional school tasks and provides them with a real challenge. This role reversal is often beneficial for both sets of students.

When working on these puzzles, students will sometimes come up with alternate solutions that may satisfy the goal, but are messy. For example, if the puzzle challenges students to move four toothpicks in a certain arrangement to make three squares, this can be done without having any single toothpicks left by themselves (the elegant solution), or it can be done with one or two toothpicks sticking out. When students first begin to work on these puzzles, you may want to accept a few messy solutions so that they don't get too frustrated. After they have gained some skill and confidence with these puzzles, they can be pushed to solve them without any toothpicks sticking out.

In addition to using their spatial skills, students will also use geometric vocabulary and logical thinking when working on these puzzles. While each puzzle may eventually be solved by trial-and-error, taking a few minutes to think logically about the problem will often reveal the solution. Another key puzzle-solving trait that students will need to develop when working on these puzzles is persistence—students can't solve a puzzle if they give up. You will need to encourage students to be persistent and to keep trying until they solve the puzzles.

As the teacher, you are encouraged to try these puzzles yourself before giving them to your students. You may find them difficult, as do many adults who are linear thinkers, but don't assume that your students will experience this same level of difficulty. You may be surprised at how well some of them do with these puzzles.

We have attempted to arrange the puzzles in this section in the order of their difficulty. However, some students may have easier times with one of the later puzzles than with some of the earlier ones.

TOOTHPICK TEASERS

Puzzle Topic
Spatial-relationship skills

Puzzle Question
How can you make exactly three congruent squares from the arrangement of toothpicks by moving and/or removing different numbers of toothpicks?

Materials
Student sheets
Flat toothpicks, 15 per student

Puzzle Background
   This activity has one challenge: to make exactly three squares from an arrangement of toothpicks. However, there are five different ways in which this same challenge must be achieved. Because of this, *Toothpick Teasers* has a special emphasis on logical thinking. Students should realize that once they have one solution, they can use the process they went through and information from that solution to solve the rest.

Puzzle Presentation
1. Each student will need a copy of the first student sheet and 15 flat toothpicks to complete this activity.
2. You may want to have students record the solutions they discover as they work on this problem. This will facilitate class discussion when students share their solutions and how they reached them. Solutions to this problem can be recorded in a variety of ways. Student sheet two has been provided as one way for students to record solutions. An alternate method might be to draw diagrams of each solution. You may use the sheet provided or allow students to come up with their own methods.

Solution Hints
   Think of the different ways you can have three squares with the number of toothpicks you will have for that teaser. Look at ways you can make those shapes by moving/removing the right number of toothpicks. Once you have solved one teaser, use that solution to help with others.

TOOTHPICK TEASERS

Arrange 15 toothpicks as shown below. In each of the teasers your challenge is to make exactly three congruent squares.

1. Remove three toothpicks and move no others.

2. Remove three toothpicks and move one other.

3. Remove three toothpicks and move two others.

4. Remove three toothpicks and move three others.

5. Remove three toothpicks and move four others.

TOOTHPICK TEASERS

Use the table on this page to record every solution you find for each of the toothpick teasers. Several of them have more than one solution, so try to get as many as you can. Record your solutions using the numbers shown in the diagram below.

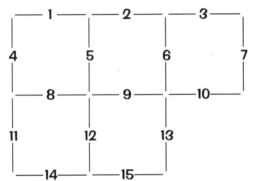

Fill in the table below with your solutions by writing the number of the teaser, the numbers of the toothpicks you removed, and the numbers of the toothpicks you moved and the spaces you moved them to. For example, if you removed toothpick 12, and then moved toothpick 6 to the space where 12 used to be, you would record that under the Move # ___ to space # ___ column as "6 to 12."

Teaser #	#s Removed	Move # ____ to space # ____
1		
2		
3		
4		
5		

TOOTHPICK PUZZLERS

Puzzle Topic
Spatial-relationship skills, geometric concepts

Puzzle Question
How can you make different numbers of squares from an arrangement of 12 toothpicks by moving or removing some of the toothpicks?

Materials
Student sheet
Flat toothpicks, 12 per student

Puzzle Background
   Toothpick Puzzlers was adapted from a set of matchstick puzzles that appear in *The Moscow Puzzles* by Boris Kordemsky (available from Dover Publications, Inc.). This puzzle is similar to *Toothpick Teasers* in that once you have solved one of the five challenges, you learn to "see" things, both visually and logically, that help solve the remaining challenges.

Puzzle Presentation
1. Students will need 12 flat toothpicks each to solve this puzzle.
2. Students need to know the meaning of congruent (same size and shape) when doing this activity.
3. This puzzle works well at a center or some other place where students can work individually for relatively short periods of time. It can be done for a few minutes each day over the course of a week allowing students to work at the puzzle in short spurts, thereby avoiding frustration if they do not solve it quickly on the first try. Doing this should allow students to experience some level of success even if they do not solve all of the different puzzles.

Solution Hint
   Remember that each square does not have to stand alone (i.e., some squares may be inside of others).

5

Toothpick Puzzlers

Begin each of the following puzzles with 12 toothpicks arranged in the pattern below.

Puzzle 1: Make two squares of different sizes by removing two toothpicks.

Puzzle 2: Make three congruent squares by moving three toothpicks.

Puzzle 3: Make three congruent squares by moving four toothpicks.

Puzzle 4: Make seven squares, not all congruent by moving two toothpicks. You may cross one toothpick over another.

Puzzle 5: Make 10 squares, not all congruent, by moving four toothpicks. You may cross one toothpick over another.

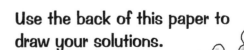

Use the back of this paper to draw your solutions.

SQUARE *Pickings*

Puzzle Topic
Spatial-relationship skills

Puzzle Question
How can you arrange the eight sticks given to form exactly three squares?

Materials
Student sheet
Flat toothpicks, 12 per student
Tape or glue

Puzzle Background
This puzzle is slightly different from the others presented in this section because it uses *double-length* toothpicks—two toothpicks taped or glued together—in addition to regular toothpicks. This makes the problem more challenging than it would otherwise be, and gives it a different feel from the rest of the toothpick puzzles. *Square Pickings* will exercise your students' spatial abilities as they work towards creating exactly three squares with their eight pieces.

Puzzle Presentation
1. Each student will need four regular-length toothpicks and four double-length toothpicks for this puzzle. Double-length toothpicks can be made by taping or gluing two toothpicks end to end. Craft sticks, ice cream sticks, or strips of paper cut to the right proportions can also be used. The only requirement is that four of the pieces are twice as long as the other four.
2. In order to maximize the math inherent in this puzzle, students need to think about the puzzle after they have found the solution. With the answer in hand, students can concentrate on the mathematics involved. For a discussion of some of the math in this activity, see the *Solutions* section.

Solution Hint
Think about the perimeter of a square and what the preimeter of three squares would be if they all had sides one toothpick in length. Compare this value to the number of toothpicks you have.

SQUARE *Pickings*

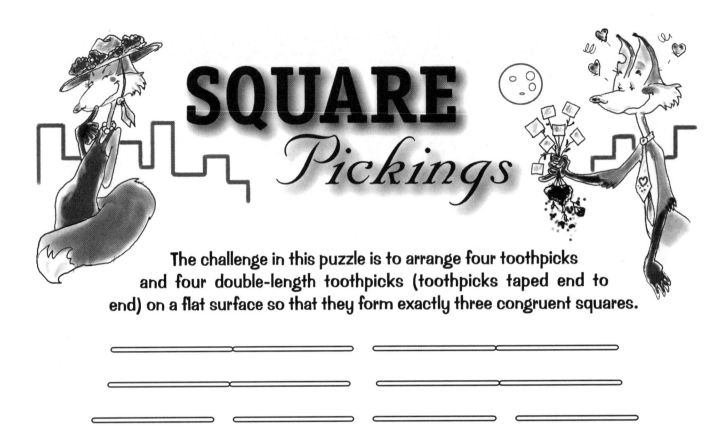

The challenge in this puzzle is to arrange four toothpicks and four double-length toothpicks (toothpicks taped end to end) on a flat surface so that they form exactly three congruent squares.

Sketch your solution in the space below.

List some of the things you noticed while doing this puzzle.

FLIPPING FISH

Puzzle Topic
Spatial-relationship skills

Puzzle Question
How can you make the toothpick fish face a different direction by moving the fewest number of toothpicks?

Materials
Student sheet
Flat toothpicks, eight per student

Puzzle Background
This puzzle has been around in various forms for a number of years. All forms begin with eight toothpicks or matches arranged in the shape of a fish. One version challenges you to move exactly three toothpicks to make the fish face the *opposite* direction. Another version challenges you to move just two toothpicks to make the fish face a *different* direction. Other versions add a small object for an eye that is moved along with the toothpicks.

Our version of the puzzle has been modified to make it more open-ended and asks students to think about their solutions. *Flipping Fish* begins by simply asking students to make a toothpick fish face another direction by moving any number of toothpicks. With this approach, there are many possible solutions, instead of the one or two possible in the classic versions. When students discover an initial solution, they are asked to examine that solution and determine if they can come up with one that moves fewer toothpicks. They are then challenged to find the minimum number of moves needed to get the fish to face a different direction and defend this number. This strategy forces them to think more deeply about the problem, and helps develop higher-order thinking skills. Finally, students are given the opportunity to communicate mathematically when they share their solutions with others.

Puzzle Presentation
1. Each student will need a copy of the student page and eight flat toothpicks for this puzzle.
2. When all students have had sufficient time to explore the puzzle and discover their solutions, close the activity with a class discussion. Encourage students to share their solutions and their justifications for those solutions.

Solution Hint
Look at *every* way the body of the fish could be recreated in a different spot.

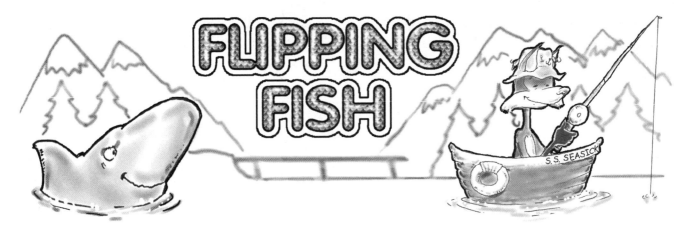

Challenge 1:

Arrange eight toothpicks on your desk in the shape of a fish, as shown below. Make the fish face a different direction by moving some of the toothpicks.

How many did you move?

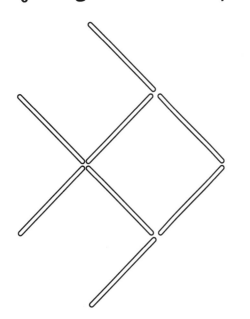

Challenge 2:

Try to get the fish to change directions by moving fewer toothpicks than you did the first time.

How many did you move?

What is the minimum number of toothpicks that must be moved to make the fish face another direction? Defend your answer.

9-Square Toothpick Challenge

Puzzle Topic
Spatial-relationship skills

Puzzle Question
How can you change the number of squares by moving or removing a given number of toothpicks from the original arrangement?

Materials
Student sheet
Flat toothpicks, 24 per student

Puzzle Background
This particular puzzle, like *Toothpick Puzzler,* is adapted from a puzzle appearing in *The Moscow Puzzles.* Our version provides ten different challenges for your students which have varying degrees of difficulty. All but one of the puzzles require students to create a different number of squares from the original arrangement by moving or removing various numbers of toothpicks. The final challenge also has students create two irregular hexagons. This is one of the most open-ended of the toothpick puzzles in this section, since almost every challenge has more than one solution. This gives students a good opportunity to compare problem-solving methods as they look at solutions that their classmates have discovered which are different from their own.

Puzzle Presentation
1. Students will each need a copy of the student sheet and 24 flat toothpicks to complete this puzzle.
2. Be sure students know that they do not need to solve the challenges in order. If they are stuck on one, they should move on to the next to avoid frustration.
3. If your students are not familiar with the concepts of congruent and irregular shapes, be sure to go over the definitions before they begin. Two shapes are congruent if they are the same size and shape. An irregular hexagon can be any shape, as long as it has six sides.

Solution Hint
Sometimes the squares will share at least part of one side in common.

9-Square Toothpick Challenge

Arrange 24 toothpicks on your desk in the shape shown below.

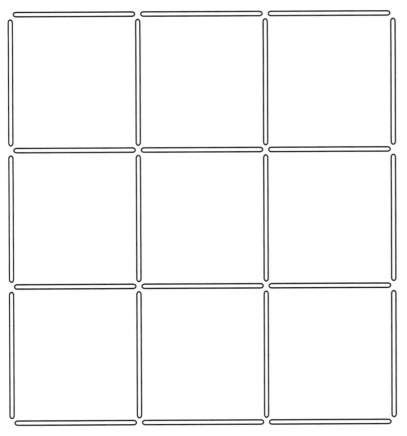

Challenges:
1. Move 12 toothpicks to make two congruent squares.
2. Remove four toothpicks leaving one large and four small squares.
3. Remove four, six, or eight toothpicks leaving five unit squares.
4. Remove eight toothpicks leaving four unit squares.
5. Remove six toothpicks leaving three squares.
6. Remove eight toothpicks leaving two squares.
7. Remove eight toothpicks leaving three squares.
8. Remove four toothpicks leaving nine squares.
9. Remove eight toothpicks leaving five squares, not all the same size.
10. Remove six toothpicks leaving two squares and two congruent irregular hexagons.

Use the back of this paper to sketch each of your solutions.

PENNING A HALF-DOZEN

Puzzle Topic
Spatial-relationship skills

Puzzle Question
How can you create six equal-sized shapes using 12 toothpicks without cutting or overlapping any of the toothpicks?

Materials
Student sheet
Flat toothpicks, 12 per student

Puzzle Background
    This puzzle comes from the collection of the great British mathematician and puzzlist, H.E. Dudeney (1847-1930). As with many matchstick puzzles, there is a story with *Penning a Half-Dozen*. This story explains that a farmer had 13 identical fence pieces which made six sheep pens, all identical in shape and size. One night a thief stole one of the fence pieces, leaving the farmer with only 12. Students are challenged to help the farmer rebuild the sheep pens so that there are still six pens of identical shape and size.

Puzzle Presentation
1. Each student will need a copy of the student page and 12 flat toothpicks for this puzzle.
2. Emphasize to students that there is a correct solution that does not overlap or cut any of the toothpicks.
3. An interesting extension for older students would be to determine the difference in area between the 13-toothpick pens and the 12-toothpick pens. Assume that each toothpick has a length of 2 units.

Solution Hint
    Don't be limited to square or rectangular pens.

A shepherd had six sheep and 13 sections of fence which were arranged into six pens of identical size and shape. The arrangement is represented below using toothpicks.

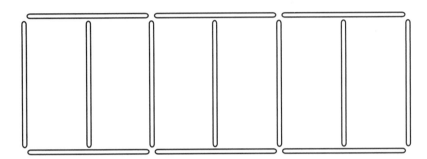

One evening someone stole one of the fence sections leaving only 12. After thinking long and hard—a quality of a persistent problem solver—the shepherd rearranged the 12 sections to form six pens of identical size and shape for the sheep.

Use 12 toothpicks to show how the shepherd made the six pens. This can be done without overlapping or cutting any of the toothpicks.

Draw your solution below.

Arrow Arrangements

Puzzle Topic
Spatial-relationship skills

Puzzle Question
How can you move a given number of toothpicks to create eight triangles or seven quadrilaterals from the arrow shape?

Materials
Student sheet
Flat toothpicks, 16 per student

Puzzle Background
This particular puzzle, like *Nine-Square Toothpick Challenge*, comes from *The Moscow Puzzles*. The puzzle is found in the section entitled "Geometry with Matches," which offers a selection of matchstick puzzles as "geometrical amusements that sharpen your mind." *Arrow Arrangements* is one of the more difficult puzzles in this section, and requires students to understand and apply some basic geometric terms such as *congruent, triangle,* and *quadrilateral*. Thus it has the benefit of not only sharpening the mind, but also giving some practice thinking about geometric shapes and concepts.

Puzzle Presentation
1. Students will each need a copy of the student sheet and 16 flat toothpicks to complete this puzzle.
2. Be sure students understand the concept of congruent triangles and quadrilaterals before they begin.

Solution Hint
Work backwards, starting with the correct number of triangles or quadrilaterals, and try to make the arrow from that arrangement.

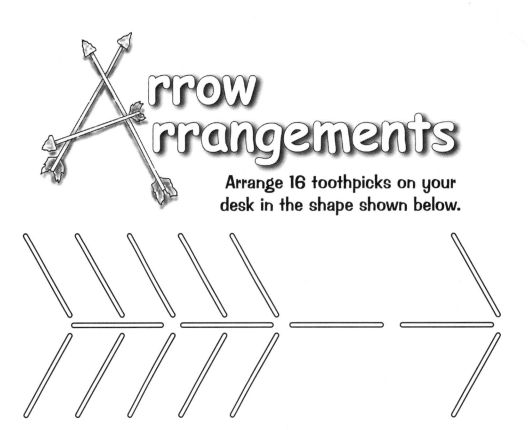

Arrow Arrangements

Arrange 16 toothpicks on your desk in the shape shown below.

Challenges:

1. Move eight toothpicks to form eight congruent triangles.
2. Move seven toothpicks to form five congruent quadrilaterals.

Record both of your solutions in the space below.

PickOut Four

Puzzle Topic
Spatial-relationship skills, geometric shapes

Puzzle Question
How can you remove four toothpicks from the arrangement to leave different combinations of shapes remaining?

Materials
Student sheet
Flat toothpicks, 16 per student

Puzzle Background
This activity consists of several related puzzles, each of which begins with 16 toothpicks arranged in the pattern shown on the student sheet. In each puzzle, four toothpicks are removed, leaving various geometric shapes. There are several *elegant* solutions for each puzzle that leave no extra toothpicks sticking out. This activity goes beyond the others in this section by providing an important opportunity to introduce or review geometric shapes and their properties. The students' interest in the activity can be used to enhance their geometric knowledge.

Puzzle Presentation
1. Each student will need 16 flat toothpicks and a copy of the student sheet for this puzzle.
2. The directions for each puzzle use geometric terms, such as congruent, parallelogram, hexagon, and trapezoid, with which your students may or may not be familiar. Be sure that students understand the meaning of the necessary terms before they attempt to solve the puzzles.
3. Some of the puzzles (2 and 5) are more difficult than others and may prove frustrating for students. They should be reminded that each puzzle has a viable solution that can be reached with a little patience and persistence.
4. Since there is more than one solution for each puzzle, having a time of class discussion can allow students to see other possibilities that they did not discover. This will also give students the opportunity to articulate their solution processes and practice their geometric vocabulary.

Solution Hint
Work backwards, taking away four toothpicks and trying to recreate the necessary shapes.

Pick Out Four

Begin each of the following puzzles with 16 toothpicks arranged in the pattern at the bottom of the page. Draw your solutions on the back of this sheet.

Puzzle 1: Remove four toothpicks and leave four congruent parallelograms.

Puzzle 2: Remove four toothpicks and leave four congruent triangles.

Puzzle 3: Remove four toothpicks and leave five congruent triangles.

Puzzle 4: Remove four toothpicks and leave a hexagon.

Puzzle 5: Remove four toothpicks and leave two congruent triangles and two parallelograms.

Puzzle 6: Remove four toothpicks and leave two congruent triangles and two congruent trapezoids.

When you have solved each of the puzzles above, create two puzzles of your own.

Puzzle 7: Remove four toothpicks and leave _____

_____

Puzzle 8: Remove four toothpicks and leave _____

_____

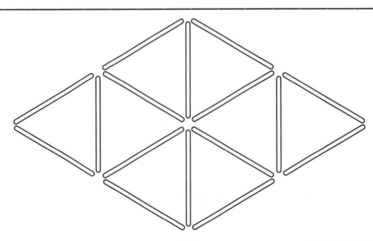

TOOTHPICK PUZZLE SOLUTIONS

Toothpick Teasers

There are several different solutions for each of the toothpick teasers. The method from the second student sheet has been used here to record one possible solution for each teaser. Additionally, diagrams of each solution are given. The dotted lines indicate the toothpicks that were removed, and the arrows indicate which toothpicks were moved, and to what location they were moved.

Teaser #	Remove #'s	Move # ___ to space # ___
1	2, 11, 14	
2	2, 13, 14	11 to 13
3	4, 13, 14	2 to 13, 11 to 4
4	2, 13, 15	12 to 13, 14 to 15, 11 to 12
5	9, 13, 15	12 to 13, 14 to 15, 11 to 12, 2 to 9

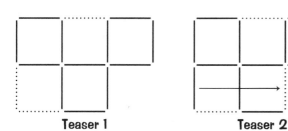

Teaser 1   **Teaser 2**

Teaser 3   **Teaser 4**

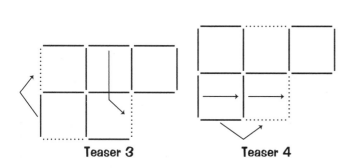

Teaser 5

Toothpick Puzzlers

The dashed lines in the diagrams indicate the toothpicks that were moved, the dotted lines indicate toothpicks that were removed.

Puzzle 1: Make two squares of different sizes by removing two toothpicks.

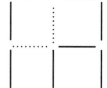

Puzzle 2: Make three congruent squares by moving three toothpicks.

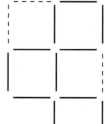

Puzzle 3: Make three congruent squares by moving four toothpicks.

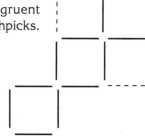

Puzzle 4: Make seven squares, not all congruent, by moving two toothpicks. You may cross one toothpick over another.

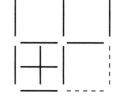

Puzzle 5: Make 10 squares, not all congruent, by moving four toothpicks. You may cross one toothpick over another.

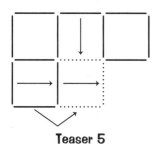

Square Pickings

This arrangement and its mirror image are the only two possible solutions using the pieces given.

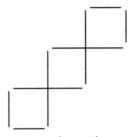

Some observations and discoveries about the math present in this puzzle:

The three squares formed in the solution are not adjacent and do not overlap, as is the case in many other toothpick puzzles. Each square has a perimeter of four toothpick lengths. The total toothpick length of the eight sticks is 12, thus proving that no valid solution may have overlapping or adjacent squares since the perimeter of the three squares equals 12. The areas of the squares are equal, so they are all congruent.

Flipping Fish

The arrows and dashed lines indicate how the toothpicks were moved in two of the possible solutions.

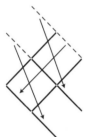 

Move three toothpicks   **Move two toothpicks**

Nine-Square Toothpick Challenge

In each diagram the dashed lines represent the toothpicks that were moved, and the dotted lines indicate toothpicks that were removed. In many cases more than one solution is possible, so students may have correct answers which are not shown here.

Challenge 1: Move 12 toothpicks to make two congruent squares.

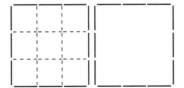

Challenge 2: Remove four toothpicks leaving one large and four small squares.

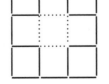

Challenge 3: Remove four, six, or eight toothpicks leaving five unit squares.

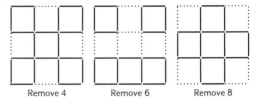

Remove 4   Remove 6   Remove 8

Challenge 4: Remove eight toothpicks leaving four unit squares.

Challenge 5: Remove six toothpicks leaving three squares.

Challenge 6: Remove eight toothpicks leaving two squares.

Challenge 7: Remove eight toothpicks leaving three squares.

Challenge 8: Remove four toothpicks leaving nine squares. (There are seven unit squares and two larger overlapping squares made of four unit squares each. These larger squares are indicated by the dashed lines.)

Challenge 9: Remove eight toothpicks leaving five squares, not all the same size.

Challenge 10: Remove six toothpicks leaving two squares and two congruent irregular hexagons.

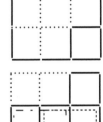

Penning a Half-Dozen

If the 12 sections of fence are arranged to form six triangular pens as shown, each pen will be congruent.

Extension

In the original arrangement, 13 toothpicks make up six rectangular pens as shown. Each pen is one half of a four-toothpick square. If a value of 2 units is assigned to the height of each pen (one toothpick), then the width of each pen is 1 unit (half of one toothpick). Using these values, it can be determined that each pen has an area of 2 units^2.

$$A = L \times W$$
$$A = 2 \text{ units} \times 1 \text{ unit}$$
$$A = 2 \text{ units}^2$$

In the new arrangement, 12 toothpicks make up six triangular pens as shown. Each pen is an equilateral triangle with sides 2 units in length. Using the Pythagorean theorem, the height of each triangle can be determined to be √3. This value can then be used to calculate the area of each pen, which is approximately 1.73 units^2.

$$a^2 + b^2 = c^2$$

$$a^2 + 1^2 = 2^2$$
$$a^2 + 1 = 4$$
$$a^2 = 3$$
$$a = \sqrt{3}$$

$$A = \frac{1}{2} b \times h$$

$$A = \frac{1}{2}(2)(\sqrt{3})$$

$$A \approx 1.73$$

The difference in area between each rectangular pen and each triangular pen, therefore, is approximately .27 units^2.

Arrow Arrangements

The dashed lines indicate the toothpicks that were moved in each solution.

Challenge 1: Move eight toothpicks to make eight congruent triangles.

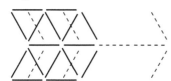

Challenge 2: Move seven toothpicks to make five congruent quadrilaterals.

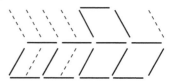

Pick Out Four

The diagrams show one possible solution for each of the six puzzles. The dotted lines indicate which toothpicks were removed.

Puzzle 1: Remove four toothpicks and leave four congruent parallelograms.

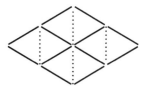

Puzzle 2: Remove four toothpicks and leave four congruent triangles.

Puzzle 3: Remove four toothpicks and leave five congruent triangles.

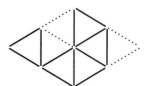

Puzzle 4: Remove four toothpicks and leave a hexagon.

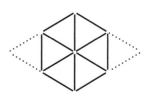

Puzzle 5: Remove four toothpicks and leave two congruent triangles and two parallelograms.

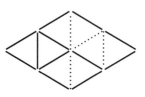

Puzzle 6: Remove four toothpicks and leave two congruent triangles and two congruent trapezoids.

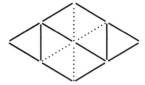

Topological Puzzles
Introduction

Topology is a branch of mathematics that emerged in the early part of the twentieth century. This mathematical field studies geometric properties that are not affected by changes in size and shape. Topologists study seemingly simple topics like knots, inside and outside, and the transformation of shapes and surfaces. Topology is related to geometry because of its study of lines, points, and figures, but unlike geometry, in topology these figures can be stretched and bent, giving topology the nickname, "rubber-sheet geometry."

At first glance, topology might not seem to have much in common with puzzles. However, several of the applications of topology lend themselves quite well to puzzling. In this section there are three different types of puzzles which are all topological in nature: networks, knots and disentanglement puzzles, and transformations.

Networks are series of points connected by paths. Leonhard Euler, *The Grandfather of Topology,* was the first to study and write on networks when he solved the famous Bridges of Königsberg problem, which involves walking across a network of seven bridges without retracing ones steps. Euler generalized the original problem into a graphic form and determined that a network may only be traveled completely without retracing any lines if there are two or fewer points where an odd number of paths intersect. More specifically, if there are two points with an odd number of paths, the network may be traveled completely without retracing any lines, but the beginning and ending points will be different. This is called an Euler path. An Euler circuit occurs when there is only one point where an odd number of paths intersect. In this case, it is possible to return to the starting point after traveling the entire network. There are only two network puzzles in this section, but they are rich in mathematical and historical background, giving you the opportunity to introduce many related topics and subjects.

Disentanglement puzzles, which abound in recreational mathematics, deal with the topological study of knots. Most appear, at first glance, to be impossible, but with careful study and persistence a solution generally appears. While students may not understand the complex mathematics involved in these puzzles, they will gain some hands-on experience with topology as they work on these puzzles.

The third type of puzzle in this section deals with the transformation of shapes and surfaces. Both of the transformation puzzles require students to take a two-dimensional sheet of paper and transform it into a shape with three-dimensional characteristics. While these puzzles are topological in nature, they also require strong spatial visualization abilities to be solved.

We have attempted to arrange these puzzles in order of difficulty. The disentanglement and transformation puzzles all build on knowledge gained in the previous puzzle(s), so it is recommended that you not do the later puzzles until the earlier ones have been mastered. This way students will gain experience and confidence solving the easier puzzles before they are challenged with the more difficult ones.

22

BRIDGE CROSSING CHALLENGE

Puzzle Topic
Network Theory

Puzzle Question
In each diagram, how can you cross every bridge once, and only once?

Materials
Student sheets

Puzzle Background
In the town of Königsberg, Prussia (now Kaliningrad, Russia), there were seven bridges over the Pregel river connecting two islands and various other parts of the city. There was a tradition in Königsberg to try and walk around the city, crossing over each of the seven bridges only once. No one was ever able to do it, and yet they were unable to prove that it could not be done. In 1735, some college students sent the problem to Leonhard Euler (1707-1783), one of the greatest mathematicians of the day. Euler was able to mathematically prove that this walk is impossible because of the number of points that were connected by an odd number of paths. Euler's study of topics like this earned him the title, *The Grandfather of Topology* because he unknowingly studied the topics that would come to be an integral part of that discipline when it was introduced over 100 years after his death.

This activity challenges students to solve some puzzles similar to the Bridges of Königsberg problem. The original problem states: *Königsberg is a city on the Pregel River that contains two islands and is joined by seven bridges. The river flows around the two islands of the town. The bridges run from the banks of the river to the two islands in the river with a bridge connecting the islands. It became town tradition to take a Sunday walk to try and cross each of the seven bridges only once. Draw the map the people must have followed in order to complete their journey.*

Each puzzle in *Bridge Crossing Challenge* asks students to draw a route that will cross every bridge once and only once. After students have solved each puzzle (or determined that it is not possible to solve), they will create a bridge crossing puzzle of their own to share with a classmate. This puzzle should help students see some of the more real-life applications of the study of topology and networks.

Puzzle Presentation
1. Each student will need a copy of the student sheets for this activity. Be sure that students use pencils so that they can make mistakes and try several different methods, if necessary.
2. Not all of the puzzles in this activity can be solved; however, students should be allowed to discover this fact for themselves.
3. When students create their own puzzles to share with a classmate, you may want to have them draw the final copy in pen so that the other students can erase pencil marks without erasing the puzzle.
4. If you would like to share some of the history of this kind of puzzle with your students, a copy of the Bridges of Königsberg has been included along with a very basic description of Euler's proof.

Solution Hint
Look at the number of bridges that go to each land mass.

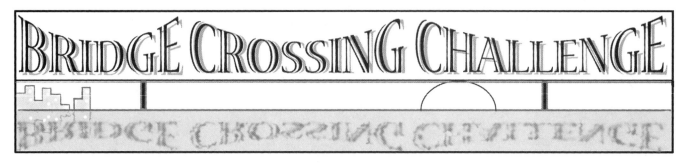

Read each scenario below and follow the directions.

There is an island in the center of Elizabeth's town that has three bridges leading to it. Elizabeth likes to take a walk from her home to the island by crossing every bridge once and only once. How can she do this? Draw Elizabeth's home where it belongs.

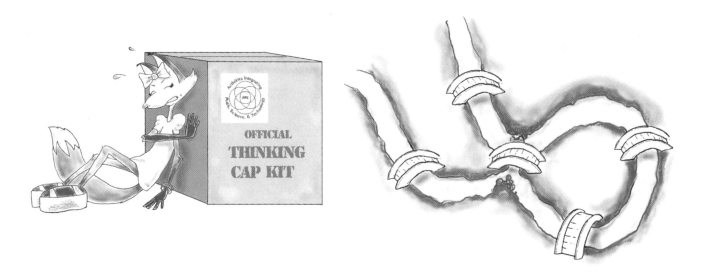

Carlos is trying to find a way to cross every bridge on the river in his town without ending up on the island. Can he do it without crossing any of the bridges more than once? Show how, numbering the bridges in the order that you cross them.

BRIDGE CROSSING CHALLENGE

BRIDGE CROSSING CHALLENGE

The Spiral River in Lin's town has nine bridges that connect five islands. Every year the Five-Island race goes through the town crossing each bridge only once. Show one route that the racers could take, numbering the bridges in the order they should be crossed.

The Revolution River creates two nearly identical islands that are each accessible by three bridges. The Euler Foundation, a new company in town, is offering $20,000 to anyone who can visit both islands by crossing each bridge once, and only once. Can you win the prize? Show how.

Draw your own bridge crossing problem in the space below and give it to a classmate to solve.

THE BRIDGES OF KÖNIGSBERG

Königsberg is a city on the **Pregel River** that contains two islands and is joined by seven bridges. The river flows around the two islands of the town. The bridges run from the banks of the river to the two islands in the river, with a bridge connecting the islands. It became town tradition to take a Sunday walk to try and cross each of the seven bridges only once. Draw the map the people must have followed in order to complete their journey.

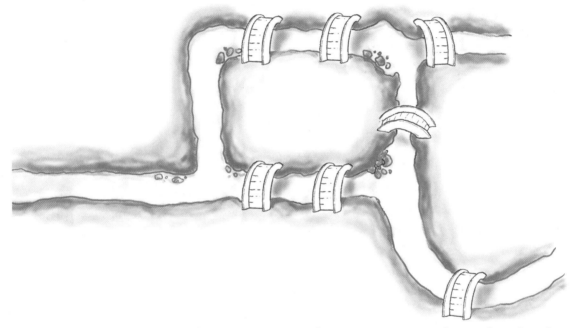

This is the original bridge crossing problem that a man named Leonhard Euler solved in the 1730s. He proved that it was impossible to cross each of the seven bridges in a single walk without retracing some of your steps. In fact, when dealing with bridges, if there are three or more pieces of land that have an odd number of bridges going to them, you will not be able to cross each bridge without retracing some steps.

How does this knowledge compare to what you discovered as you solved the puzzles?

Draw two bridge-crossing puzzles on the back of this page, one that is possible, and one that is not. Give them to a classmate and have the classmate determine which can be solved and which cannot without actually doing either one.

NAVIGATING NETWORKS

Puzzle Topic
Topology, networks

Puzzle Question
Which of the networks can be traced completely without lifting your pencil, and why?

Materials
Student sheet

Puzzle Background
This problem bears many similarities to *Bridge Crossing Challenge* because it has students explore networks. In this case, however, the networks have been reduced to their simplest form—a series of points connected by lines rather than bridges and land masses. In this context, students should be able to apply their discoveries from *Bridge Crossing Challenge* as well as the things they learn in this activity to reach the generalization that Euler discovered for traveling closed networks without retracing any lines.

Puzzle Presentation
1. Be sure that students use pencils to do this activity so that they can erase their lines and try again if they are unsuccessful on their first attempt.
2. As an extension, students can be challenged to construct their own networks; both ones which can be traveled and ones which cannot.

Solution Hint
Look at the number of odd and even vertices in each network.

NAVIGATING NETWORKS

Your challenge is to determine which of the networks below can be traced. Begin by placing your pencil at any point on the network and move along the lines until you have traced the entire figure. You may not trace over lines more than once. Mark the vertices where you begin and end, and record whether the network is traceable by writing "yes" or "no" in the space provided.

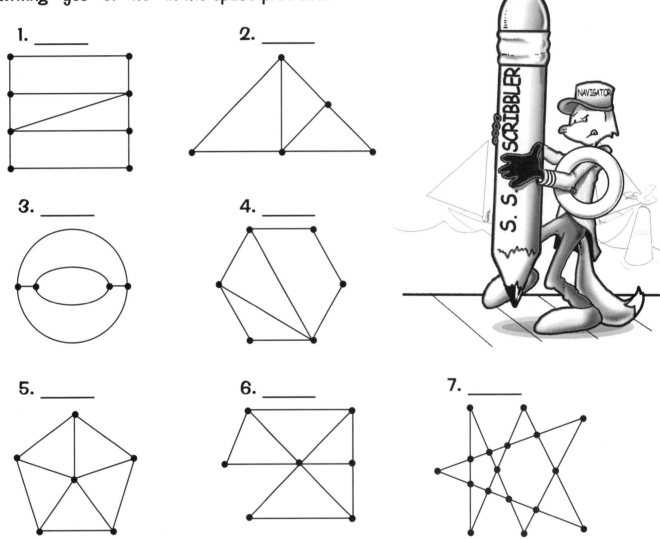

Which of the networks above could be traced?

What do these networks have in common?

Write a generalization about the characteristics of networks that can be traced.

Rings 'n' Strings

Puzzle Topic
Topology

Puzzle Question
How can you remove your object from the string without cutting or untying the string?

Materials
Student sheet
Objects with holes in them
String

Puzzle Background
   Rings 'n' Strings is the first activity in this section of topological disentanglement puzzles. It has been carefully selected as the first disentanglement puzzle for several reasons. First, it is fairly easy and shouldn't frustrate students too much. Second, its solution involves an important topological move that can sometimes be applied in other rope puzzles. It is recommended that you give your students this activity before asking them to attempt any of the rope puzzles which occur later in this section.

Puzzle Presentation
1. To do this puzzle with your students you will need a number of objects with holes in them. These objects need not be identical. Things like chart rings, masking tape, bracelets, coffee mugs, and student scissors work well. You should have at least one object per group, but you may want more. Each group will also need a piece of string or yarn about 60-70 cm long.
2. It is recommended that you make a sample puzzle in front of the class to introduce the activity and clarify the instructions. Students will need to take their string, fold it in half, and run it through the hole in their object. Next, the loose ends are brought through the loop and pulled tight. The string is then tied around some large object such as the leg of a chair or a desk so that it cannot be taken off. The challenge is to remove the object from the string without cutting or untying the string.
3. Once students have mastered the initial challenge, the next challenge is to put the object back onto the string without untying it or removing it from the chair, desk, etc.

Solution Hint
   Think about what you did to get the string through the ring initially.

Rings 'n' Strings

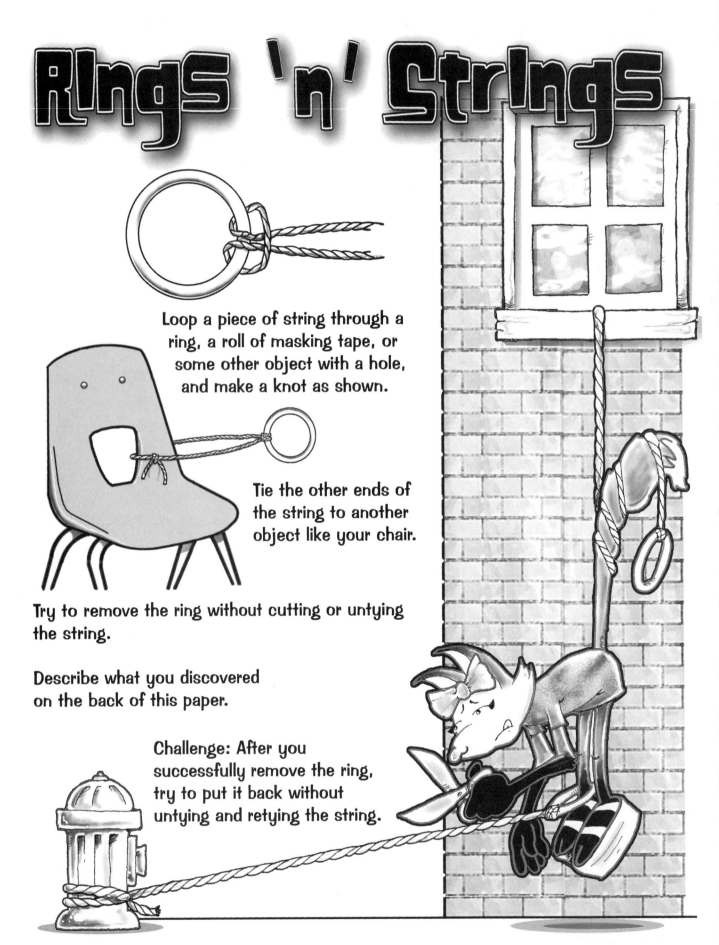

Loop a piece of string through a ring, a roll of masking tape, or some other object with a hole, and make a knot as shown.

Tie the other ends of the string to another object like your chair.

Try to remove the ring without cutting or untying the string.

Describe what you discovered on the back of this paper.

Challenge: After you successfully remove the ring, try to put it back without untying and retying the string.

STRINGING the RING

Puzzle Topic
Topology

Puzzle Question
How does a loop of beaded chain get knotted around a ring when the ring is dropped through the chain?

Materials
Student sheet
Metal rings
Beaded chain, about one meter per puzzle

Puzzle Background

This puzzle shows one way which topology can be applied outside of mathematics to provide amusement and entertainment. *Stringing the Ring* is a magic trick which works because of topological principles. In this trick, a closed loop of beaded chain is dangled from one hand. A solid metal ring is brought up between the loop of chain and dropped. Instead of falling to the ground, the ring *magically* knots itself in the bottom of the loop of chain. The challenge for students is to discover how the ring gets knotted around the chain when it is dropped. Once they have discovered the secret, they will be able to practice the *trick* to share with their friends and family.

Puzzle Presentation

1. Each puzzle needs a piece of beaded chain and a metal ring. This chain can be purchased at hardware stores, and is typically used for pull cords on ceiling fans or lamps. A more lightweight version can also be purchased at craft stores in the homemade jewelry section. The chain needs to be a little less than one meter long (about two and a half to three feet). Metal rings can also be found in craft or hardware stores. A good size for the rings is 5-6 cm (2-2.5 in) in diameter.
2. If beaded chain and solid rings are unavailable, string or yarn and chart rings or ring-like objects such as rolls of masking tape can be substituted; however, this will affect the ease of performing the trick.
3. If you have enough rings for each student, allow everyone to have their own puzzle. If not, make a few puzzles and place them at a center or have students work on the activity in groups.
4. There are two parts to this activity. The first part is fairly simple and is designed to help students understand how the ring gets knotted around the chain. Once students have done this, they will be ready for the second part of the activity, which involves applying their knowledge to the trick and performing it.
5. The second part of the activity may take some time for students to master. Encourage them to persevere until they are able to consistently perform the trick. To extend the activity, experiment with the length of the chain, the size of the ring, etc. to find the best combination for performing.

Solution Hint

When performing the trick, think about ways to make the ring rotate as it falls off your fingers. Pay attention to the way your fingers are oriented in relation to the chain.

STRINGING the RING

Magicians sometimes use mathematics to do magic tricks. One such trick is to get a ring dropped around the outside of a loop of beaded chain to become tied to that loop with a knot. While some skill is involved in performing this trick, the real secret to doing it is to figure out the underlying mathematics of how the knot gets tied.

To help you do this, place the ring and chain on a flat surface as shown.

While holding one end of the loop, grab the ring and slowly pull it in the opposite direction. If you hold the correct end and grab the ring in exactly the right place, you should be able to knot the ring to the chain.

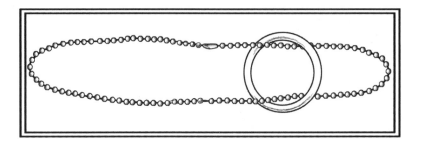

Now that you've watched the trick happen horizontally and slowly, try it vertically. Be prepared because this will happen much more quickly. Study the illustration on the left. This shows the starting point of the ring and loop. Your challenge is to drop the ring in such a way that the ring becomes tied to the loop as illustrated at the top of the page.

Once you have figured out how the trick works, you will need to practice it until you can perform it consistently. Good Luck!

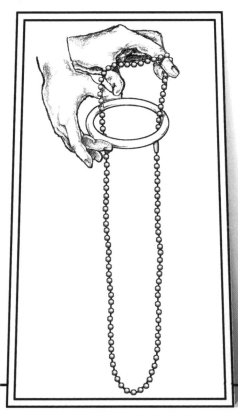

Knotty puzzle

Puzzle Topic
Topology

Puzzle Question
How can you tie an overhand knot in the center of a piece of string without letting go of the ends of the string with your hands?

Materials
Student sheet
String or yarn, one meter per puzzle

Puzzle Background
   This puzzle picks up on the area of topology that deals with knots, but also challenges students' logical thinking skills. Students are asked to tie an overhand knot in a piece of string. The catch is that this must be done by picking up the string by the ends and not letting go until after the knot has been tied. Students must learn to think logically and topologically in order to discover the solution to this puzzle.

Puzzle Presentation
1. Each puzzle needs a piece of string or yarn about one meter in length. Each student may have their own, or you may wish to set up one or two for the class to work on at a center.
2. In order for students to all experience the joy of solving this puzzle for themselves, you may want to assign it as homework or have students work on it when they are alone so that they are more likely to solve it without looking at other students' methods.

Solution Hint
   Think about how you pick up the piece of string.

Knotty puzzle

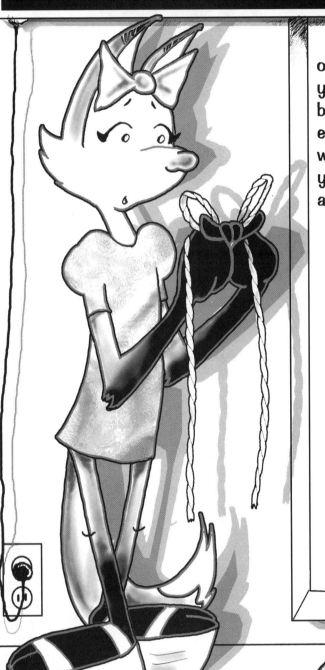

The challenge in this puzzle is to tie an overhand knot in the middle of a piece of yarn. The catch is that you must do this by picking up the ends of the yarn, one in each hand, and tie the knot in the middle without letting go of either end of the yarn. Describe your solution using words and/or pictures below.

Ready or Knot

How to tie the knot and stay sane

Möbius Mysteries

Puzzle Topic
Topology

Puzzle Question
How can you explain the apparent paradox of the double Möbius strips?

Materials
Scratch paper
Scissors
Tape
Student sheets

Puzzle Background
The Möbius loop is a topological surface first discovered by August Ferdinand Möbius in 1858. Möbius was a mathematician and professor of astronomy whose work in topology revolutionized the field of non-Euclidean geometry. A Möbius loop can be constructed by connecting two ends of a strip of paper after giving one end a half twist. This results in a baffling surface which has only one side and one edge.

The Möbius loop has been immortalized by artists like M.C. Escher, who used it in his print *Moebius Strip II*, which depicts ants marching in an endless line around a Möbius loop. It also has practical applications in the industrial world, where the large belts in some machinery have been designed with a half twist so that both *sides* get equal wear.

This puzzle presents a fascinating variation of the Möbius loop in which two apparently disconnected loops turn out to be joined together. Students will be challenged to explain this phenomenon as they explore topology using the Möbius loop.

Puzzle Presentation
1. This puzzle works best if you construct a model in front of the class, move the pencil between the *two* loops to show that they are not connected, and then try to pull them apart, showing that they are, in fact, connected.
2. When moving the pencil between the *two* loops, you will find that after one rotation the pencil will be facing the opposite direction than it was when you started. It is necessary to make two complete rotations to return the pencil to its original orientation. This realization is an important part of explaining the puzzle, and students should be allowed to make the discovery for themselves without having it pointed out to them.
3. Once you have demonstrated the puzzle for the class, give students the necessary materials and have them construct their own version of the puzzle. It is better if the paper students are using is plain so that it is more of a challenge to distinguish between *front* and *back*.

Solution Hint
Coloring each side of each strip of paper a different color before the band is assembled can help students see which strips are being attached to each other.

Möbius Mysteries

Cut two identical strips of paper that are about 11 inches long and one inch wide.

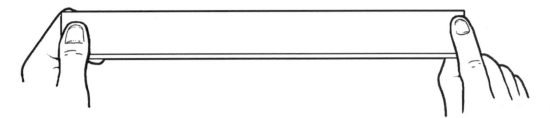

Place one strip on top of the other, holding at the ends between your thumb and first finger.

Give the strips a half twist and bring the ends together.

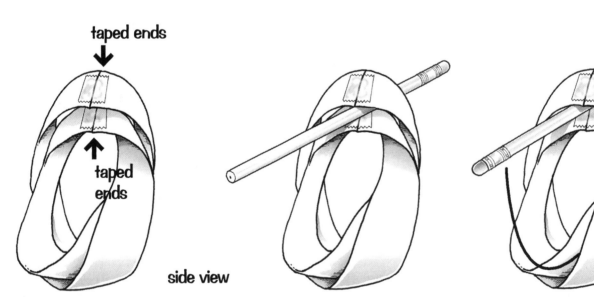

taped ends

taped ends

side view

Tape the ends, together—top to top and bottom to bottom. You should now have two Möbius loops nested right next to each other.

Take a pencil and place it between the two loops.

Move the pencil around the loop one time until it returns to the place you began.

Möbius Mysteries

Answer these questions after you have made your loops and followed the directions of the first student page.

1. What direction is the tip of the pencil facing now?

2. Is this the same or different than the direction it was facing when you began?

3. Move the pencil around the loop one more time. Now what direction is it facing?

4. Pull the two loops apart. What happens?

5. How can you explain this?

the GREAT ESCAPE

Puzzle Topic
Topology

Puzzle Question
How can you remove the string from Ima Fox without cutting it or untaping the penny?

Materials
Student sheet
Cardstock
Scissors
Tape
Hole punch
String, one meter per student
Pennies, one per student

Puzzle Background
   This puzzle (published previously as *Leprechaun on the Loose*) is our version of a classic disentanglement puzzle. It challenges students to remove a piece of string from a fox without cutting the string or removing the penny which is taped to the ends of the string. As students work on *The Great Escape*, they will get practice with their patience as well as their spatial manipulation abilities.

Puzzle Presentation
1. Because this puzzle is easily made from inexpensive materials, each student should have one. For each puzzle you will need a sheet of cardstock or oak tag, a one meter piece of string, and a penny. Plastic chips or other small objects that are too large to fit through the holes in the puzzle can be substituted for pennies.
2. It is recommended that you make a sample copy of the puzzle before giving it to your students to familiarize yourself with the construction process. This not only enables you to give students guidance as they make the puzzle, it allows you to try the puzzle yourself.

Solution Hint
   Think about the way you solved *Rings 'n' Strings* and how what you learned there could apply to this puzzle.

the GREAT ESCAPE

Ima Fox is a famous escape artist. Her most daring feat ever was escaping from 20 feet of steel cable padlocked five times inside a safe underwater—and she did it all in less than three minutes! Your challenge is to help Ima out of her latest tangle. Remove the string that holds her without cutting it or untaping the penny. If you are successful, try to get the string back on.

Cut out the picture of Ima Fox and use a hole punch to make holes in the three places indicated. Take a one-meter piece of string and fold it in half to make a loop. Insert the loop down through the top left hole and bring it back up through the top right hole. Hold the loose ends of the string together and thread them through the loop and then down through the bottom hole. Tape the loose ends to a penny.

Tangled Hearts

Puzzle Topic
Topology

Puzzle Question
How can you remove the small heart from the puzzle without taking off the pennies or cutting the string?

Materials
Student sheets
Cardstock
Scissors
Tape
String, 80 cm per student
Pennies, two per student

Puzzle Background
   Tangled Hearts is very similar to *Rings 'n' Strings* and *The Great Escape*, but it is the most difficult of the three, and should not be given to students until they have been exposed to the earlier, simpler puzzles. Like all disentanglement puzzles, this one may appear at first glance to be impossible. However, with careful study and perseverance, a solution can be discovered which allows you to remove the small heart from the puzzle without cutting the string or removing the pennies. Once the small heart has been removed, the additional challenge is to put the heart back on the puzzle without untaping the pennies, a task that can prove more difficult than removing it.

Puzzle Presentation
1. Since these puzzles are made from such inexpensive materials, each student should have his or her own puzzle to solve.
2. Before presenting this activity to your class, you should make a sample copy of the puzzle to familiarize yourself with the construction process. This will allow you to better assist your students as they attempt to construct their own puzzles.
3. Each puzzle requires a large heart and a small heart, an 80 cm piece of string and two pennies. Other objects of a similar size may be substituted for pennies. The instructions for assembly are on the first student sheet. The second student sheet has two copies of the hearts needed to make one puzzle. This page should be copied onto cardstock or oak tag to give the puzzle more durability.
4. If the string begins to get too tangled as students attempt to solve the puzzle, untape the pennies and reconstruct the puzzle to get it untangled.

Solution hint
   Modify the techniques you used on *The Great Escape* to suit this puzzle.

Tangled Hearts

Follow the directions below to make your heart puzzle.

1. Cut out the two hearts on the next page and punch out the holes.

2. Cut an 80 cm length of string and lay it across the large heart as shown.

3. Thread the two ends of the string through the bottom hole in the large heart from underneath.

4. Thread both ends through the hole in the small heart. Thread one end of the string through the right hole in the large heart and the other end through the left hole.

5. Finish your heart by taping a penny, or other similar-sized object, to each of the two loose ends of the string.

Tangled Hearts

Each puzzle needs a large heart and a small heart.

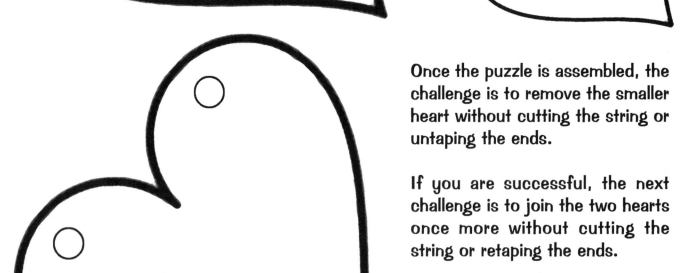

Once the puzzle is assembled, the challenge is to remove the smaller heart without cutting the string or untaping the ends.

If you are successful, the next challenge is to join the two hearts once more without cutting the string or retaping the ends.

(Note: If your string becomes too tangled, untape the ends and reconstruct the puzzle according to the directions on the previous page.)

Linking Loops

Puzzle Topic
Topology

Puzzle Question
How can you detach yourself from your partner without cutting the strings that connect you or taking them off your wrists?

Materials
Student sheet
Piece of string 150 cm long, one per student

Puzzle Background
   This puzzle is a classic in the field of topology which has been around since at least 1960, when it appeared in a California State Series booklet on topology. Despite its different appearance, the principles involved are identical to those used in *The Great Escape* and *Tangled Hearts*. This activity should give students a chance to apply, in a new way, the methods and techniques they have already discovered.

Puzzle Presentation
1. Students will need to work in pairs for this activity. It is suggested that you pair boys with boys and girls with girls since students will likely try all manner of acrobatics and contortions to separate themselves from their partners.
2. Each student will need a piece of string about 150 cm long. This string should be at least the thickness of kite string so that it will not break easily or cut into students wrists if pulled tight.
3. The loops that students tie in the ends of their string should fit loosely around their wrists.
4. Be sure that all pairs are properly connected before they begin to try solving the puzzle.
5. You may want to bring a camera on the day you do this puzzle to capture the interesting and often humerous positions in which students will likely place themselves while trying to separate their strings.

Solution Hint
   Think about how you could apply the methods used to solve *The Great Escape* or *Tangled Hearts* to this puzzle.

Linking Loops

Instructions:

1. Take your piece of string and tie a loop in each end so that your hand can fit easily through the loop with room to spare.
2. Put your left hand through one of the loops.
3. Link your string with your partner's string, and place your right hand through the remaining loop as illustrated.

Challenge: You and your partner should now be joined by your strings. Try to detach yourself from your partner without cutting either string or removing your hands from the loops at any time. Good luck!

©2001 AIMS Education Foundation

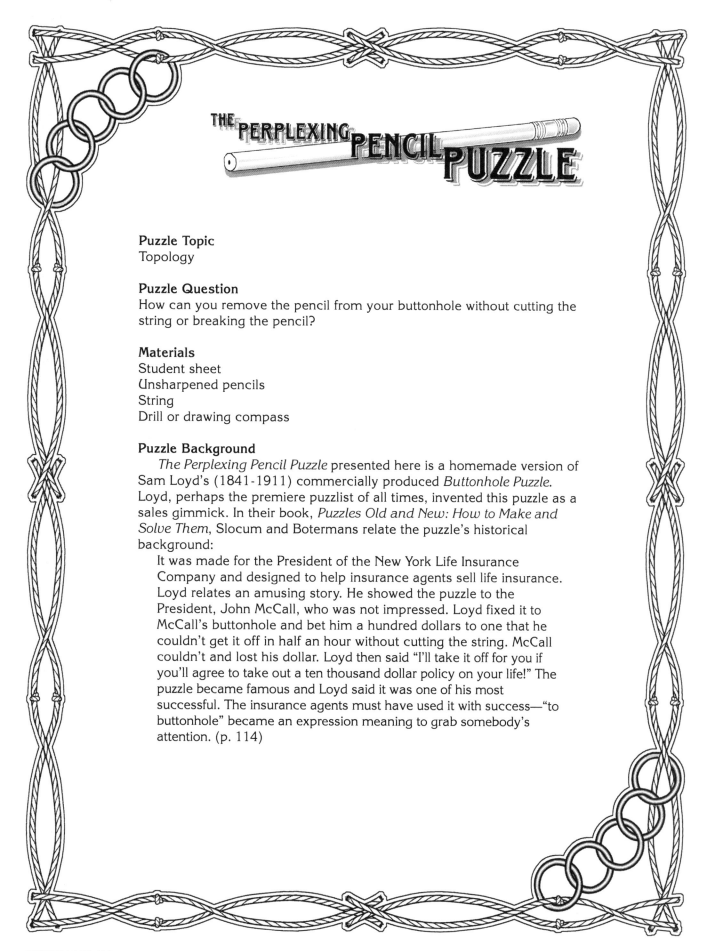

THE PERPLEXING PENCIL PUZZLE

Puzzle Topic
Topology

Puzzle Question
How can you remove the pencil from your buttonhole without cutting the string or breaking the pencil?

Materials
Student sheet
Unsharpened pencils
String
Drill or drawing compass

Puzzle Background
    The Perplexing Pencil Puzzle presented here is a homemade version of Sam Loyd's (1841-1911) commercially produced *Buttonhole Puzzle*. Loyd, perhaps the premiere puzzlist of all times, invented this puzzle as a sales gimmick. In their book, *Puzzles Old and New: How to Make and Solve Them*, Slocum and Botermans relate the puzzle's historical background:

> It was made for the President of the New York Life Insurance Company and designed to help insurance agents sell life insurance. Loyd relates an amusing story. He showed the puzzle to the President, John McCall, who was not impressed. Loyd fixed it to McCall's buttonhole and bet him a hundred dollars to one that he couldn't get it off in half an hour without cutting the string. McCall couldn't and lost his dollar. Loyd then said "I'll take it off for you if you'll agree to take out a ten thousand dollar policy on your life!" The puzzle became famous and Loyd said it was one of his most successful. The insurance agents must have used it with success—"to buttonhole" became an expression meaning to grab somebody's attention. (p. 114)

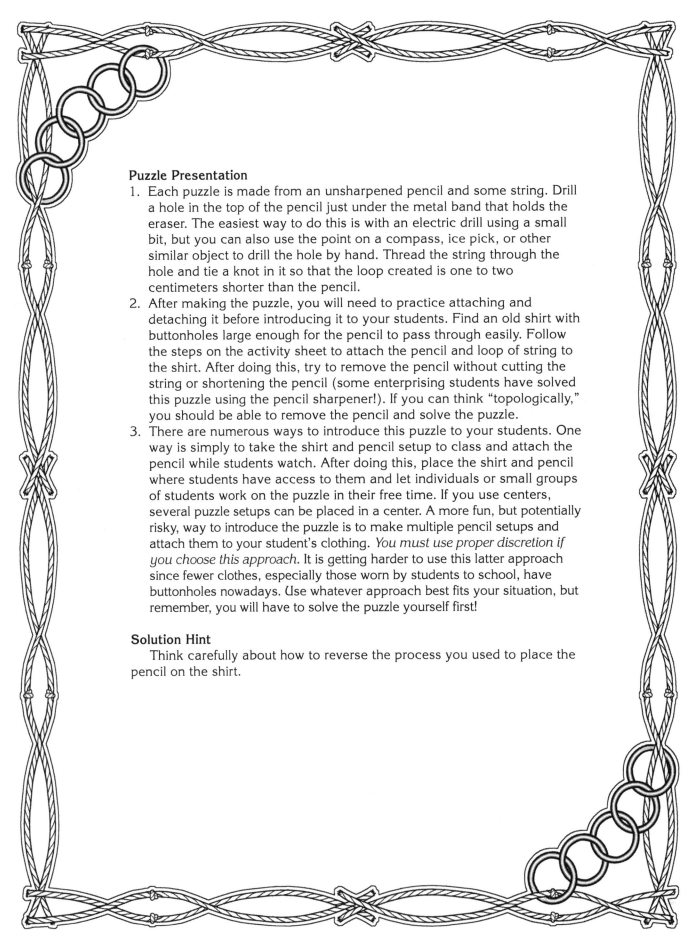

Puzzle Presentation

1. Each puzzle is made from an unsharpened pencil and some string. Drill a hole in the top of the pencil just under the metal band that holds the eraser. The easiest way to do this is with an electric drill using a small bit, but you can also use the point on a compass, ice pick, or other similar object to drill the hole by hand. Thread the string through the hole and tie a knot in it so that the loop created is one to two centimeters shorter than the pencil.

2. After making the puzzle, you will need to practice attaching and detaching it before introducing it to your students. Find an old shirt with buttonholes large enough for the pencil to pass through easily. Follow the steps on the activity sheet to attach the pencil and loop of string to the shirt. After doing this, try to remove the pencil without cutting the string or shortening the pencil (some enterprising students have solved this puzzle using the pencil sharpener!). If you can think "topologically," you should be able to remove the pencil and solve the puzzle.

3. There are numerous ways to introduce this puzzle to your students. One way is simply to take the shirt and pencil setup to class and attach the pencil while students watch. After doing this, place the shirt and pencil where students have access to them and let individuals or small groups of students work on the puzzle in their free time. If you use centers, several puzzle setups can be placed in a center. A more fun, but potentially risky, way to introduce the puzzle is to make multiple pencil setups and attach them to your student's clothing. *You must use proper discretion if you choose this approach.* It is getting harder to use this latter approach since fewer clothes, especially those worn by students to school, have buttonholes nowadays. Use whatever approach best fits your situation, but remember, you will have to solve the puzzle yourself first!

Solution Hint

Think carefully about how to reverse the process you used to place the pencil on the shirt.

THE PERPLEXING PENCIL PUZZLE

To make this puzzle, drill a small hole through a new pencil just under the metal band at the top. Thread a piece of string through the hole and tie a knot in it to create a loop that is shorter than the pencil.

Next, find an old shirt with buttonholes large enough for the pencil to fit through freely. Place the loop around the buttonhole as shown in the illustration. Pull the fabric surrounding the buttonhole up through the loop until the tip of the pencil can go through the buttonhole from underneath. Then pull the pencil through and the loop will form an overhand knot around the buttonhole.

Now that the pencil is attached, all you have to do is remove it and you've solved the puzzle. Good luck!

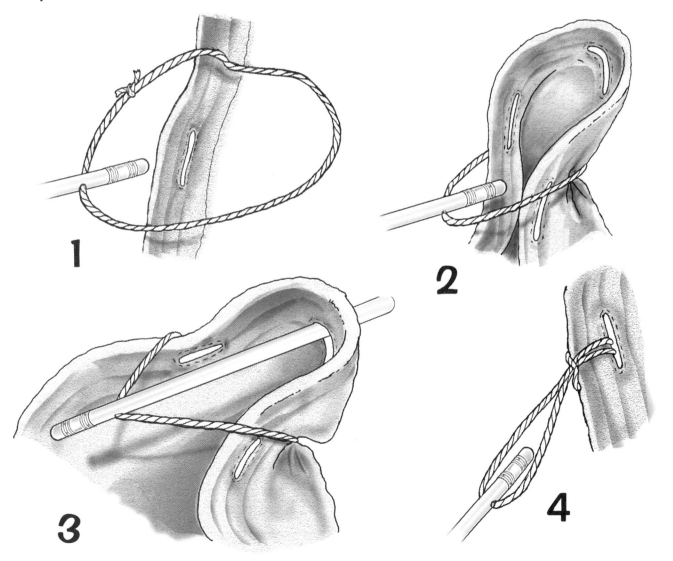

cut and fold challenge

Puzzle Topic
Topology, spatial visualization

Puzzle Question
How can you make the shape known as a *hypersquare* from a single sheet of paper by only cutting and folding?

Materials
Scratch paper
Scissors
Student sheet, optional
Bulletin board space, optional

Puzzle Background
   The Cut and Fold Challenge asks students to make the three-dimensional shape pictured on the next page from a single sheet of paper. The idea for this puzzle came from Martin Gardner's column in the November 1978 issue of *Scientific American*. Gardner traced the origins of the shape, which has come to be called a *hypersquare*, to an entrance exam from the school of architecture at the University of Leningrad. While this puzzle can be very difficult for people who are not strong in spatial-visualization skills, it is also very rewarding to finally discover the secret of the puzzle and arrive at the solution. At first glance, this puzzle might appear to have nothing to do with topology; however, keep in mind that topology studies the transformation of shapes and surfaces. In this case a two-dimensional piece of paper is transformed into an object with three-dimensional characteristics. This transformation is topological in nature, but also challenges students to exercise their spatial-visualization skills.

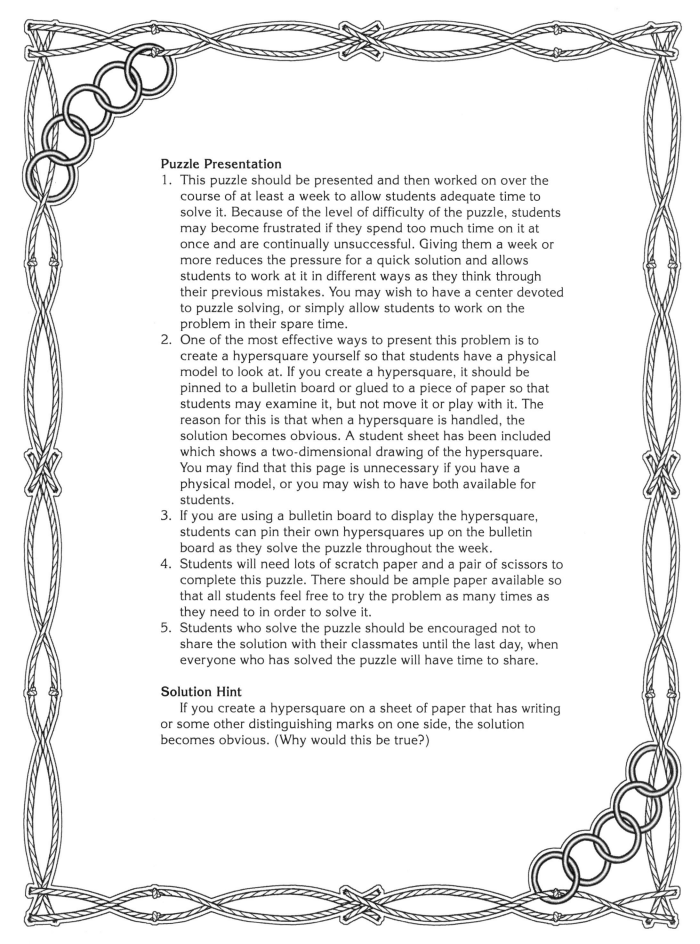

Puzzle Presentation

1. This puzzle should be presented and then worked on over the course of at least a week to allow students adequate time to solve it. Because of the level of difficulty of the puzzle, students may become frustrated if they spend too much time on it at once and are continually unsuccessful. Giving them a week or more reduces the pressure for a quick solution and allows students to work at it in different ways as they think through their previous mistakes. You may wish to have a center devoted to puzzle solving, or simply allow students to work on the problem in their spare time.

2. One of the most effective ways to present this problem is to create a hypersquare yourself so that students have a physical model to look at. If you create a hypersquare, it should be pinned to a bulletin board or glued to a piece of paper so that students may examine it, but not move it or play with it. The reason for this is that when a hypersquare is handled, the solution becomes obvious. A student sheet has been included which shows a two-dimensional drawing of the hypersquare. You may find that this page is unnecessary if you have a physical model, or you may wish to have both available for students.

3. If you are using a bulletin board to display the hypersquare, students can pin their own hypersquares up on the bulletin board as they solve the puzzle throughout the week.

4. Students will need lots of scratch paper and a pair of scissors to complete this puzzle. There should be ample paper available so that all students feel free to try the problem as many times as they need to in order to solve it.

5. Students who solve the puzzle should be encouraged not to share the solution with their classmates until the last day, when everyone who has solved the puzzle will have time to share.

Solution Hint

If you create a hypersquare on a sheet of paper that has writing or some other distinguishing marks on one side, the solution becomes obvious. (Why would this be true?)

cut and fold challenge

This part of the shape should stick up at right angles to the desk.

These parts of the shape should lie flat on the desk.

FOOTPRINT STAMP

Your challenge in this puzzle is to make the three-dimensional shape pictured above from a single sheet of paper. You must do it by cutting and folding without using any tape or glue.

Puzzle Topic
Topology, spatial visualization

Puzzle Question
How can you make the bands shown by cutting and folding pieces of paper and then taping them into loops?

Materials
Student sheet
Cash register tape or scratch paper
Scissors
Tape

Puzzle Background
Baffling Bands introduces two puzzling paper structures that, at first glance, seem impossible to make. Both structures are related to the paper figure called the *hypersquare,* which is the subject of the previous activity, *Cut and Fold Challenge.* While the relation of this activity to topology might not immediately be seen, it is closely connected to the Möbius band, the *one-sided* loop popularized by the drawings of M.C. Escher. By constructing these baffling bands, students will experience yet another facet of topology while exercising their spatial-visualization and problem-solving skills.

Puzzle Presentation
1. If your students have not yet done the *Cut and Fold Challenge*, they should do so before attempting this activity. *Baffling Bands* is a more challenging version of the hypersquare, and if students do not have a base formed by exposure to the easier problem, they will likely encounter frustration as they attempt to solve this problem.
2. Students may go through quite a bit of paper while working on this problem. While lengths of cash-register tape are ideal for this activity, strips cut long ways from 8.5" x 11" scratch paper will also work. Either way, students should be encouraged to recycle their scraps and mistakes.
3. Spatial visualization problems like *Baffling Bands* are often very frustrating for adults and students alike. You need to think about how your students handle frustration and let this guide you as you plan a way to use this problem in your classroom. One of the best ways to reduce frustration is by introducing problems such as this one after students have had success with several easier problems of the same nature.

Solution Hints
Think about how you solved the *Cut and Fold Challenge* and how that could be applied here. To solve the extra challenge, think about how this puzzle is related to a Möbius loop.

baffling bands

Study the drawings.
Each shows a band made from a
strip of paper that has been cut,
folded, and taped together. Try to
make each band.

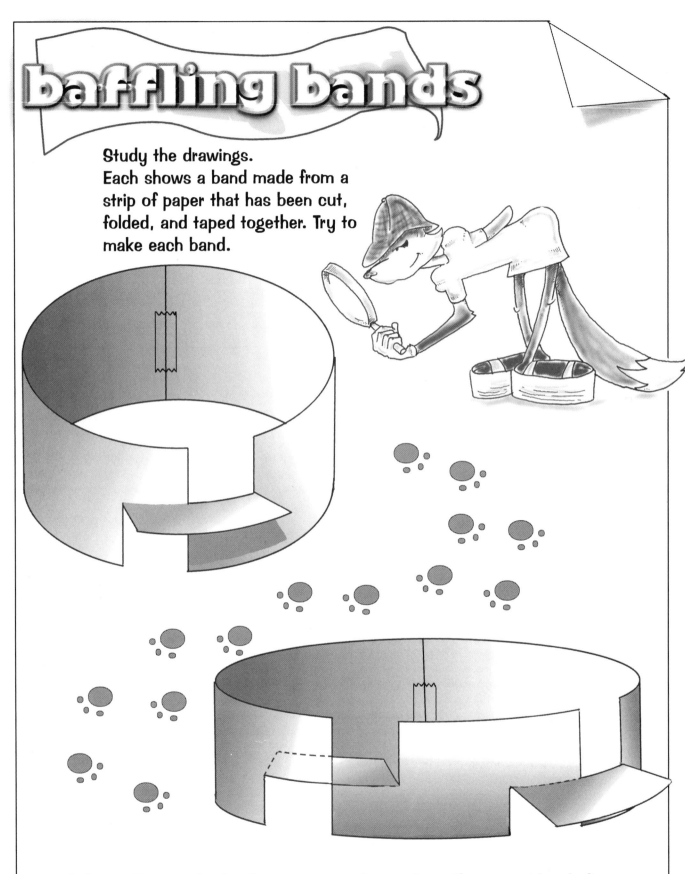

Extra Challenge: Try to make the above structures by starting with an uncut band of paper.

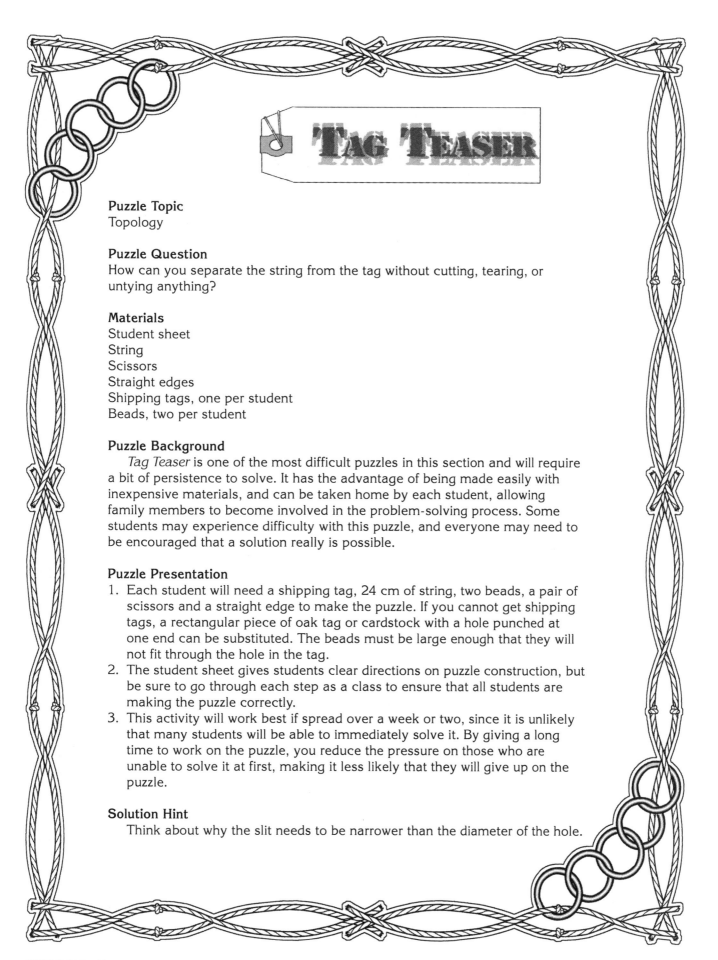

Tag Teaser

Puzzle Topic
Topology

Puzzle Question
How can you separate the string from the tag without cutting, tearing, or untying anything?

Materials
Student sheet
String
Scissors
Straight edges
Shipping tags, one per student
Beads, two per student

Puzzle Background
    Tag Teaser is one of the most difficult puzzles in this section and will require a bit of persistence to solve. It has the advantage of being made easily with inexpensive materials, and can be taken home by each student, allowing family members to become involved in the problem-solving process. Some students may experience difficulty with this puzzle, and everyone may need to be encouraged that a solution really is possible.

Puzzle Presentation
1. Each student will need a shipping tag, 24 cm of string, two beads, a pair of scissors and a straight edge to make the puzzle. If you cannot get shipping tags, a rectangular piece of oak tag or cardstock with a hole punched at one end can be substituted. The beads must be large enough that they will not fit through the hole in the tag.
2. The student sheet gives students clear directions on puzzle construction, but be sure to go through each step as a class to ensure that all students are making the puzzle correctly.
3. This activity will work best if spread over a week or two, since it is unlikely that many students will be able to immediately solve it. By giving a long time to work on the puzzle, you reduce the pressure on those who are unable to solve it at first, making it less likely that they will give up on the puzzle.

Solution Hint
    Think about why the slit needs to be narrower than the diameter of the hole.

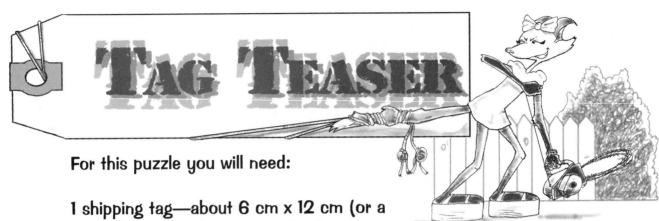

Tag Teaser

For this puzzle you will need:

1 shipping tag—about 6 cm x 12 cm (or a similar rectangle cut out of oak tag)
24 cm piece of string
2 beads, each larger than the hole in the tag
scissors
ruler or other straight edge

To make the puzzle,
1. Fold the tag in half vertically.
2. Place the ruler as shown, parallel to the edge of the tag so that you can see the top of the hole. Draw a line here,
starting about 1 cm from the hole and going all the way to the fold.

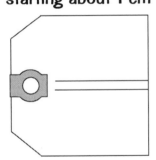

3. Move the ruler down until it is just above the bottom of the hole. Draw a second line parallel to the first. Be sure the distance between the lines is less than the diameter of the hole (see diagram to the left).
4. Starting at the fold, cut along both lines. Be sure you do not cut into the hole.

5. Unfold the tag. Thread one end of the string down through the hole, up through one of the slits, over the strip between the slits, down through the other slit, and back up through the hole.
6. Pull the ends of the string so that they are even. Tie a bead to each end of the string. (Make sure that you cannot pass the bead through the hole in the tag.)

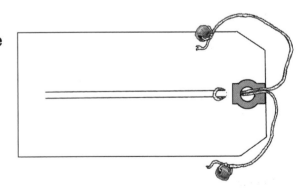

Now the puzzle is ready to be solved. All you have to do is separate the string from the tag without removing the beads, cutting the string, or tearing the tag.

Bridge Crossing Challenge

One possible solution is shown for each puzzle. In each case, there is more than one correct solution.

Puzzle One

Puzzle Two

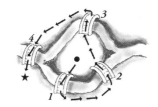

Puzzle Three

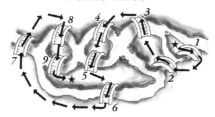

Puzzle Four: Impossible

Navigating Networks

The networks which can be traveled are shown below with one possible path indicated by arrows. The first arrow is darker than the rest. Each is marked with a starting and ending point. In every case, more than one solution is possible. Numbers three, five, and six cannot be traced.

1.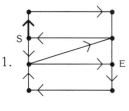

2.

4.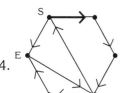

7.

3.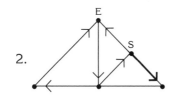

Stringing the Ring

The way this puzzle works can be easily seen by doing it slowly. As the ring falls, it rotates, causing the chain to loop around it and form a knot. The real trick here is how to get the chain to consistently knot itself around the ring. Only one method will be described here, there are several that will work equally well with enough practice.

Place the ring around the loop of chain. Be sure that the fingers that are holding the ring are at right angles to the fingers holding the loop of chain. As you hold the ring, let one edge rest on the top of your index finger, and support the opposite edge with your thumb. Let go of the ring by moving only your thumb, or only your index finger. This causes the ring to rotate just the right amount to tie itself up in the loop. With practice, this technique should work every time.

Rings 'n' Strings

To remove the ring

Take the end of the loop that goes through the ring and spread it apart. Slip the ring through this opening in the string. The ring should now be able to slip off the string.

To replace the ring

Slip the ring around the string. Pull the end of the string wide and slip the ring through this opening. The ring should now be knotted on the string.

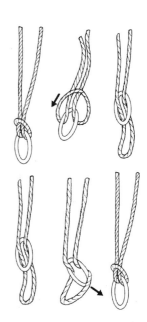

A Knotty Puzzle

Before you pick up the piece of string, cross your arms. Pick up one end of the yarn with the hand on top of your arm, and the other end with the hand under your arm. When you uncross your arms (while still holding the string) you will create an overhand knot in the middle of the piece of string.

Möbius Mysteries

In order to understand what is happening with the two strips of paper, it is important to examine how they are taped together. Before the two strips are twisted and taped together, they are placed one on top of the other. Each strip in the beginning configuration has a left and right end. (It might help to label these ends beforehand: TL, TR, BL, & BR.) When the strips are given a half twist and their ends joined, the right end of the top strip ends up being taped to the left end of the bottom strip. Likewise, the left end of the top strip ends up being taped to the right end of the bottom strip. In this way the finished product appears to be two separate Möbius loops nested within each other when in actuality they form one large loop with two half twists. This means that when a pencil is inserted between the two pieces of paper, it must travel twice around the loop to return to its original orientation.

The Great Escape

To remove the string

Take the loop which you initially created by folding the string in half and push it through the hole between the fox's feet. Once it is through the hole, push the penny through the loop. At this point, you can pull the string and it will come off the fox.

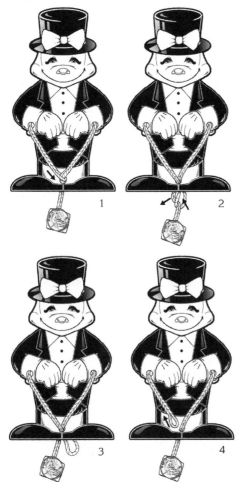

To return the string

Place the loop up through the hole between the feet, down through one of the holes by the hands, and up through the other hole by the hands. Put the loop through the hole between the feet again, and push the penny through the loop, just as you did to remove it. When the loop is pulled back up through the bottom hole, the puzzle will be reassembled as it was originally.

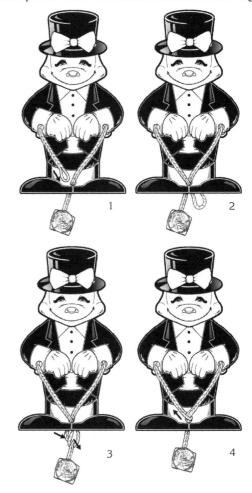

Tangled Hearts

Step 1: Take the loop in the end of the string and place it through one of the holes at the top of the heart.

Step 2: Slip the penny through the loop and pull the loop back through the hole.

Step 3: Slip the loop through the other hole at the top of the heart. Slip the penny through the loop.

Step 4: Pull the loop back through the hole. You should now be able to remove the small heart.

To replace the small heart, simply repeat these steps in reverse.

Linking Loops

Step 1: Take your string and slip it through the bottom part of the loop on one of your partner's wrists. Be sure to come from behind, slipping the string through towards your partner's fingers.

Step 2: Have your partner place his or her hand through the loop created by your string so that your string is resting on the top of his or her hand.

Step 3: Pull your string out of your partner's loop. If you have done it properly, you should now be disentangled.

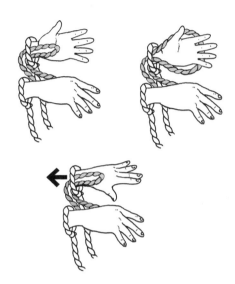

The Perplexing Pencil Puzzle

To solve this puzzle, you must reverse the process you used to attach the pencil, and loop to the buttonhole. To do this, loosen the knot so that the loop surrounds the buttonhole. Pull the material around the buttonhole up through the loop so that the material is several centimeters above the loop. Next, poke the eraser end of the pencil through the buttonhole. Once the pencil is through the buttonhole, pull on it from below and it should come out quite easily. If there is not enough slack in the string to free the pencil, pull more material up through the loop and try again.

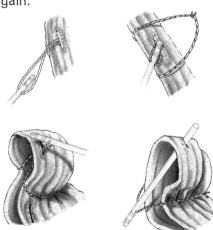

Cut and Fold Challenge

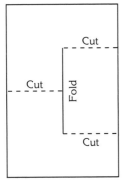

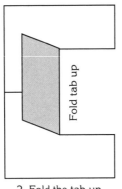

1. Cut the paper as indicated by the dashed lines.

2. Fold the tab up as indicated.

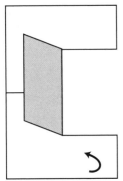

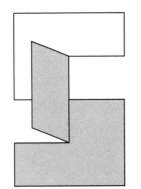

3. Rotate the bottom right corner 180°.

4. This is your completed hypersquare.

Baffling Bands
Band One

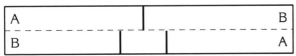

The strip of paper is cut in three places as shown. The paper is then twisted and joined together so that the letters match up A to A and B to B. Depending on the way the paper is twisted, the band will look like the picture on the student page, or its mirror image.

Band Two

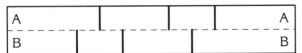

The strip of paper is cut with two sets of cuts instead of one. The sets of cuts can be made opposite of each other, as shown, or both oriented the same way. The paper is twisted two times so that the letters match up. Again, depending on how the paper is twisted, the band will be like the picture, or its mirror image.

Extra Challenge
Band One

To create the first band starting with an uncut loop of paper, simply tape the band together with a twist already in it. Make the cuts as you would in the original challenge, and the strip will untwist itself to form the band.

Band Two

Tape the loop of paper together and make the same cuts as in the original challenge. Twist the section between the top far left cut and the bottom far right cut. This will create the second band. (You may need to crease the band in places before twisting.)

Tag Teaser

The secret to solving *Tag Teaser* is to use the narrow strip cut in the tag. Since this strip is cut narrower than the hole in the tag, it can be maneuvered through the hole. When this is done, the string and beads are easily removed by pulling them through the loop created by the strip. This process can be reversed to put the puzzle back together.

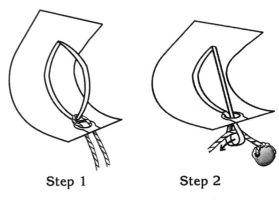

Step 1   **Step 2**

Step 3

Logical Thinking Problems
Introduction

Although logic is an important topic in mathematics, it is often avoided by teachers and textbooks alike. This section seeks to remedy this omission and build students' skills and confidence in the area of logic.

Logical reasoning is an essential skill, not only in mathematics, but in all areas of life. Students unconsciously use inductive and deductive reasoning on a daily basis as they consider the likelihood of events occurring based on past experience or form a general conclusion from specific examples. The activities in this section will help students develop those skills and think more clearly about using them in appropriate situations.

There are several different types of logic problems in this section. Some are paradoxical in nature and seem impossible until the flaw in the line of thought is discovered. Others belong to the classic category of puzzles which involve getting people or items across a river or divide with certain restrictions. Many of the puzzles are solved more easily with the use of manipulatives, therefore you may want to make them available for students.

As with the other sections, we have attempted to arrange the puzzles in order of difficulty. However, this order can be followed loosely, as some students may find the later problems easier than the earlier ones.

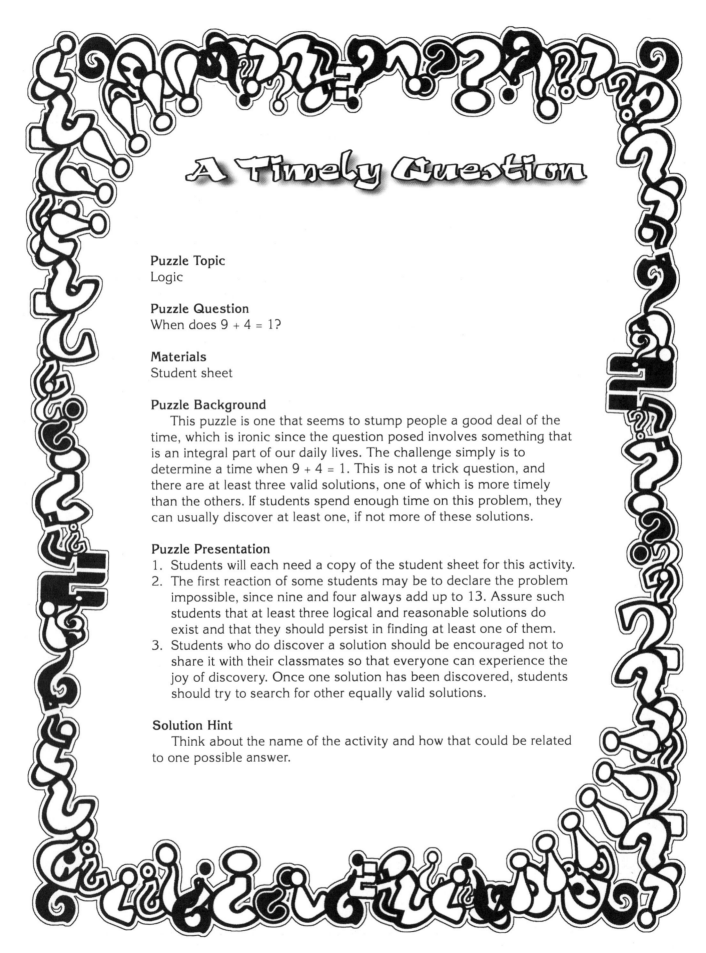

A Timely Question

Puzzle Topic
Logic

Puzzle Question
When does 9 + 4 = 1?

Materials
Student sheet

Puzzle Background
This puzzle is one that seems to stump people a good deal of the time, which is ironic since the question posed involves something that is an integral part of our daily lives. The challenge simply is to determine a time when 9 + 4 = 1. This is not a trick question, and there are at least three valid solutions, one of which is more timely than the others. If students spend enough time on this problem, they can usually discover at least one, if not more of these solutions.

Puzzle Presentation
1. Students will each need a copy of the student sheet for this activity.
2. The first reaction of some students may be to declare the problem impossible, since nine and four always add up to 13. Assure such students that at least three logical and reasonable solutions do exist and that they should persist in finding at least one of them.
3. Students who do discover a solution should be encouraged not to share it with their classmates so that everyone can experience the joy of discovery. Once one solution has been discovered, students should try to search for other equally valid solutions.

Solution Hint
Think about the name of the activity and how that could be related to one possible answer.

A Timely Question

The challenge in this activity is to find at least one reasonable answer to the question below. This is not a trick question—there are at least two simple, logical answers. If you spend some time thinking about this question, you should be able to come up with one or more solutions. Use the space on the chalkboard to explain your answer(s). Have a good time!

WHEN DOES 9 + 4 = 1 ?

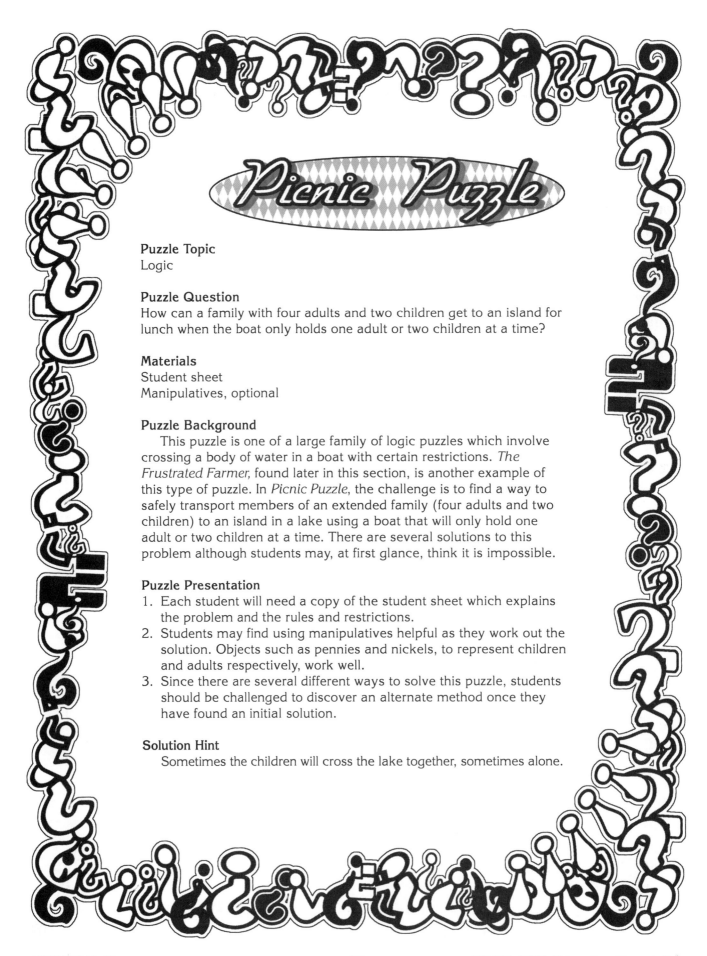

Picnic Puzzle

Puzzle Topic
Logic

Puzzle Question
How can a family with four adults and two children get to an island for lunch when the boat only holds one adult or two children at a time?

Materials
Student sheet
Manipulatives, optional

Puzzle Background
This puzzle is one of a large family of logic puzzles which involve crossing a body of water in a boat with certain restrictions. *The Frustrated Farmer,* found later in this section, is another example of this type of puzzle. In *Picnic Puzzle,* the challenge is to find a way to safely transport members of an extended family (four adults and two children) to an island in a lake using a boat that will only hold one adult or two children at a time. There are several solutions to this problem although students may, at first glance, think it is impossible.

Puzzle Presentation
1. Each student will need a copy of the student sheet which explains the problem and the rules and restrictions.
2. Students may find using manipulatives helpful as they work out the solution. Objects such as pennies and nickels, to represent children and adults respectively, work well.
3. Since there are several different ways to solve this puzzle, students should be challenged to discover an alternate method once they have found an initial solution.

Solution Hint
Sometimes the children will cross the lake together, sometimes alone.

Picnic Puzzle

While hiking in the woods, a family (grandma, grandpa, mom, dad, and two school-aged children) comes to a small lake. In the middle of the lake is a beautiful island that would be the perfect place for their picnic. On the shore nearby is a boat with one paddle. Next to the boat is a sign that says visitors are welcome to use the boat if they return it to the same spot when they are through using it. The boat, however, is so small that it can only hold one adult or two children at a time. Is there a way that the family can use the boat to get everyone to the island for their picnic? Show how this could be done using words and/or pictures.

The Frustrated Farmer

Puzzle Topic
Logic

Puzzle Question
How can a farmer get a cat, a mouse, and a block of cheese safely across the river in a boat by taking only one thing across at a time?

Materials
Student sheets
Dowels or pencils, optional
Scrap lumber, optional
Butcher paper, optional

Puzzle Background
   This is one of a family of puzzles which has been around for many years and has varying degrees of difficulty. These puzzles usually have three common characteristics. First, they all involve getting something across a river (or pond) in a boat. Second, one or more of the things in each puzzle is in danger of being eaten if the puzzle-solver is careless enough to leave it in the wrong company. Lastly, the puzzles are intended to be done as thought problems, without any manipulatives. By modifying this last characteristic however, the problem becomes much easier to solve and can even be done by younger students.
   In this particular puzzle, a farmer must transport a cat, a mouse, and a block of cheese across a river in a row boat. She can only take one thing in the boat with her at a time. If the cat is left alone with the mouse (on either side of the river), it will eat the mouse. Likewise, if the mouse is left alone with the block of cheese, it will eat the cheese. Students must determine a way to get the cat, the mouse, and the cheese across the river safely.

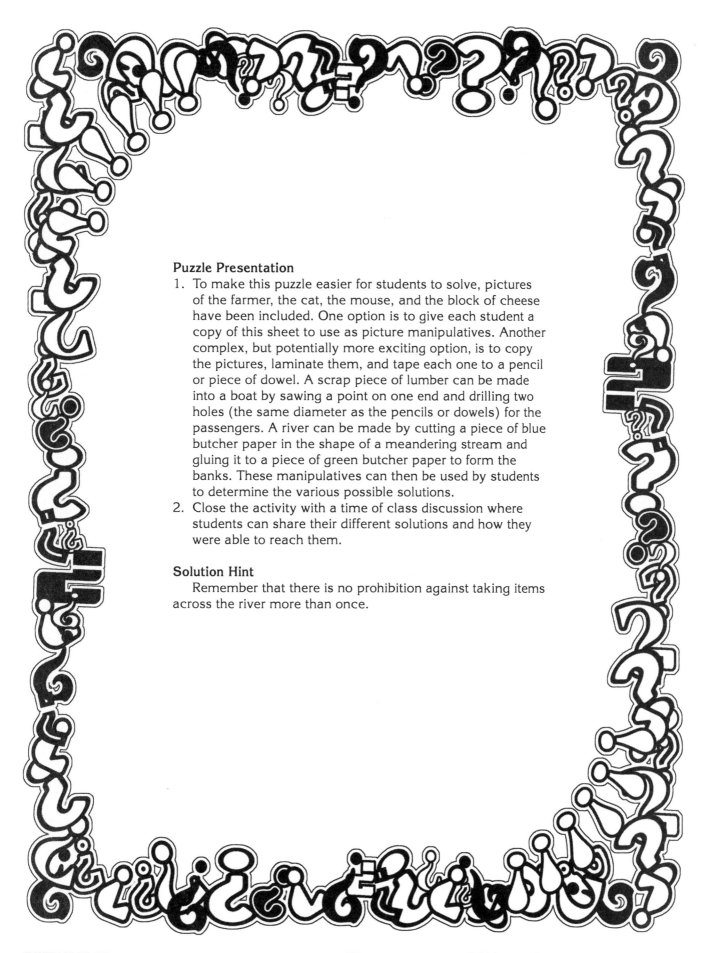

Puzzle Presentation

1. To make this puzzle easier for students to solve, pictures of the farmer, the cat, the mouse, and the block of cheese have been included. One option is to give each student a copy of this sheet to use as picture manipulatives. Another complex, but potentially more exciting option, is to copy the pictures, laminate them, and tape each one to a pencil or piece of dowel. A scrap piece of lumber can be made into a boat by sawing a point on one end and drilling two holes (the same diameter as the pencils or dowels) for the passengers. A river can be made by cutting a piece of blue butcher paper in the shape of a meandering stream and gluing it to a piece of green butcher paper to form the banks. These manipulatives can then be used by students to determine the various possible solutions.

2. Close the activity with a time of class discussion where students can share their different solutions and how they were able to reach them.

Solution Hint

Remember that there is no prohibition against taking items across the river more than once.

The Frustrated Farmer

In this puzzle you must help a farmer get a cat, a mouse, and a block of cheese safely across a river in a boat. The farmer may only take one thing at a time in the boat. She cannot leave the cat and the mouse together on either side of the river, or the cat will eat the mouse. Likewise, she cannot leave the mouse alone with the block of cheese, or the mouse will eat the cheese. How can the farmer get everything across the river without anything being eaten?

Use the space below to show how you helped the farmer solve her problem. You may use pictures and/or words.

The Frustrated Farmer

A Royal Riddle

Puzzle Topic
Logic

Puzzle Question
How can you get each royal couple across the gorge without leaving any prince alone with a princess who is not his own?

Materials
Student sheet
Manipulatives, optional

Puzzle Background
This puzzle is an adaptation of a classic logic puzzle that has been around for many years. In the original puzzle, three couples are trying to cross a river in a boat which only holds two people at a time. Each wife has an objection to her husband being alone with any other woman in the boat or on either side of the river. The challenge is to get all six people across the river without violating the wishes of the wives. In our modified version the challenge is the same, but the story is told in a slightly different way. There is also the option of using manipulatives to make the task easier for students.

Puzzle Presentation
1. Each student will need a copy of the student sheet for this activity.
2. If your students need the aid of manipulatives you can have them cut out the figures on the second student sheet or create manipulatives of their own design.

Solution Hint
The same person may need to cross the gorge several times.

A Royal Riddle

Snow White, Sleeping Beauty, Cinderella, and their respective Prince Charmings were taking a walk together through the enchanted forest. They came to a place where a deep gorge blocked their path back to the palace. The only way to cross the gorge was on a rope that could hold up to two people at a time. The gorge was so wide that the rope could not be swung back across; someone had to ride it going both ways. The only problem was that each princess was unwilling to let her prince be alone with either of the other princesses on the rope swing or on either side of the gorge. How can they all make it across the gorge safely?

Describe your solution using words and/or pictures in the space below.

A Royal Riddle

Snow White's Prince Charming

Sleeping Beauty's Prince Charming

Cinderella's Prince Charming

Snow White

Sleeping Beauty

Cinderella

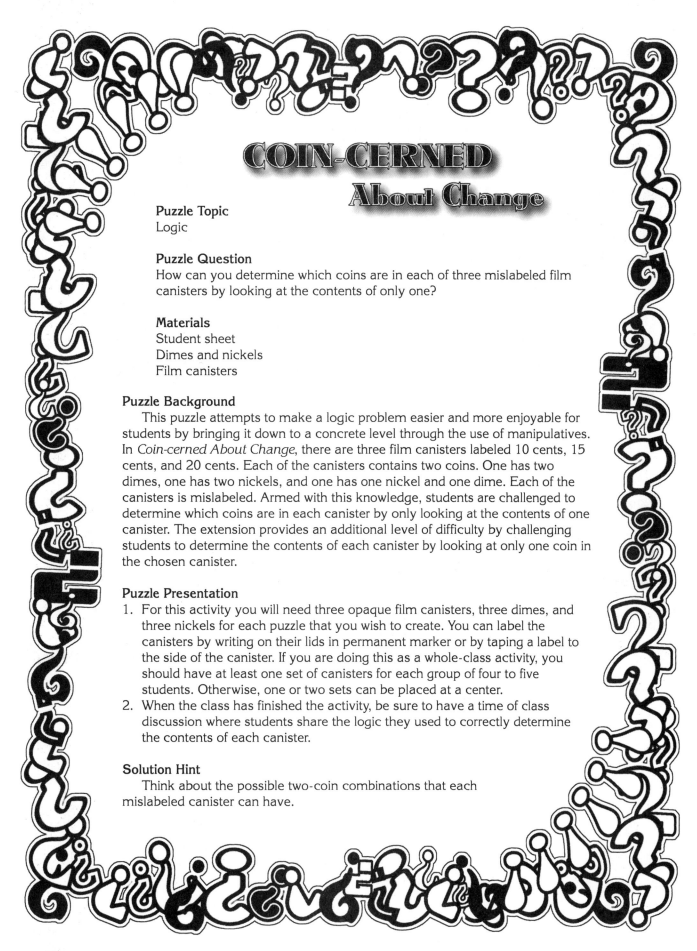

COIN-CERNED
About Change

Puzzle Topic
Logic

Puzzle Question
How can you determine which coins are in each of three mislabeled film canisters by looking at the contents of only one?

Materials
Student sheet
Dimes and nickels
Film canisters

Puzzle Background

This puzzle attempts to make a logic problem easier and more enjoyable for students by bringing it down to a concrete level through the use of manipulatives. In *Coin-cerned About Change*, there are three film canisters labeled 10 cents, 15 cents, and 20 cents. Each of the canisters contains two coins. One has two dimes, one has two nickels, and one has one nickel and one dime. Each of the canisters is mislabeled. Armed with this knowledge, students are challenged to determine which coins are in each canister by only looking at the contents of one canister. The extension provides an additional level of difficulty by challenging students to determine the contents of each canister by looking at only one coin in the chosen canister.

Puzzle Presentation

1. For this activity you will need three opaque film canisters, three dimes, and three nickels for each puzzle that you wish to create. You can label the canisters by writing on their lids in permanent marker or by taping a label to the side of the canister. If you are doing this as a whole-class activity, you should have at least one set of canisters for each group of four to five students. Otherwise, one or two sets can be placed at a center.
2. When the class has finished the activity, be sure to have a time of class discussion where students share the logic they used to correctly determine the contents of each canister.

Solution Hint

Think about the possible two-coin combinations that each mislabeled canister can have.

COIN-CERNED About Change

One of the three canisters you have contains two nickels, one contains two dimes, and one contains one nickel and one dime. Each canister has been labeled incorrectly. The challenge is to determine what each canister holds by examining the contents of only one. Explain in words and/or pictures how you would do this.

Extra challenge: Try to find a way to correctly determine what coins are in each canister by looking at only one coin from one canister. How would you do this?

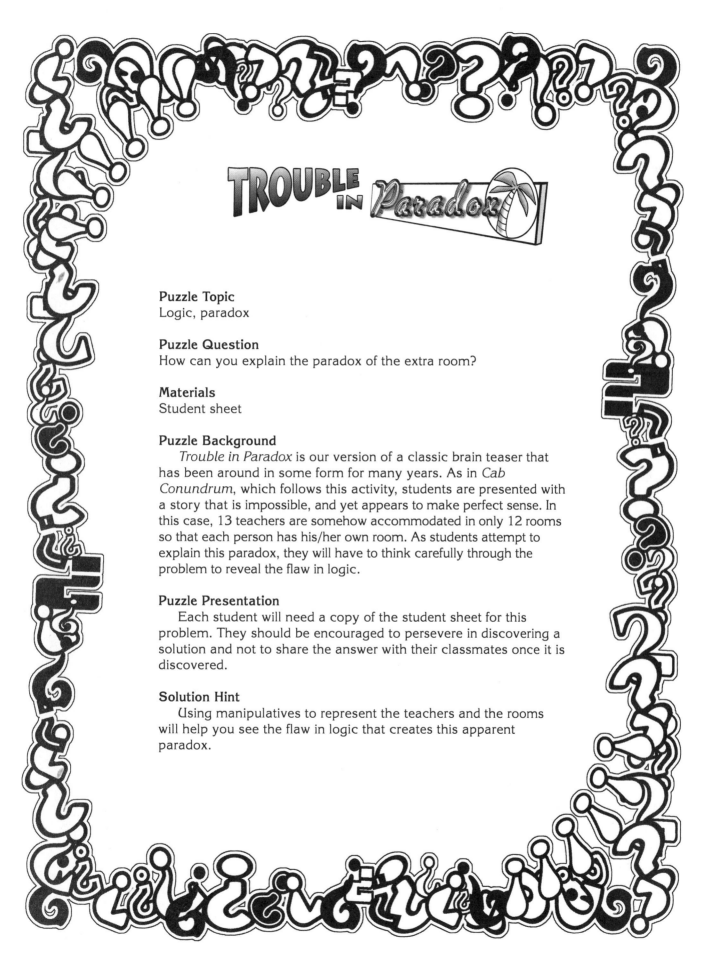

TROUBLE IN Paradox

Puzzle Topic
Logic, paradox

Puzzle Question
How can you explain the paradox of the extra room?

Materials
Student sheet

Puzzle Background
   Trouble in Paradox is our version of a classic brain teaser that has been around in some form for many years. As in *Cab Conundrum*, which follows this activity, students are presented with a story that is impossible, and yet appears to make perfect sense. In this case, 13 teachers are somehow accommodated in only 12 rooms so that each person has his/her own room. As students attempt to explain this paradox, they will have to think carefully through the problem to reveal the flaw in logic.

Puzzle Presentation
   Each student will need a copy of the student sheet for this problem. They should be encouraged to persevere in discovering a solution and not to share the answer with their classmates once it is discovered.

Solution Hint
   Using manipulatives to represent the teachers and the rooms will help you see the flaw in logic that creates this apparent paradox.

TROUBLE IN Paradox

Thirteen teachers are in Paradox, New York attending a math conference. When they arrive at the Enigma Hotel to check in, they are told that only 12 rooms are available. Since their school had made reservations for 13 rooms, the teachers are a bit upset that they will have to find another place to stay. As they are preparing to leave and find another hotel, the manager comes out and asks if there is a problem. When she hears of their situation she assures them that the Enigma Hotel has enough space to accommodate each teacher in his or her own room. She takes two of the teachers to room #1 and promises to come back in a few minutes and take one of them to another room. She takes the third teacher to room #2, the fourth teacher to room #3, the fifth teacher to room #4 and so on, taking the twelfth teacher to room #11. She then returns to room #1 and escorts the extra teacher waiting there to room #12. All of the teachers are now happily settled in their own rooms. Is this possible? Why or why not?

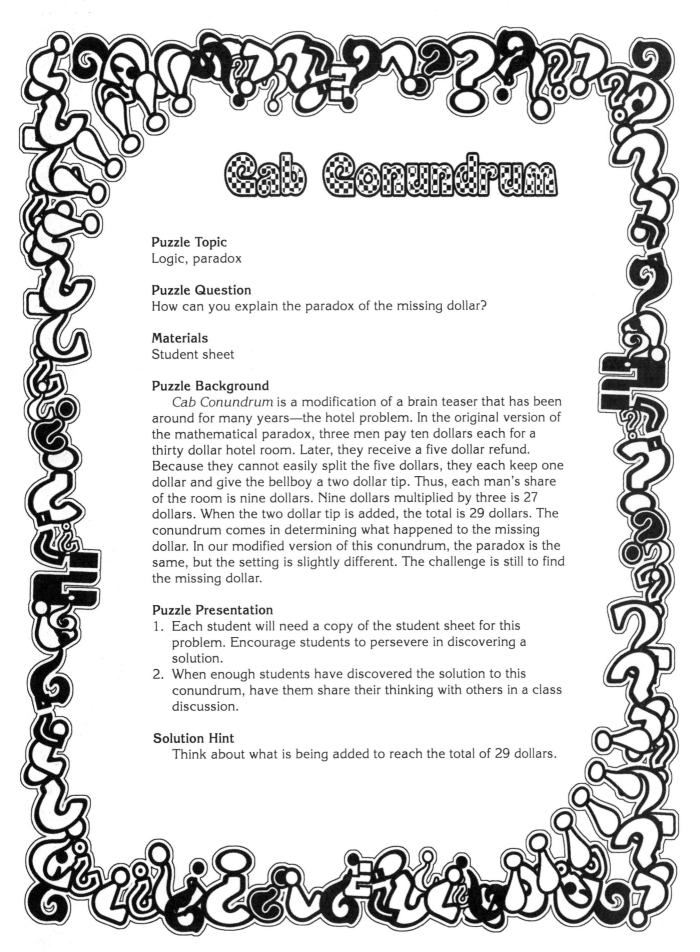

Cab Conundrum

Puzzle Topic
Logic, paradox

Puzzle Question
How can you explain the paradox of the missing dollar?

Materials
Student sheet

Puzzle Background
    Cab Conundrum is a modification of a brain teaser that has been around for many years—the hotel problem. In the original version of the mathematical paradox, three men pay ten dollars each for a thirty dollar hotel room. Later, they receive a five dollar refund. Because they cannot easily split the five dollars, they each keep one dollar and give the bellboy a two dollar tip. Thus, each man's share of the room is nine dollars. Nine dollars multiplied by three is 27 dollars. When the two dollar tip is added, the total is 29 dollars. The conundrum comes in determining what happened to the missing dollar. In our modified version of this conundrum, the paradox is the same, but the setting is slightly different. The challenge is still to find the missing dollar.

Puzzle Presentation
1. Each student will need a copy of the student sheet for this problem. Encourage students to persevere in discovering a solution.
2. When enough students have discovered the solution to this conundrum, have them share their thinking with others in a class discussion.

Solution Hint
    Think about what is being added to reach the total of 29 dollars.

Cab Conundrum

Three men agree to share a cab from the airport into town. When they arrive, the meter reads $25. Each man gives the driver a $10 bill. She hands them five $1 bills as change. Each man takes one of the $1 bills. They give the driver the remaining two $1 bills as a tip.

Each man has now spent nine dollars, and the driver has two dollars, bringing the total to $29 ($3 \times 9 = 27$, $27 + 2 = 29$). What happened to the other dollar?

Your challenge is to explain this paradox.

LOGICAL THINKING PUZZLE SOLUTIONS

A Timely Question

There are a few very common instances when $9 + 4 = 1$. One is on a clock. Nine o'clock plus four hours equals one o'clock. Another is in a calendar year. September (9) plus four months (4) equals January (1). A third possible solution is that nine plus four equals one baker's dozen. Your students may come up with other creative and equally valid responses to this question.

Picnic Puzzle

One of the several possible solutions is described below. In order to get the family off of the island, the same steps can be followed by reversing the island and the shore.

1. Both children get in the boat and row to the island. One child stays on the island, and the other one rows the boat back to shore.
2. The father rows the boat to the island, and the child that was on the island rows back to shore.
3. Both children get back in the boat and row to the island. Again, one stays and the other rows the boat back to shore.
4. The mother rows the boat to the island, and the child that was on the island rows back to shore.
5. Both children get in the boat and row to the island. One child stays on the island, and the other rows the boat back to shore.
6. The grandmother gets in the boat and rows to the island. The child that was on the island rows the boat back to shore.
7. Both children once again get into the boat and row to the island. One child stays on the island, the other rows the boat back to shore.
8. The grandfather gets in and rows the boat to the island. The child that was on the island rows back to shore.
9. The child that was on shore gets back into the boat, and they both row across the lake to their family on the island—very hungry for lunch after all that rowing!

The Frustrated Farmer

There are few different solutions to this problem, depending on which order the cat and the cheese are taken across. One possible solution is described here. Assuming that the farmer is starting on the left bank of the river, follow these steps:

1. Take the mouse across to the right bank, leaving the cat and the cheese on the left bank.
2. Return to the left bank and take the cheese across to the right bank, leaving the cat on the left bank.
3. Leave the cheese on the right bank, but take the mouse back across to the left bank.
4. Take the cat across to the right bank, leaving the mouse on the left bank.
5. Return for the mouse and take it across to the right bank. Now the farmer, the cat, the mouse, and the cheese are all on the right bank of the river.

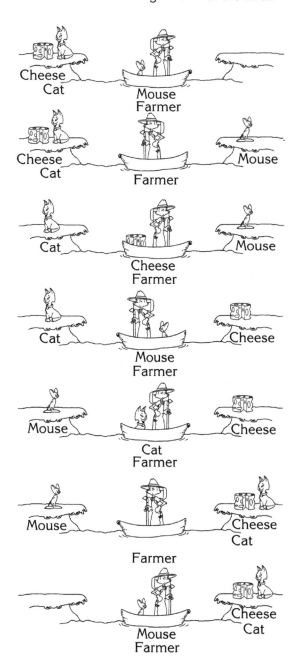

A Royal Riddle

There are many possible solutions to this problem. Only one possibility is presented here.

        SW = Snow White
     PCSW = Snow White's Prince Charming
        SB = Sleeping Beauty
     PCSB = Sleeping Beauty's Prince Charming
         C = Cinderella
      PCC = Cinderella's Prince Charming

1. SW and PCSW swing across. PCSW swings back.
2. SB and PCSB swing across. PCSB swings back.
3. C and PCC swing across. PCC swings back.
4. PCC and PCSB swing across. PCSB swings back.
5. PCSB and PCSW swing across. All of the couples are safely across.

Coin-cerned about Change

The logic for the original problem is as follows:

When you look at the contents of one canister, you can follow a process of elimination to identify the contents of the other two canisters. This is possible because each canister is mislabeled, which means that only two of the three possible coin combinations can be inside a given canister. For example, two dimes could be in either the canister labeled *15 cents*, or the canister labeled *10 cents*. Likewise two nickels could be in the *15 cents* or *20 cents* containers, and a dime and a nickel could be in either the *10 cents* or *20 cents* containers. The table below shows the different canisters and their possible contents.

Canister	Possible Contents	
10 cents	one nickel, one dime	two dimes
15 cents	two nickels	two dimes
20 cents	two nickels	one nickel, one dime

When you open a canister and look at its contents, you eliminate the combination you discover from the other canister where it could have occurred. For example, if you discover two dimes in the *15 cents* canister, you know that that combination cannot occur in the *10 cents* canister.

Canister	Possible Contents	
10 cents	one nickel, one dime	two dimes
15 cents	two nickels	two dimes
20 cents	two nickels	one nickel, one dime

From there it follows that since one nickel and one dime is the only possible combination for the *10 cents* canister, it cannot be in the *20 cents* canister.

Canister	Possible Contents	
10 cents	one nickel, one dime	two dimes
15 cents	two nickels	two dimes
20 cents	two nickels	one nickel, one dime

This process of elimination leads you to the conclusion that the *10 cents* canister contains one nickel and one dime, the *15 cents* canister contains two dimes, and the *20 cents* canister contains two nickels. Regardless of which canister you start with or what combination you see, this same process will work.

Canister	Possible Contents	
10 cents	one nickel, one dime	two dimes
15 cents	two nickels	two dimes
20 cents	two nickels	one nickel, one dime

Extension

When you can only look at one of the coins in one of the containers, the logic changes slightly from that explained above.

When you can only look at one coin, you *must* look at one of the coins in the *15 cents* canister because the only possibilities for this canister are two nickels or two dimes. This lets you be sure which combination you are seeing by only looking at one coin. If you see a dime, you know that you are seeing part of the two dimes combination, therefore the canister labeled *10 cents* must contain one nickel and one dime. It then follows that the canister labeled *20 cents* contains two nickels. If you see a nickel, you know that you are seeing part of the two nickels combination, therefore the canister labeled *20 cents* must contain one nickel and one dime. It then follows that the canister labeled *10 cents* contains two dimes.

If you chose either the *10 cents* or *20 cents* canister when you can only look at one coin, you cannot always be sure which combination it contains. If you look at the *10 cents* canister and see a dime, you could be seeing part of the two dimes combination, or part of the one nickel, one dime combination. Likewise, if you look at the *20 cents* canister and see a nickel, you could be seeing part of the two nickels combination, or a part of the one nickel, one dime combination.

Trouble in Paradox

The reason this paradox seems to work is that it makes you forget about one of the 13 teachers. When the manager puts the twelfth teacher in room #11 there is still one more teacher waiting for a room. However, the phrasing makes you think that the thirteenth teacher is waiting in the first room, when it is actually the second teacher. The paradox is illustrated in the diagram below.

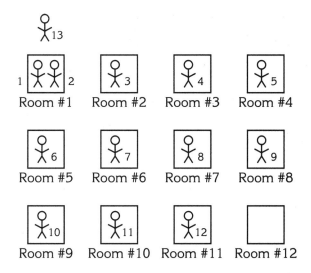

Cab Conundrum

To explain this paradox, you need only to add up the amounts. The fare was $25, the tip was two dollars, and each man kept one dollar. This adds up to $30. The error in reasoning is caused by the sentence that says, "Each man has now spent nine dollars and the driver has two dollars for a total of $29." Actually the first part of this sentence is correct—each man does spend nine dollars, since the total cost of the cab ride is $27 (the $25 fare and the $2 tip). The error comes in the second part of the sentence. What needs to be added to this 27 dollars is the three dollars that the men keep, not the two dollar tip—the tip was accounted for in the cost of the ride.

Dissection Puzzles
Introduction

Dissection puzzles are geometric in nature and come in two general forms. One of these forms originated in China with a square dissection puzzle. This puzzle made its way to America and Europe early in the 19th century with the name *Chinese Puzzle Game*. This particular puzzle has maintained its popularity even in modern times. Somewhere along the way it picked up the name *tangram*. Many similar dissection puzzles were invented in the wake of the popular tangram. Each of these puzzles contains several geometric pieces that can be put together edge to edge, without overlapping, to form a number of interesting shapes. Ideally these puzzles should be run on cardstock for greater durability. Students can also be given envelopes in which to keep their puzzles while they are not working on them.

In the other form of dissection puzzles, which also has a rich historical tradition, the challenge is to start with a larger geometric shape and break it up into smaller (often congruent) shapes. This type of puzzle provides opportunities to build geometric concepts like similarity, congruence, perimeter, and area.

Since both types of dissection puzzles exercise students' spatial visualization abilities as they manipulate shapes and divide regions, they might prove frustrating at first. However, as students work with these puzzles they will gain experience and confidence. To keep students from getting too frustrated, an attempt has been made to organize this section so that the puzzles generally increase in difficulty as the section progresses.

SHAPE MAKERS

Puzzle Topic
Dissection

Puzzle Question
How can you rearrange the 12 puzzle pieces to make a square, a right triangle, a parallelogram, and a trapezoid?

Materials
Student sheets
Scissors

Puzzle Background

As the first activity in the section, *Shape Makers* is the easiest of the dissection puzzles in which a series of smaller shapes must be rearranged to form a larger shape. In this case, four squares and eight triangles must be reassembled to create a large square, a large triangle, a parallelogram, and a trapezoid. While the main challenge in *Shape Makers* is fairly simple, it has many possibilities for more challenging extensions.

The second student sheet provides some of these extensions, showing three additional irregular shapes which can be created using the 12 puzzle pieces. Once students discover how to make these shapes, they are challenged to create some shapes of their own and record them. These student-created shapes can be traded with classmates so that students can try to solve puzzles that their friends have created. This gives the students more ownership of the puzzle and an extra incentive to try and create a shape that will stump others in the class.

Puzzle Presentation

1. Each student will need a pair of scissors and a copy of the student sheets to complete this activity.
2. You may wish to provide students with scratch paper on which they can draw their own shapes to be made with the puzzle pieces. This will allow them to create many shapes and trade them easily with their classmates. (Be sure that students only draw the outline of the shape, not the individual pieces.)
3. If desired, set up a section of bulletin board on which students can post the shapes that they create. These shapes can be taken down and solved by other students as time permits.

Solution Hint

Don't forget that each triangular shape is equivalent to one half of each square shape.

81

SHAPE MAKERS

The squares and triangles that make up the rectangle below can be cut out and rearranged to form the four geometric shapes shown at the bottom of the page. Cut out the 12 pieces and reassemble them to form these four shapes. Make a record of each solution.

Square

Right Triangle

Parallelogram

Trapezoid

SHAPE MAKERS

Once you have solved the puzzle and made the four regular geometric shapes, try to make the three irregular shapes below using the same pieces.

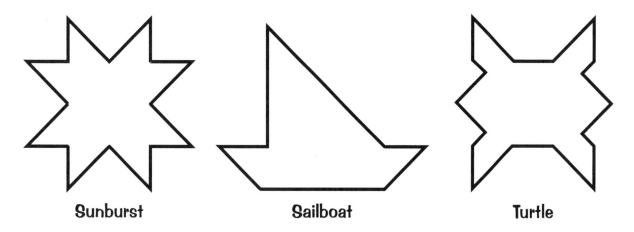

Sunburst   Sailboat   Turtle

Draw your solutions in the space below.

What other shapes can you make with your puzzle pieces? Draw pictures below of two more shapes you can create.

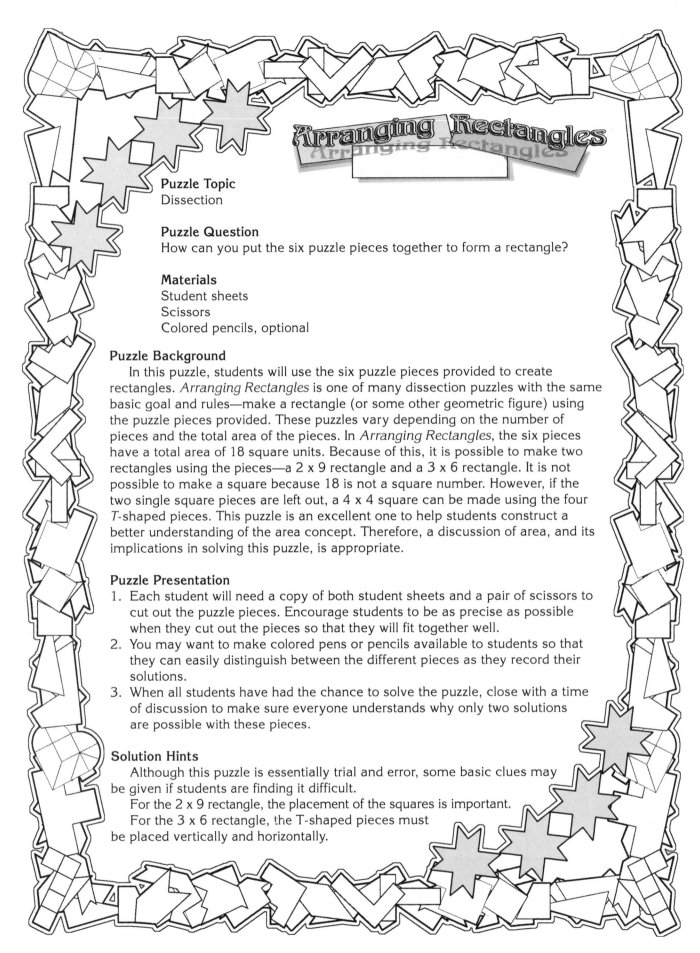

Arranging Rectangles

Puzzle Topic
Dissection

Puzzle Question
How can you put the six puzzle pieces together to form a rectangle?

Materials
Student sheets
Scissors
Colored pencils, optional

Puzzle Background

In this puzzle, students will use the six puzzle pieces provided to create rectangles. *Arranging Rectangles* is one of many dissection puzzles with the same basic goal and rules—make a rectangle (or some other geometric figure) using the puzzle pieces provided. These puzzles vary depending on the number of pieces and the total area of the pieces. In *Arranging Rectangles*, the six pieces have a total area of 18 square units. Because of this, it is possible to make two rectangles using the pieces—a 2 x 9 rectangle and a 3 x 6 rectangle. It is not possible to make a square because 18 is not a square number. However, if the two single square pieces are left out, a 4 x 4 square can be made using the four *T*-shaped pieces. This puzzle is an excellent one to help students construct a better understanding of the area concept. Therefore, a discussion of area, and its implications in solving this puzzle, is appropriate.

Puzzle Presentation

1. Each student will need a copy of both student sheets and a pair of scissors to cut out the puzzle pieces. Encourage students to be as precise as possible when they cut out the pieces so that they will fit together well.
2. You may want to make colored pens or pencils available to students so that they can easily distinguish between the different pieces as they record their solutions.
3. When all students have had the chance to solve the puzzle, close with a time of discussion to make sure everyone understands why only two solutions are possible with these pieces.

Solution Hints

Although this puzzle is essentially trial and error, some basic clues may be given if students are finding it difficult.

For the 2 x 9 rectangle, the placement of the squares is important.

For the 3 x 6 rectangle, the T-shaped pieces must be placed vertically and horizontally.

Arranging Rectangles

Cut out the six pieces below. Put them together to form a rectangle. See how many different rectangles you can make. Record each solution you find on the grid paper on the next page. When you have found all the solutions you can, answer the questions below the grid.

Arranging Rectangles

Record each solution you find in the grid below.

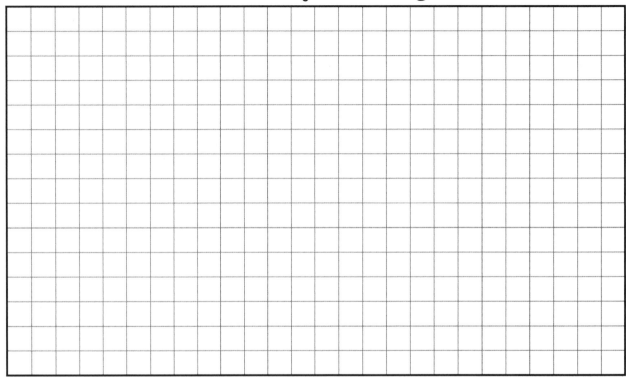

1. How many different rectangles did you discover?

2. Do you think you have found them all? Why or why not?

3. Is it possible to make a square using these pieces? Justify your answer.

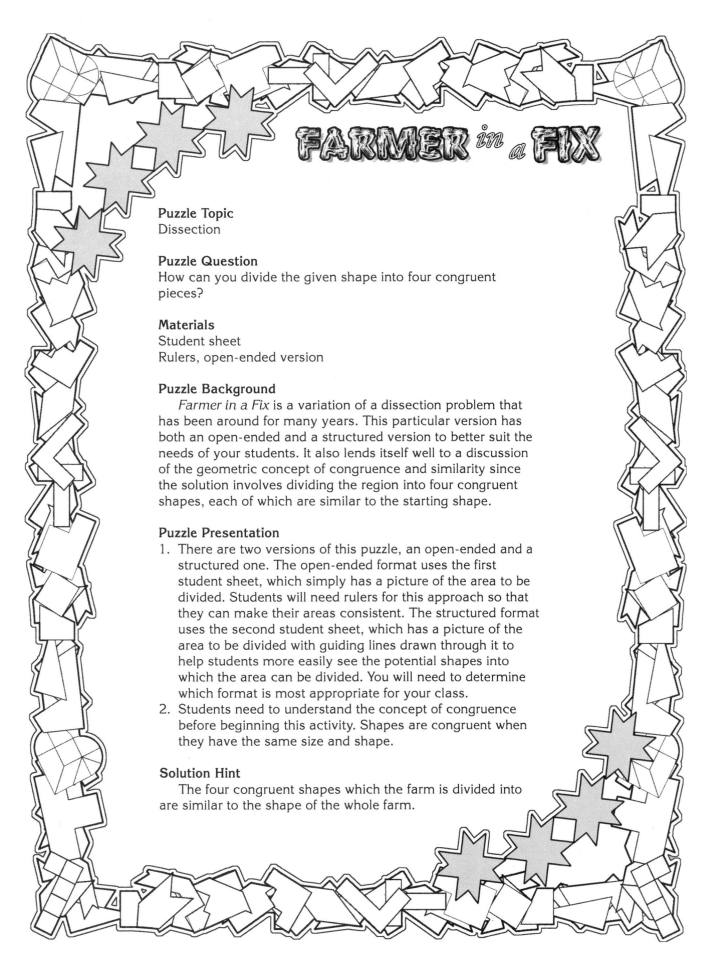

FARMER in a FIX

Puzzle Topic
Dissection

Puzzle Question
How can you divide the given shape into four congruent pieces?

Materials
Student sheet
Rulers, open-ended version

Puzzle Background
Farmer in a Fix is a variation of a dissection problem that has been around for many years. This particular version has both an open-ended and a structured version to better suit the needs of your students. It also lends itself well to a discussion of the geometric concept of congruence and similarity since the solution involves dividing the region into four congruent shapes, each of which are similar to the starting shape.

Puzzle Presentation
1. There are two versions of this puzzle, an open-ended and a structured one. The open-ended format uses the first student sheet, which simply has a picture of the area to be divided. Students will need rulers for this approach so that they can make their areas consistent. The structured format uses the second student sheet, which has a picture of the area to be divided with guiding lines drawn through it to help students more easily see the potential shapes into which the area can be divided. You will need to determine which format is most appropriate for your class.
2. Students need to understand the concept of congruence before beginning this activity. Shapes are congruent when they have the same size and shape.

Solution Hint
The four congruent shapes which the farm is divided into are similar to the shape of the whole farm.

FARMER in a FIX

Felicia is in a fix. She is ready to retire and turn over the farm to her four children. She wants to be as fair as possible to each child, so she decides to divide the farm into four congruent (equal size and shape) sections—one for each child. Help Felicia out of her fix by drawing in lines on the farm's outline below to divide it into four congruent pieces.

Felicia is in a fix. She is ready to retire and turn over the farm to her four children. She wants to be as fair as possible to each child, so she decides to divide the farm into four congruent (equal size and shape) sections—one for each child. Help Felicia out of her fix by showing her how to divide the farm into four congruent pieces using the outline shown below.

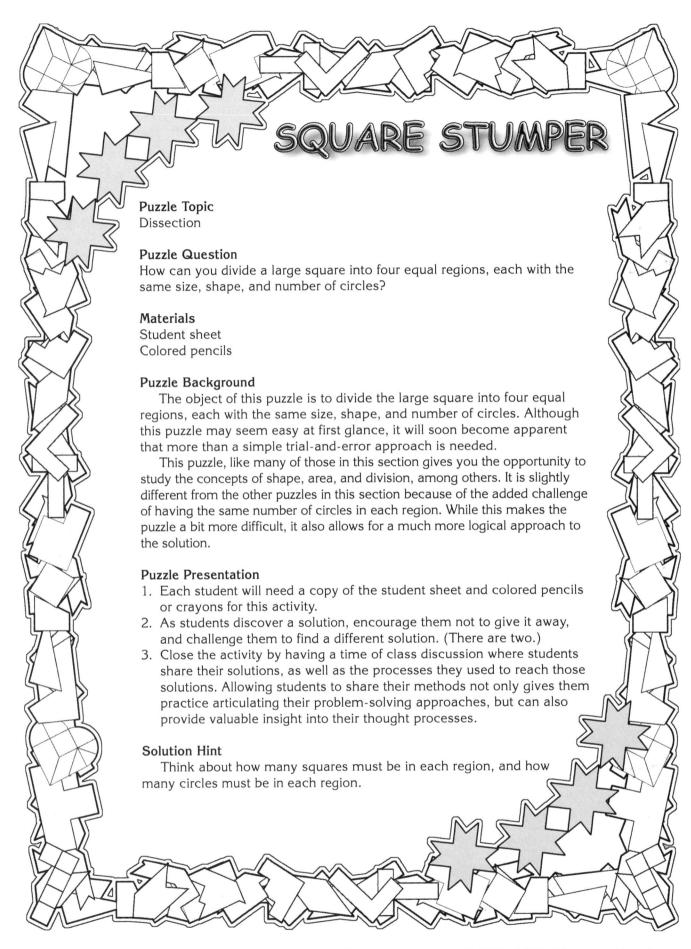

SQUARE STUMPER

Puzzle Topic
Dissection

Puzzle Question
How can you divide a large square into four equal regions, each with the same size, shape, and number of circles?

Materials
Student sheet
Colored pencils

Puzzle Background
   The object of this puzzle is to divide the large square into four equal regions, each with the same size, shape, and number of circles. Although this puzzle may seem easy at first glance, it will soon become apparent that more than a simple trial-and-error approach is needed.

   This puzzle, like many of those in this section gives you the opportunity to study the concepts of shape, area, and division, among others. It is slightly different from the other puzzles in this section because of the added challenge of having the same number of circles in each region. While this makes the puzzle a bit more difficult, it also allows for a much more logical approach to the solution.

Puzzle Presentation
1. Each student will need a copy of the student sheet and colored pencils or crayons for this activity.
2. As students discover a solution, encourage them not to give it away, and challenge them to find a different solution. (There are two.)
3. Close the activity by having a time of class discussion where students share their solutions, as well as the processes they used to reach those solutions. Allowing students to share their methods not only gives them practice articulating their problem-solving approaches, but can also provide valuable insight into their thought processes.

Solution Hint
   Think about how many squares must be in each region, and how many circles must be in each region.

SQUARE STUMPER

The square below can be divided into four equal regions, each with the same size, shape, and number of circles. Identify the four regions by coloring each one differently.

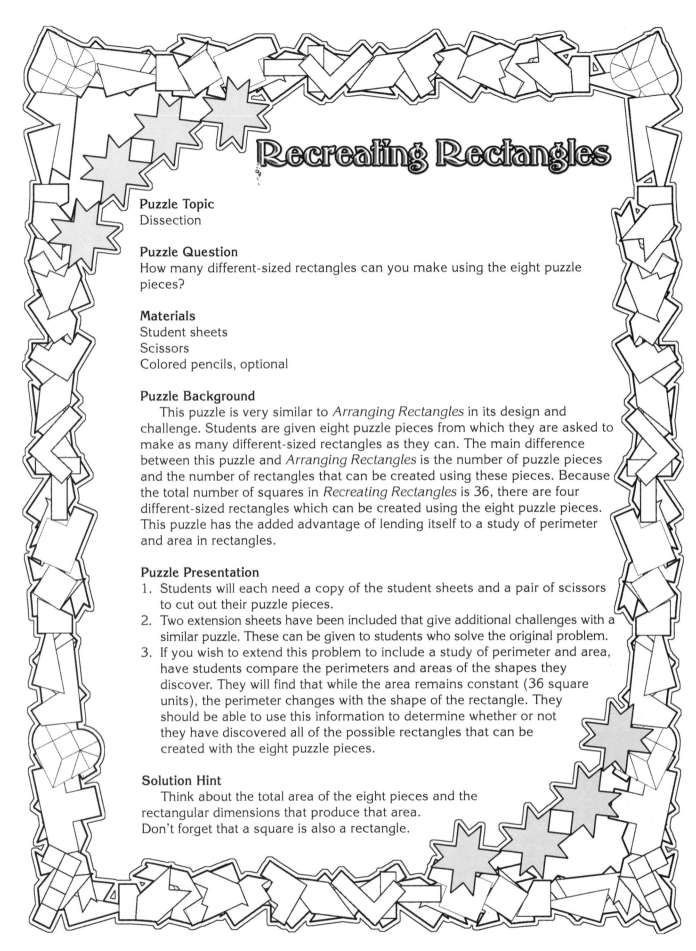

Recreating Rectangles

Puzzle Topic
Dissection

Puzzle Question
How many different-sized rectangles can you make using the eight puzzle pieces?

Materials
Student sheets
Scissors
Colored pencils, optional

Puzzle Background
This puzzle is very similar to *Arranging Rectangles* in its design and challenge. Students are given eight puzzle pieces from which they are asked to make as many different-sized rectangles as they can. The main difference between this puzzle and *Arranging Rectangles* is the number of puzzle pieces and the number of rectangles that can be created using these pieces. Because the total number of squares in *Recreating Rectangles* is 36, there are four different-sized rectangles which can be created using the eight puzzle pieces. This puzzle has the added advantage of lending itself to a study of perimeter and area in rectangles.

Puzzle Presentation
1. Students will each need a copy of the student sheets and a pair of scissors to cut out their puzzle pieces.
2. Two extension sheets have been included that give additional challenges with a similar puzzle. These can be given to students who solve the original problem.
3. If you wish to extend this problem to include a study of perimeter and area, have students compare the perimeters and areas of the shapes they discover. They will find that while the area remains constant (36 square units), the perimeter changes with the shape of the rectangle. They should be able to use this information to determine whether or not they have discovered all of the possible rectangles that can be created with the eight puzzle pieces.

Solution Hint
Think about the total area of the eight pieces and the rectangular dimensions that produce that area.
Don't forget that a square is also a rectangle.

Recreating Rectangles

Carefully cut out the shapes below and put them together to make as many different-sized rectangles as you can. Each rectangle should use all eight pieces. You can flip pieces over if necessary. Draw a picture of each solution you discover on the next page.

Extra Challenge: Once you have discovered a few solutions using the rules above, try to get a solution without flipping any of the pieces over. Record your discoveries.

Recreating Rectangles

Record each solution you discover in the grid below. You may want to use different colors to distinguish between the different pieces in each rectangle.

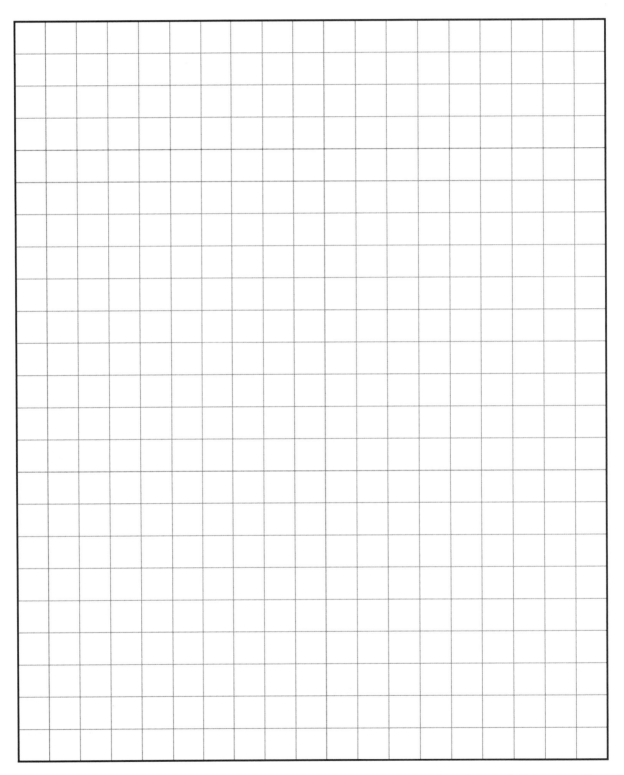

94

Recreating Rectangles

Extension

Carefully cut out the shapes below and put them together to make each of the rectangles you discovered in the first part of the activity in a different way. See how many different solutions you can discover for each possible rectangle. You can flip pieces over if necessary. Draw a picture of each solution you discover on the grid paper.

Extra Challenge: Once you have discovered a few solutions using the rules above, try to get a solution without flipping any of the pieces over. Record your discoveries on the grid paper.

PUZZLE PLAY   95   © 2001 AIMS Education Foundation

Recreating Rectangles

Now that you have successfully discovered all four rectangles that can be made using either set of puzzle pieces, try making the shapes below using the nine pieces from the extension. You can flip your pieces over if necessary.

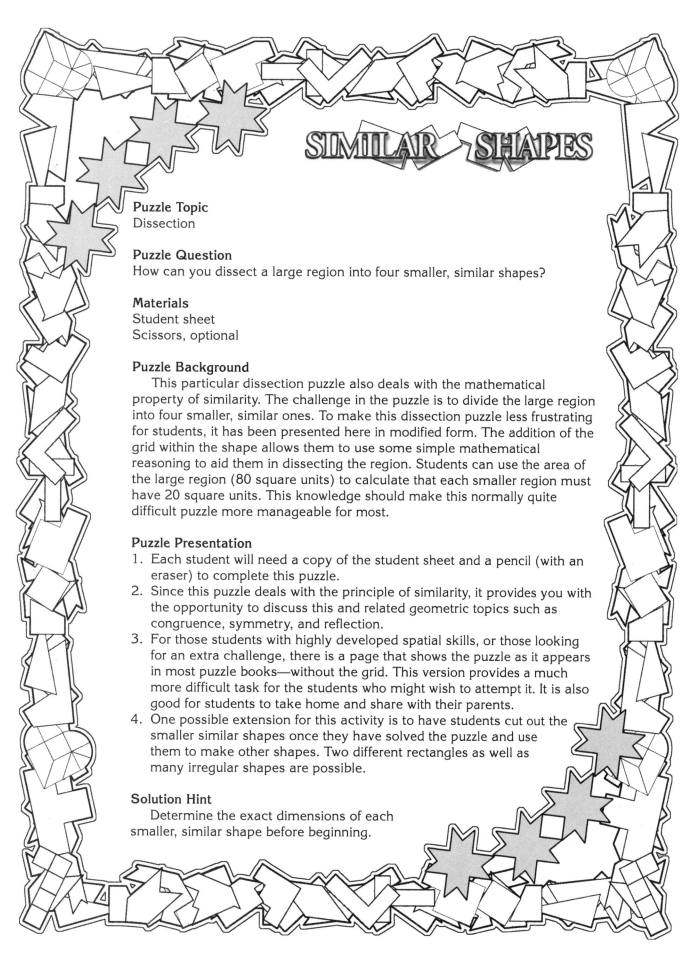

Puzzle Topic
Dissection

Puzzle Question
How can you dissect a large region into four smaller, similar shapes?

Materials
Student sheet
Scissors, optional

Puzzle Background
This particular dissection puzzle also deals with the mathematical property of similarity. The challenge in the puzzle is to divide the large region into four smaller, similar ones. To make this dissection puzzle less frustrating for students, it has been presented here in modified form. The addition of the grid within the shape allows them to use some simple mathematical reasoning to aid them in dissecting the region. Students can use the area of the large region (80 square units) to calculate that each smaller region must have 20 square units. This knowledge should make this normally quite difficult puzzle more manageable for most.

Puzzle Presentation
1. Each student will need a copy of the student sheet and a pencil (with an eraser) to complete this puzzle.
2. Since this puzzle deals with the principle of similarity, it provides you with the opportunity to discuss this and related geometric topics such as congruence, symmetry, and reflection.
3. For those students with highly developed spatial skills, or those looking for an extra challenge, there is a page that shows the puzzle as it appears in most puzzle books—without the grid. This version provides a much more difficult task for the students who might wish to attempt it. It is also good for students to take home and share with their parents.
4. One possible extension for this activity is to have students cut out the smaller similar shapes once they have solved the puzzle and use them to make other shapes. Two different rectangles as well as many irregular shapes are possible.

Solution Hint
Determine the exact dimensions of each smaller, similar shape before beginning.

SIMILAR SHAPES

In mathematics, two figures that have the same shape, but not necessarily the same size, are similar. The challenge in this puzzle is to show how to divide the large shape below into four smaller, similar shapes.

SIMILAR SHAPES

In mathematics, two figures that have the same shape, but not necessarily the same size, are similar. The challenge in this puzzle is to draw in lines to divide the large shape below into four smaller, similar shapes.

© 2001 AIMS Education Foundation

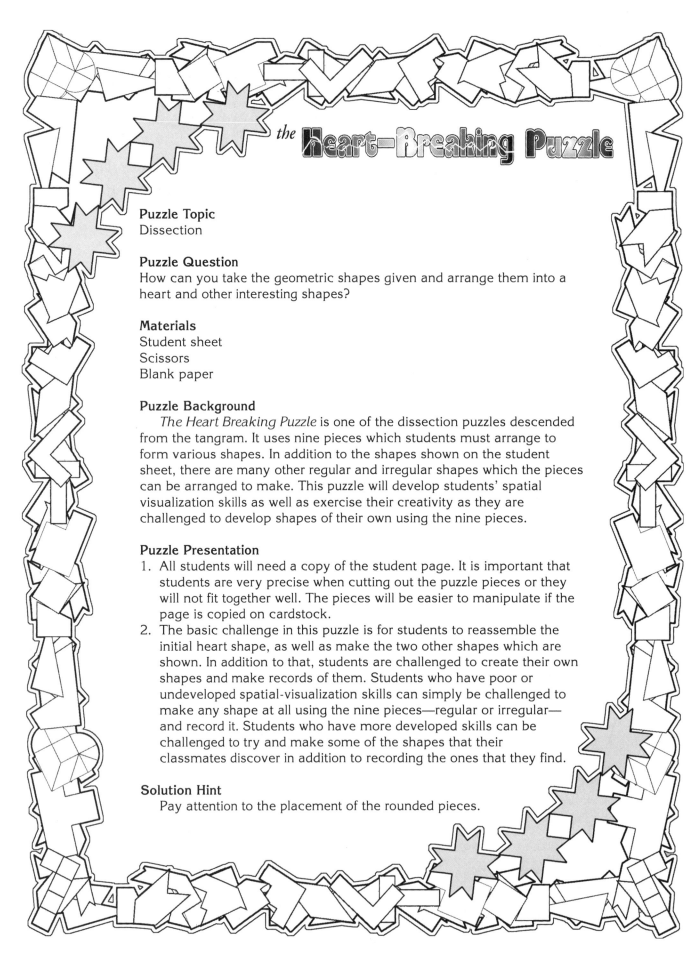

the Heart-Breaking Puzzle

Puzzle Topic
Dissection

Puzzle Question
How can you take the geometric shapes given and arrange them into a heart and other interesting shapes?

Materials
Student sheet
Scissors
Blank paper

Puzzle Background
   The Heart Breaking Puzzle is one of the dissection puzzles descended from the tangram. It uses nine pieces which students must arrange to form various shapes. In addition to the shapes shown on the student sheet, there are many other regular and irregular shapes which the pieces can be arranged to make. This puzzle will develop students' spatial visualization skills as well as exercise their creativity as they are challenged to develop shapes of their own using the nine pieces.

Puzzle Presentation
1. All students will need a copy of the student page. It is important that students are very precise when cutting out the puzzle pieces or they will not fit together well. The pieces will be easier to manipulate if the page is copied on cardstock.
2. The basic challenge in this puzzle is for students to reassemble the initial heart shape, as well as make the two other shapes which are shown. In addition to that, students are challenged to create their own shapes and make records of them. Students who have poor or undeveloped spatial-visualization skills can simply be challenged to make any shape at all using the nine pieces—regular or irregular— and record it. Students who have more developed skills can be challenged to try and make some of the shapes that their classmates discover in addition to recording the ones that they find.

Solution Hint
   Pay attention to the placement of the rounded pieces.

100

the Heart-Breaking Puzzle

Carefully cut out the pieces of the heart puzzle. Use all nine pieces to make as many interesting shapes as you can, including the two shown below. The pieces must be placed edge to edge and can't overlap. Make a record of your shapes by drawing their outlines on a separate sheet of paper. Once you have found as many interesting shapes as you can, try to reassemble the heart.

LIVE & In Person!
singing that
#1 hit
"Heartbreaking
Puzzle"
*available for weddings

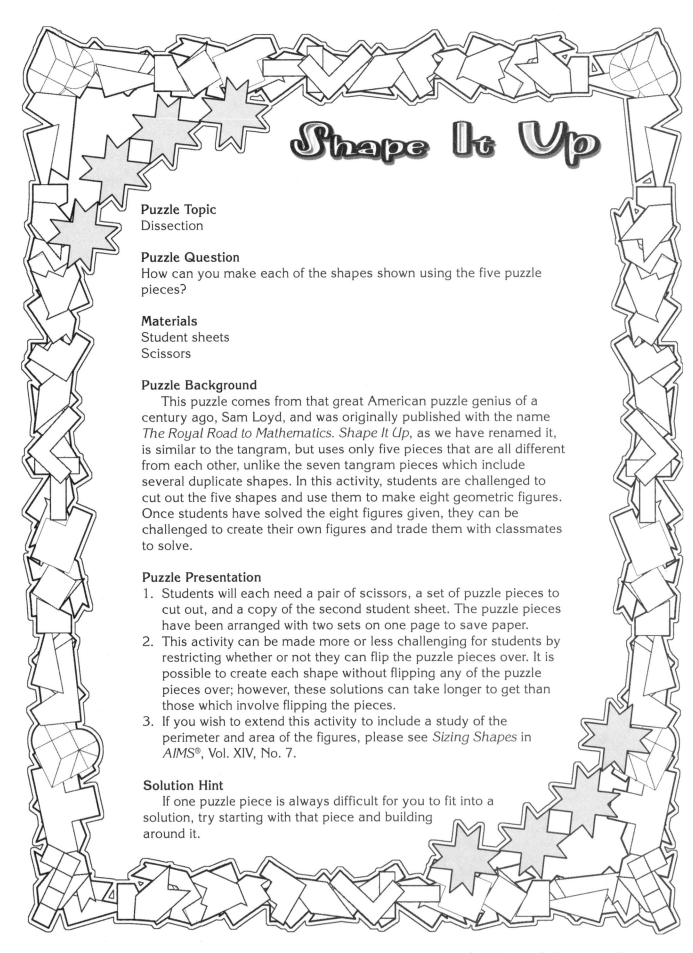

Shape It Up

Puzzle Topic
Dissection

Puzzle Question
How can you make each of the shapes shown using the five puzzle pieces?

Materials
Student sheets
Scissors

Puzzle Background
This puzzle comes from that great American puzzle genius of a century ago, Sam Loyd, and was originally published with the name *The Royal Road to Mathematics. Shape It Up*, as we have renamed it, is similar to the tangram, but uses only five pieces that are all different from each other, unlike the seven tangram pieces which include several duplicate shapes. In this activity, students are challenged to cut out the five shapes and use them to make eight geometric figures. Once students have solved the eight figures given, they can be challenged to create their own figures and trade them with classmates to solve.

Puzzle Presentation
1. Students will each need a pair of scissors, a set of puzzle pieces to cut out, and a copy of the second student sheet. The puzzle pieces have been arranged with two sets on one page to save paper.
2. This activity can be made more or less challenging for students by restricting whether or not they can flip the puzzle pieces over. It is possible to create each shape without flipping any of the puzzle pieces over; however, these solutions can take longer to get than those which involve flipping the pieces.
3. If you wish to extend this activity to include a study of the perimeter and area of the figures, please see *Sizing Shapes* in *AIMS*®, Vol. XIV, No. 7.

Solution Hint
If one puzzle piece is always difficult for you to fit into a solution, try starting with that piece and building around it.

Shape It Up

.5 lbs   .5 lbs

Carefully cut out the five shapes below. Use them to make each of the figures on the next page.

Carefully cut out the five shapes. Use them to make each of the figures on the next page.

Shape It Up

Make each of the following figures with your five pieces. Each figure must use all five pieces. Make a record of each solution you discover by sketching the pieces in the outlines as they belong. You may also use the space at the bottom of the paper and the back of the paper to record solutions, since several of the figures have more than one.

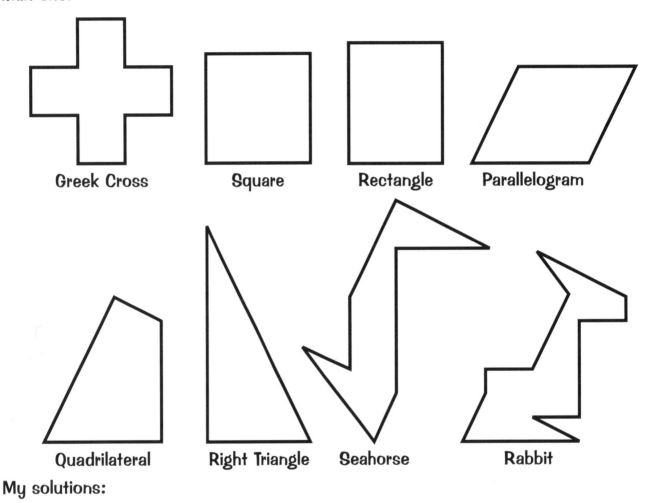

Greek Cross   Square   Rectangle   Parallelogram

Quadrilateral   Right Triangle   Seahorse   Rabbit

My solutions:

Extra challenge: Create some more irregular shapes like the Seahorse and the Rabbit. Make a picture of each, and trade them with your classmates to solve.

.5 lbs ———— .5 lbs

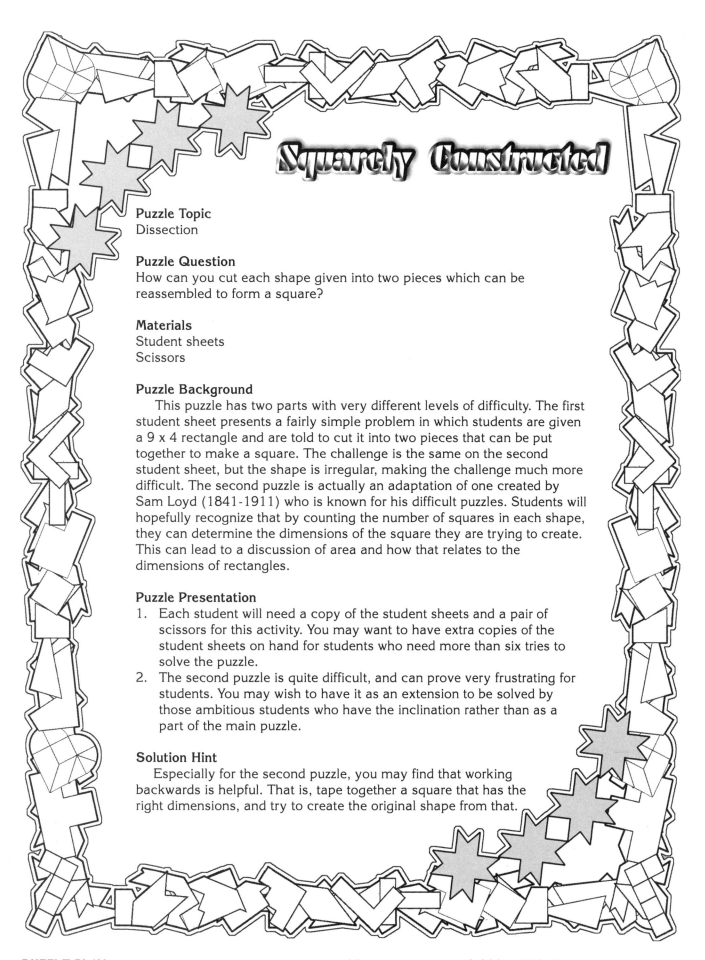

Squarely Constructed

Puzzle Topic
Dissection

Puzzle Question
How can you cut each shape given into two pieces which can be reassembled to form a square?

Materials
Student sheets
Scissors

Puzzle Background
This puzzle has two parts with very different levels of difficulty. The first student sheet presents a fairly simple problem in which students are given a 9 x 4 rectangle and are told to cut it into two pieces that can be put together to make a square. The challenge is the same on the second student sheet, but the shape is irregular, making the challenge much more difficult. The second puzzle is actually an adaptation of one created by Sam Loyd (1841-1911) who is known for his difficult puzzles. Students will hopefully recognize that by counting the number of squares in each shape, they can determine the dimensions of the square they are trying to create. This can lead to a discussion of area and how that relates to the dimensions of rectangles.

Puzzle Presentation
1. Each student will need a copy of the student sheets and a pair of scissors for this activity. You may want to have extra copies of the student sheets on hand for students who need more than six tries to solve the puzzle.
2. The second puzzle is quite difficult, and can prove very frustrating for students. You may wish to have it as an extension to be solved by those ambitious students who have the inclination rather than as a part of the main puzzle.

Solution Hint
Especially for the second puzzle, you may find that working backwards is helpful. That is, tape together a square that has the right dimensions, and try to create the original shape from that.

105

Squarely Constructed 1

Cut one of the rectangles below into two pieces that fit together to make a square. The cuts must be along the lines of the grid. If you do not succeed the first time, try again using what you have learned.

© 2001 AIMS Education Foundation

Squarely Constructed II

Cut out one of the grids below. Make cuts to divide the grid into two pieces that will fit together to make a square. The cuts must be along the lines of the grid. If you do not succeed the first time, try again using what you have learned.

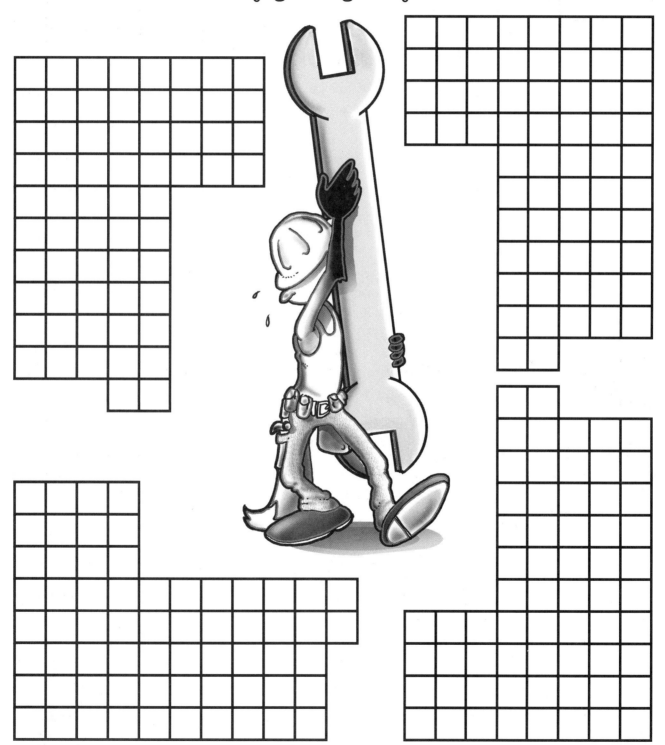

the INFINITE I

Puzzle Topic
Dissection

Puzzle Question
How many different shapes can you make using the four puzzle pieces?

Materials
Student sheets
Cardstock
Scissors

Puzzle Background
    This puzzle is a modification of the classic T Puzzle, in which people are challenged to assemble four puzzle pieces to make only one shape, a block T. *The Infinite I* uses the same shapes as the T Puzzle with one exception. The larger of the two quadrilateral pieces has been lengthened so that its longest side is the same length as the longest side of the irregular, five-sided piece. This slight modification makes it possible to construct all sorts of interesting shapes that can't be made with the original T Puzzle pieces. This puzzle will strengthen the spatial-visualization abilities of students as they work to find many different combinations of the four pieces.

Puzzle Presentation
1. The puzzle pieces for this activity are printed with four sets on one page to conserve paper. This page should be photocopied onto cardstock or a similar type of paper to give the puzzle pieces more durability. When cutting out their puzzles, students must be careful to cut exactly along the lines so that the pieces will fit together properly.
2. Each student will need a copy of the first student sheet and one set of puzzle pieces from the second sheet for this activity. You may want to give students envelopes to keep their pieces in while they are not using them. This will prevent the pieces from getting lost and will also allow students to take the puzzles home and share them with their families.
3. You may wish to have students sketch the outlines of each different shape that they create on separate pieces of paper. This will allow students to share their creations with classmates, and challenge others to find the solutions.

Solution Hint
    You may need to flip some of the pieces over.

the INFINITE I

Father of Infinite I

Use the four puzzle pieces to make as many interesting shapes as you can. Make a record of each shape you create by drawing it below. For an additional challenge, try to make some of the shapes pictured on this sheet.

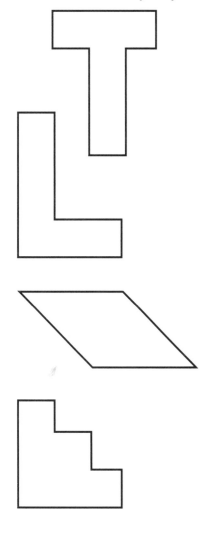

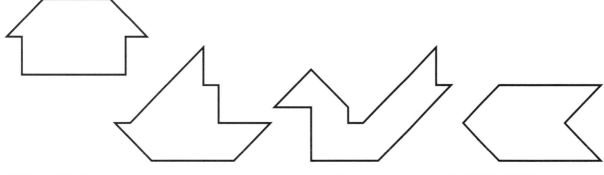

This page has the pieces to make four puzzles. They have been placed side by side to make them easier to cut out.

Dissection Puzzle Solutions

Shape Makers

Most of the figures have multiple correct solutions. One possibility for each is shown below.

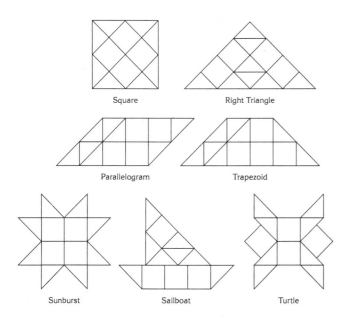

Square   Right Triangle

Parallelogram   Trapezoid

Sunburst   Sailboat   Turtle

Arranging Rectangles

The two possible rectangles which can be made with the six pieces are shown below.

2 x 9 rectangle

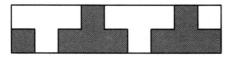

3 x 6 rectangle

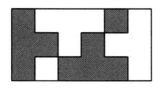

(Square solution possible using only 4 of the 6 pieces.)

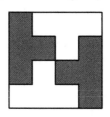

Farmer in a Fix

Felicia's farm must be divided as shown below in order to be fair to all four of her children.

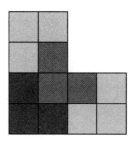

Square Stumper

There are two solutions to *Square Stumper* which each use a different shaped region. Both regions consist of four squares and three circles. The shape of each region is shown below.

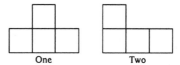

One   Two

The darkened lines show how the regions divide the square.

One   Two

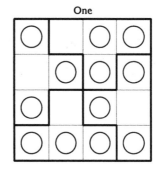
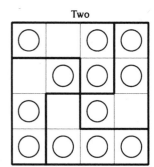

Recreating Rectangles

One possible solution for each rectangle is shown below. None of the pieces were flipped over to reach these solutions.

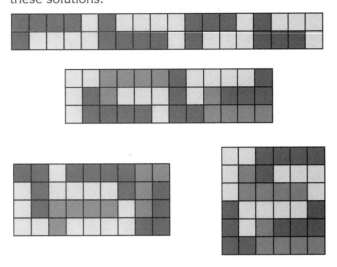

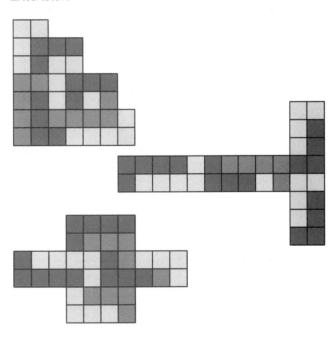

Extension

Similar Shapes

The puzzle shape is shown below divided into four smaller, similar shapes.

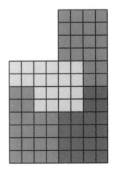

Heart Breaking Puzzle

The solutions to the two shapes shown on the student sheet as well as a few other possibilities are shown below.

Shape It Up

At least one possible solution for each shape is shown below. All of these solutions were reached without flipping any of the pieces over.

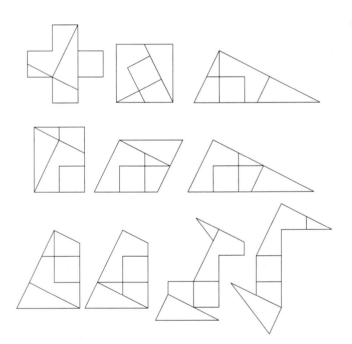

Squarely Constructed

The cuts for each shape and how the pieces fit together to form a square are shown below.

Squarely Constructed I

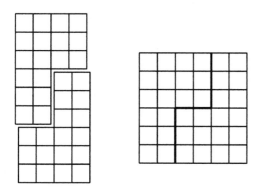

Squarely Constructed II

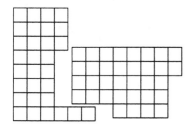 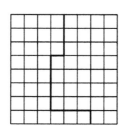

The Infinite I

The solutions to a few of the shapes shown on the first student sheet are shown below. Keep in mind that this is only a small sample of the shapes that can be created using these puzzle pieces.

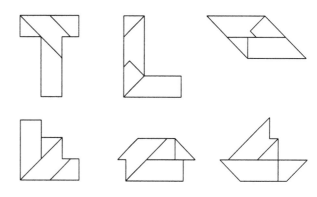

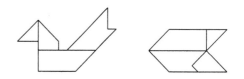

Three-Dimensional Puzzles

Introduction

The puzzles in this section are unique in that they are three-dimensional in nature. In one way, they are like the jigsaw puzzles we grew up with as children since they have specific pieces that fit together a certain way to form the final product. Instead of a picture, however, these puzzles create a geometric solid instead—either a cube or a tetrahedron. (A few of the cube puzzles can also form other interesting shapes.)

Unlike many of the other puzzles in this book which can be done as whole-class activities, the puzzles here are perhaps better suited for use at centers or placed in a classroom *Puzzle Corner* where they can be worked on over an extended period of time. There are several reasons for this. One reason is the cost of the puzzles, which may not allow students to have their own individual puzzles on which to work. (Although they are teacher- or student-constructed, the materials for each puzzle range in cost from one to two dollars. However, some of the puzzles, like the Soma Cube, are so versatile and motivating that it might be worth the cost to provide each student with a puzzle.) Another reason for placing these puzzles in a center is that most of them have multiple solutions and can engage students for an extended period of time. In addition, a few of the puzzles toward the end of this section are quite challenging and won't likely be solved quickly.

When presenting these puzzles, it is important that you carefully consider the puzzle-solving abilities of your students, since the puzzles vary greatly in their difficulty levels. The first few puzzles in the section are fairly easy, while the last few are extremely challenging. It is important that students build some confidence by solving the earlier puzzles before they tackle the latter ones.

Because much of what is involved in solving these puzzles is trial and error, and because there are often multiple solutions, several of the teacher's pages in this section do not include a *Solution Hint*. If students are having a difficult time finding a solution, tell them to put the puzzle away and try it again another time. (It is amazing how often students will spend a lot of time unsuccessfully on a puzzle, put it away in frustration, and then solve it almost immediately a few days later when they try it again.)

As with all of the puzzles in this book, please work on these puzzles yourself before presenting them to your students. DO NOT look at the solutions unless it is absolutely necessary! If you don't have strong spatial-manipulation skills, you will benefit greatly from trying these puzzles on your own and struggling with them until you finally discover a solution. You will also be able to more accurately judge the difficulty level of each puzzle and evaluate its appropriateness for use with your students.

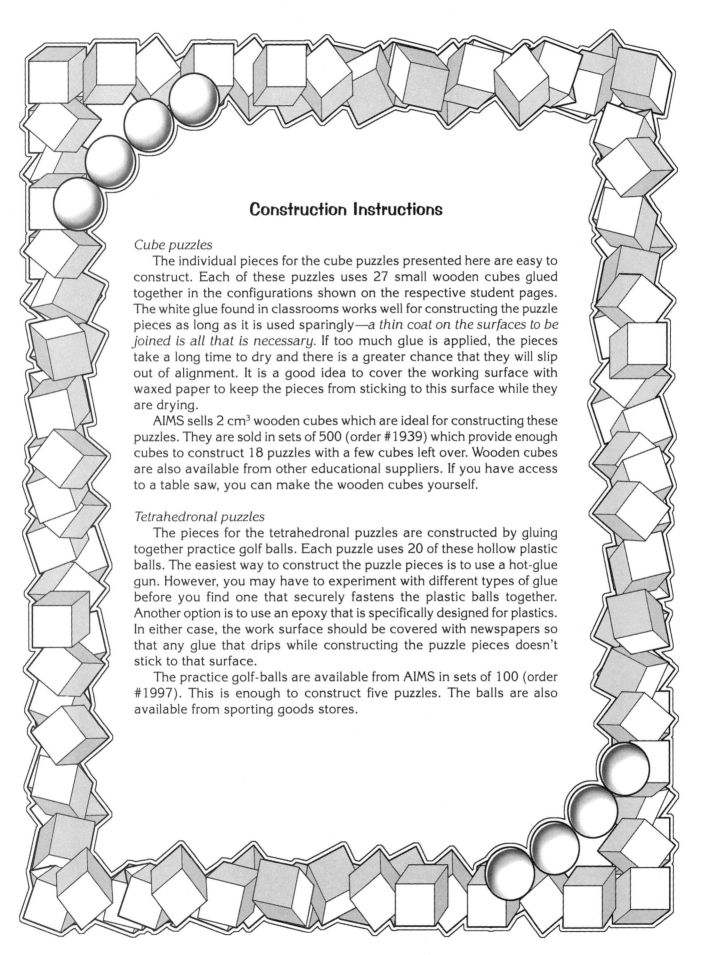

Construction Instructions

Cube puzzles

The individual pieces for the cube puzzles presented here are easy to construct. Each of these puzzles uses 27 small wooden cubes glued together in the configurations shown on the respective student pages. The white glue found in classrooms works well for constructing the puzzle pieces as long as it is used sparingly—*a thin coat on the surfaces to be joined is all that is necessary*. If too much glue is applied, the pieces take a long time to dry and there is a greater chance that they will slip out of alignment. It is a good idea to cover the working surface with waxed paper to keep the pieces from sticking to this surface while they are drying.

AIMS sells 2 cm^3 wooden cubes which are ideal for constructing these puzzles. They are sold in sets of 500 (order #1939) which provide enough cubes to construct 18 puzzles with a few cubes left over. Wooden cubes are also available from other educational suppliers. If you have access to a table saw, you can make the wooden cubes yourself.

Tetrahedronal puzzles

The pieces for the tetrahedronal puzzles are constructed by gluing together practice golf balls. Each puzzle uses 20 of these hollow plastic balls. The easiest way to construct the puzzle pieces is to use a hot-glue gun. However, you may have to experiment with different types of glue before you find one that securely fastens the plastic balls together. Another option is to use an epoxy that is specifically designed for plastics. In either case, the work surface should be covered with newspapers so that any glue that drips while constructing the puzzle pieces doesn't stick to that surface.

The practice golf-balls are available from AIMS in sets of 100 (order #1997). This is enough to construct five puzzles. The balls are also available from sporting goods stores.

TRICUBE TEASER

Puzzle Topic
Geometric solids, cubes

Puzzle Question
How can you assemble the nine tricube pieces to make a 3 x 3 x 3 cube?

Materials
Student sheets
Puzzle pieces
Colored dot stickers, optional
Permanent marker, optional

Puzzle Background
    Tricube Teaser was developed by Kevin Holmes in the 1980s under the name *The Nine Tricubes*. This puzzle consists of nine identical tricube shapes which can be arranged 111 different ways to form a 3 x 3 x 3 cube. Because there are so many solutions, this puzzle is one of the easiest cube construction puzzles. This is why it is the first one presented in this section. It is a good puzzle to use with your class at the beginning of the year as they are developing their problem-solving skills and gaining confidence in their abilities—the multiple solutions make the chances of success almost certain for your students. Because the original puzzle is so easy, an optional extension is included on the third student page to present to students who aren't challenged by the original puzzle.

Puzzle Presentation
1. See the *Introduction* for construction instructions.
2. The challenge in this puzzle, like all the other cube puzzles in this section, is to assemble the pieces to form a 3 x 3 x 3 cube. This challenge is presented on the first student page.
3. The second student sheet shows students some additional shapes that can be created using the tricube pieces.
4. The third student sheet, which is optional, has students make a checkered cube by using puzzle pieces with every other cube marked. There are several ways students can do this. Permanent felt-tip markers can be used to color the cubes, but this can be messy. A better option is to use colored dot or star stickers. However, this option requires a lot of stickers, since each puzzle has 64 faces that need to be marked.

TRICUBE TEASER

Glue together the 27 cubes your teacher has given you to form nine of the tricubes shown below. Once your pieces are completely dry, assemble them to form the 3 x 3 x 3 cube illustrated here. See how many different ways you can do this.

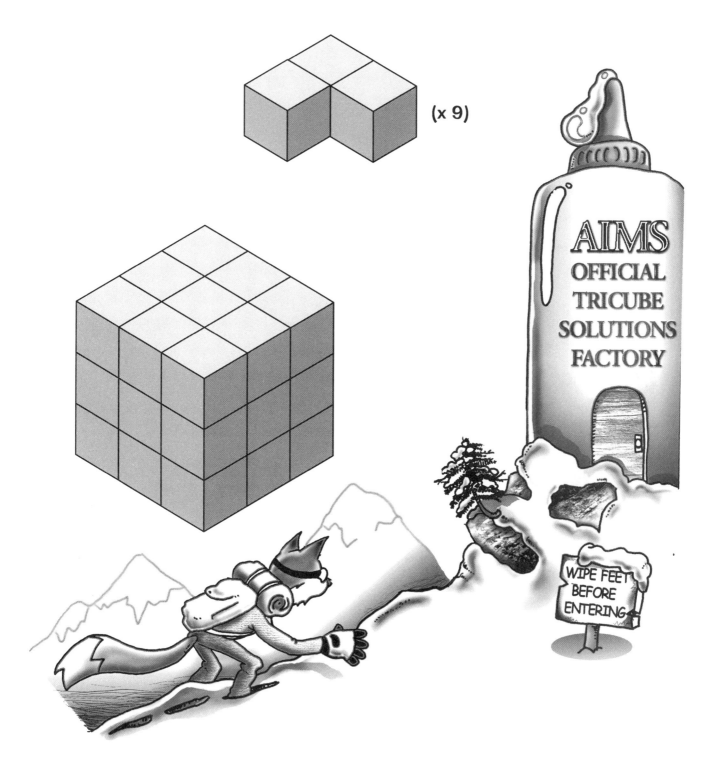

(x 9)

AIMS
OFFICIAL
TRICUBE
SOLUTIONS
FACTORY

WIPE FEET
BEFORE
ENTERING

117

TRICUBE TEASER

Try to make each of the shapes shown below using your nine puzzle pieces. When you have created all of these shapes, invent some of your own.

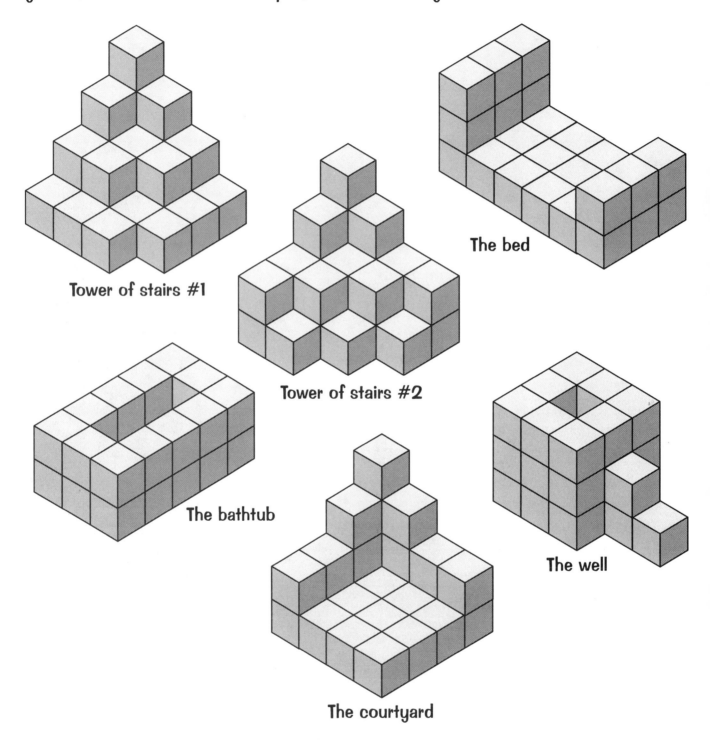

Tower of stairs #1

Tower of stairs #2

The bed

The bathtub

The courtyard

The well

Note: For the well, the hole goes all the way to the bottom layer. For the bathtub, the hole in the center does not go all the way to the bottom.

TRICUBE TEASER

Extra Challenge: Mark your pieces as shown below using a marker or stickers. When you have marked all nine pieces, try to assemble the cube so that each side is checkered as shown. After you have solved the cube, try the striped wall and create some shapes of your own that are checkered or striped.

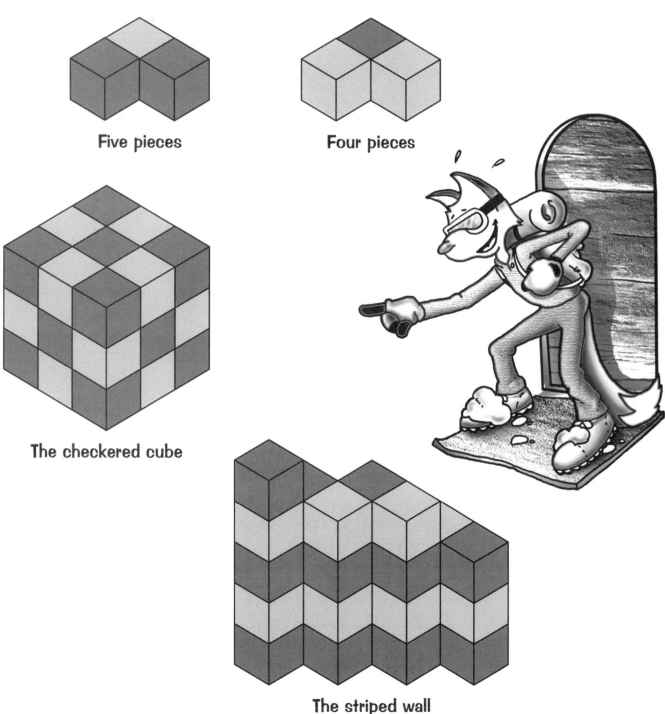

Five pieces

Four pieces

The checkered cube

The striped wall

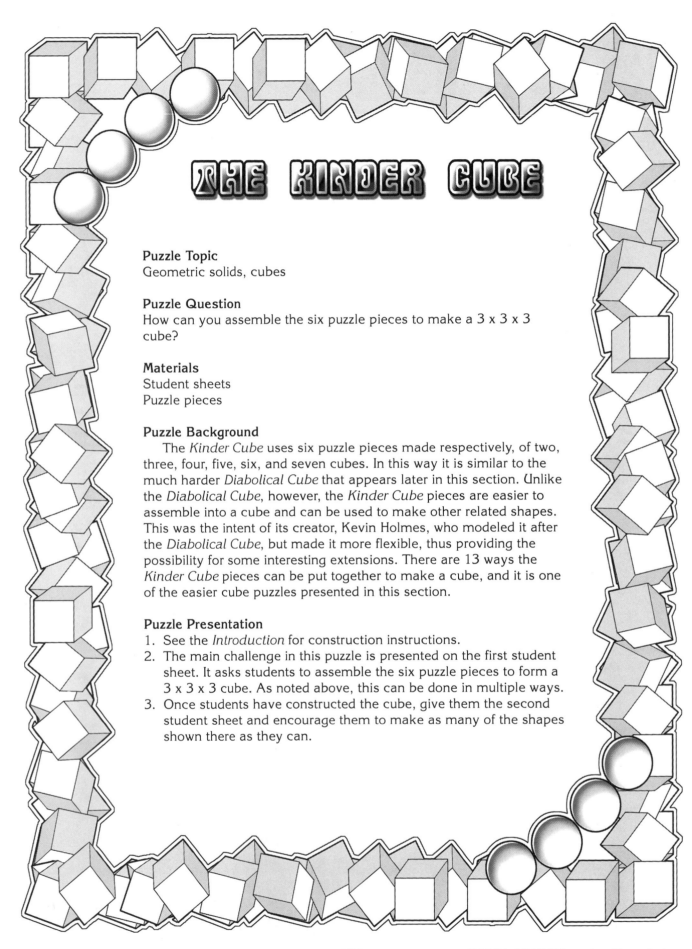

THE KINDER CUBE

Puzzle Topic
Geometric solids, cubes

Puzzle Question
How can you assemble the six puzzle pieces to make a 3 x 3 x 3 cube?

Materials
Student sheets
Puzzle pieces

Puzzle Background
    The *Kinder Cube* uses six puzzle pieces made respectively, of two, three, four, five, six, and seven cubes. In this way it is similar to the much harder *Diabolical Cube* that appears later in this section. Unlike the *Diabolical Cube*, however, the *Kinder Cube* pieces are easier to assemble into a cube and can be used to make other related shapes. This was the intent of its creator, Kevin Holmes, who modeled it after the *Diabolical Cube*, but made it more flexible, thus providing the possibility for some interesting extensions. There are 13 ways the *Kinder Cube* pieces can be put together to make a cube, and it is one of the easier cube puzzles presented in this section.

Puzzle Presentation
1. See the *Introduction* for construction instructions.
2. The main challenge in this puzzle is presented on the first student sheet. It asks students to assemble the six puzzle pieces to form a 3 x 3 x 3 cube. As noted above, this can be done in multiple ways.
3. Once students have constructed the cube, give them the second student sheet and encourage them to make as many of the shapes shown there as they can.

THE KINDER CUBE

Glue together the 27 cubes your teacher has given you to form the shapes shown below.

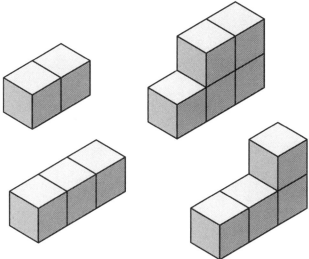

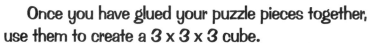

Once you have glued your puzzle pieces together, use them to create a 3 x 3 x 3 cube.

THE KINDER CUBE

Try to make each of the shapes below using the number of puzzle pieces indicated.

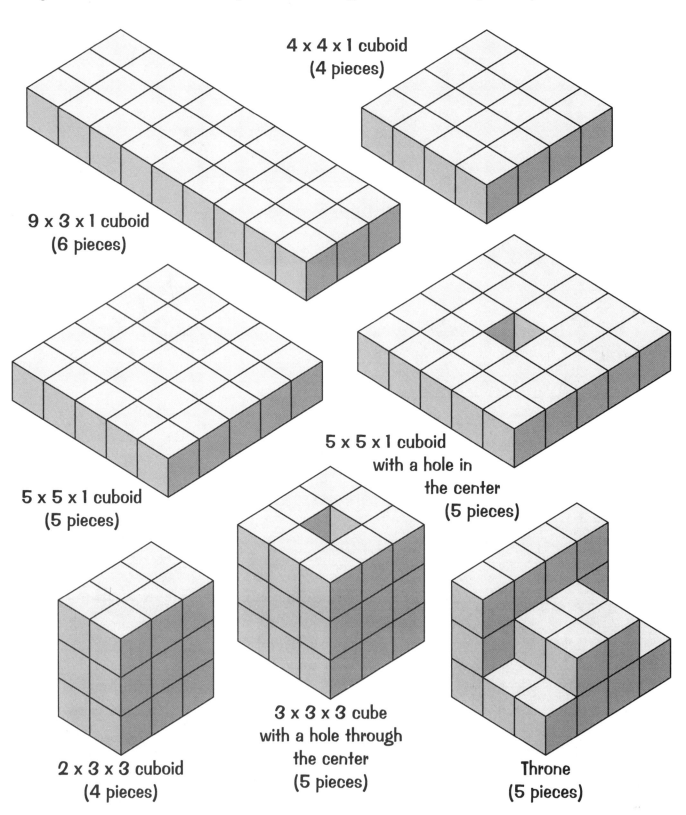

4 x 4 x 1 cuboid
(4 pieces)

9 x 3 x 1 cuboid
(6 pieces)

5 x 5 x 1 cuboid
(5 pieces)

5 x 5 x 1 cuboid
with a hole in
the center
(5 pieces)

2 x 3 x 3 cuboid
(4 pieces)

3 x 3 x 3 cube
with a hole through
the center
(5 pieces)

Throne
(5 pieces)

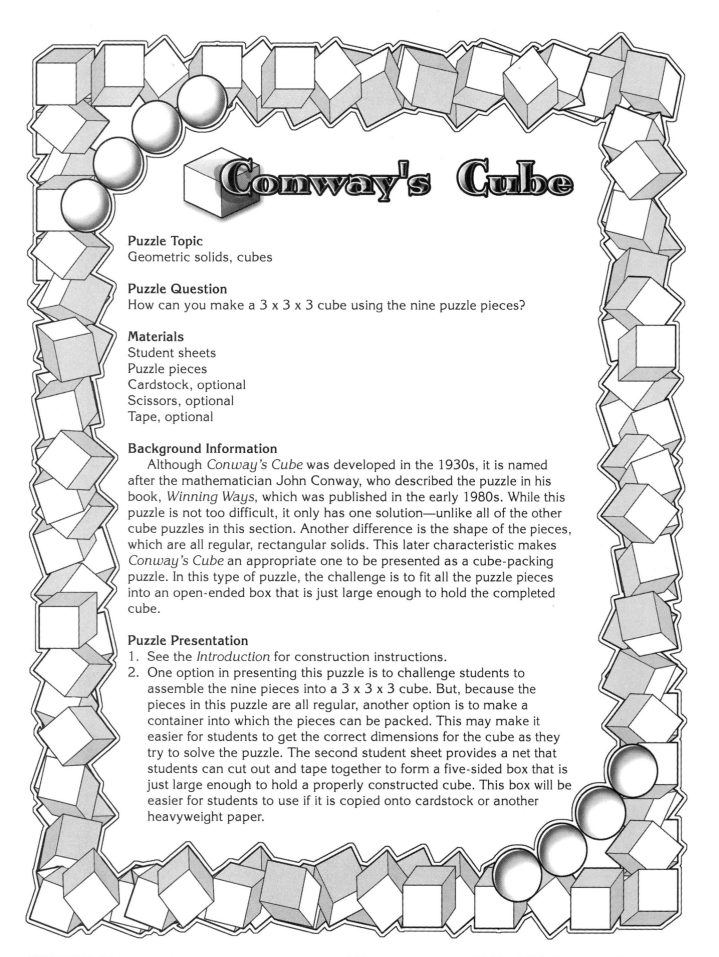

Conway's Cube

Puzzle Topic
Geometric solids, cubes

Puzzle Question
How can you make a 3 x 3 x 3 cube using the nine puzzle pieces?

Materials
Student sheets
Puzzle pieces
Cardstock, optional
Scissors, optional
Tape, optional

Background Information
Although *Conway's Cube* was developed in the 1930s, it is named after the mathematician John Conway, who described the puzzle in his book, *Winning Ways*, which was published in the early 1980s. While this puzzle is not too difficult, it only has one solution—unlike all of the other cube puzzles in this section. Another difference is the shape of the pieces, which are all regular, rectangular solids. This later characteristic makes *Conway's Cube* an appropriate one to be presented as a cube-packing puzzle. In this type of puzzle, the challenge is to fit all the puzzle pieces into an open-ended box that is just large enough to hold the completed cube.

Puzzle Presentation
1. See the *Introduction* for construction instructions.
2. One option in presenting this puzzle is to challenge students to assemble the nine pieces into a 3 x 3 x 3 cube. But, because the pieces in this puzzle are all regular, another option is to make a container into which the pieces can be packed. This may make it easier for students to get the correct dimensions for the cube as they try to solve the puzzle. The second student sheet provides a net that students can cut out and tape together to form a five-sided box that is just large enough to hold a properly constructed cube. This box will be easier for students to use if it is copied onto cardstock or another heavyweight paper.

Conway's Cube

Using three single cubes, and six tetracubes, create a *3 x 3 x 3* cube as shown below.

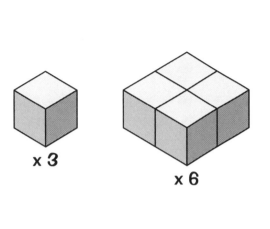

x 3

x 6

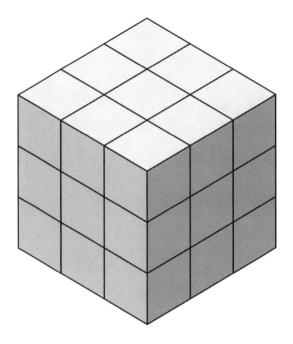

Conway's Cube

The shape below is called a "net" because when it is cut out and folded up it will make a three-dimensional shape. Cut out the net, fold each flap up along the dashed lines, and tape the sides together to make a box with no top. Assemble your cube in this box, and store your puzzle there when you are not using it.

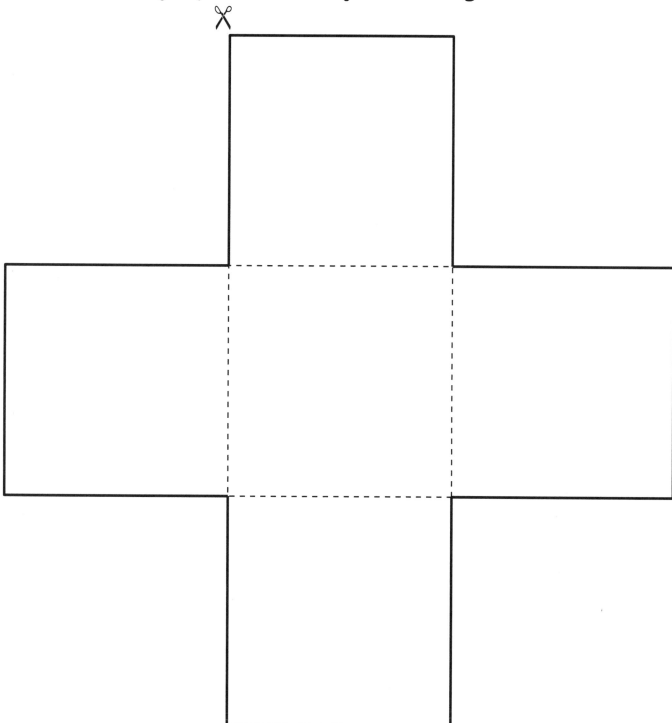

PERPLEXING PYRAMIDS I & II

Puzzle Topic
Geometric solids, tetrahedrons

Puzzle Question
How can you arrange the four puzzle pieces so that they form a tetrahedron (triangular-based pyramid)?

Materials
Student sheets
Puzzle pieces
Triangular puzzle base (optional—see *Puzzle Presentation*)

Puzzle Background
The two puzzles in this activity require students to create a tetrahedron, or triangular-based pyramid, using plastic golf balls which have been glued together in different shapes. The two tetrahedron puzzles presented here are much easier than the *Troublesome Tetrahedron* puzzle that appears later in this section. However, both puzzles may still require persistence on the part of students. These puzzles will also give students an opportunity to use their problem-solving skills.

Puzzle Presentation
1. See the *Introduction* for construction information.
2. Place these puzzles in a center or the classroom *Puzzle Corner*.
3. The plastic golf balls used for the puzzle pieces may be too slippery to assemble on smooth surfaces. To solve this problem, make a triangular base for each puzzle using three pieces of cardboard (1" x 8.5") taped together like a pool-ball rack.

Solution Hints
For the first puzzle, think how you could make two identical shapes with the four pieces, then try to fit these two shapes together to form a pyramid.

For the second puzzle, not all of the smaller pyramids will be oriented the same way.

PERPLEXING PYRAMID

Assemble these four pieces to form a triangular-based pyramid (tetrahedron). Top and side views are shown below.

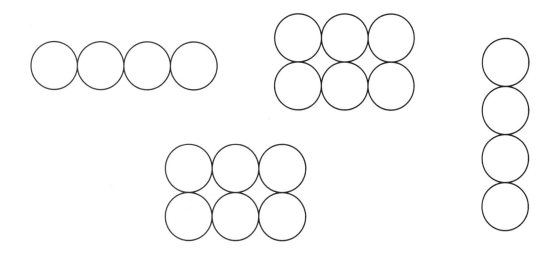

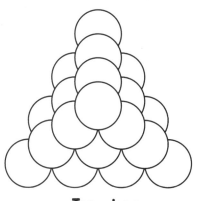

Top view

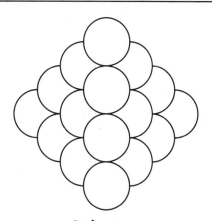

Side view

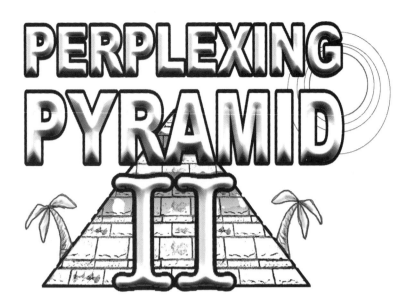

PERPLEXING PYRAMID II

Assemble these five pieces to form a triangular-based pyramid (tetrahedron). Top and side views are shown below.

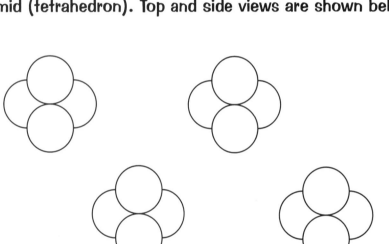

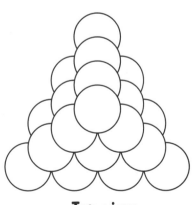

Top view

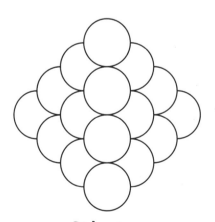

Side view

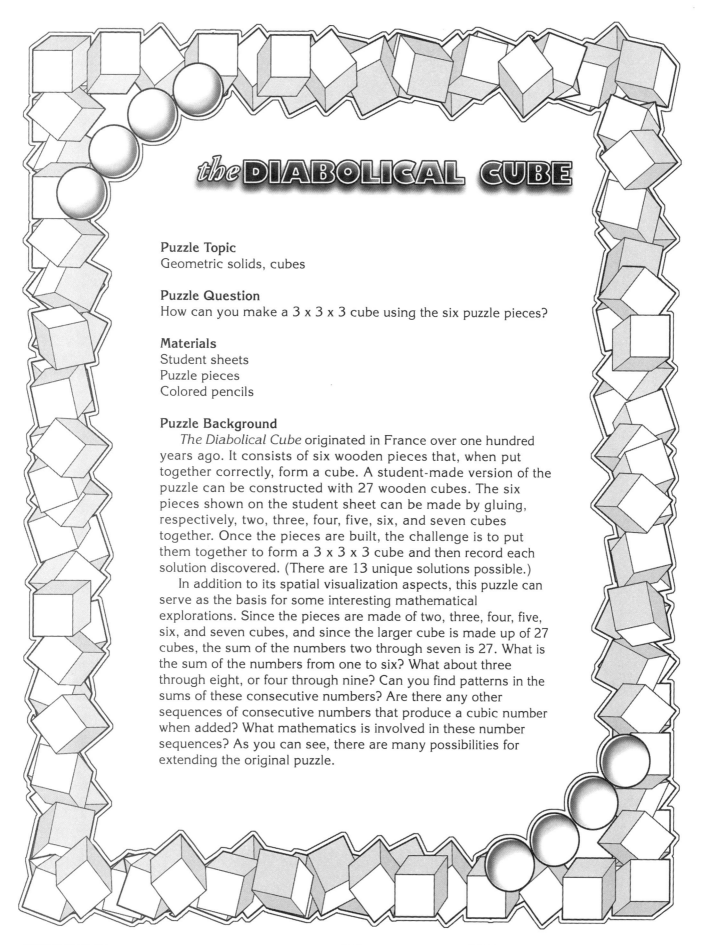

the DIABOLICAL CUBE

Puzzle Topic
Geometric solids, cubes

Puzzle Question
How can you make a 3 x 3 x 3 cube using the six puzzle pieces?

Materials
Student sheets
Puzzle pieces
Colored pencils

Puzzle Background
The Diabolical Cube originated in France over one hundred years ago. It consists of six wooden pieces that, when put together correctly, form a cube. A student-made version of the puzzle can be constructed with 27 wooden cubes. The six pieces shown on the student sheet can be made by gluing, respectively, two, three, four, five, six, and seven cubes together. Once the pieces are built, the challenge is to put them together to form a 3 x 3 x 3 cube and then record each solution discovered. (There are 13 unique solutions possible.)

In addition to its spatial visualization aspects, this puzzle can serve as the basis for some interesting mathematical explorations. Since the pieces are made of two, three, four, five, six, and seven cubes, and since the larger cube is made up of 27 cubes, the sum of the numbers two through seven is 27. What is the sum of the numbers from one to six? What about three through eight, or four through nine? Can you find patterns in the sums of these consecutive numbers? Are there any other sequences of consecutive numbers that produce a cubic number when added? What mathematics is involved in these number sequences? As you can see, there are many possibilities for extending the original puzzle.

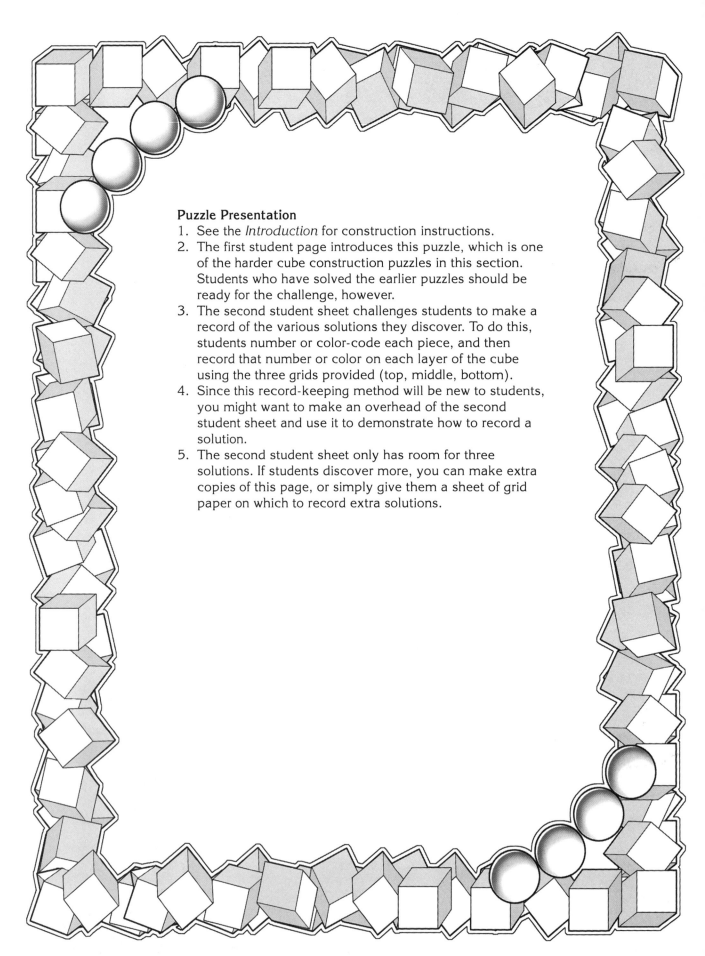

Puzzle Presentation
1. See the *Introduction* for construction instructions.
2. The first student page introduces this puzzle, which is one of the harder cube construction puzzles in this section. Students who have solved the earlier puzzles should be ready for the challenge, however.
3. The second student sheet challenges students to make a record of the various solutions they discover. To do this, students number or color-code each piece, and then record that number or color on each layer of the cube using the three grids provided (top, middle, bottom).
4. Since this record-keeping method will be new to students, you might want to make an overhead of the second student sheet and use it to demonstrate how to record a solution.
5. The second student sheet only has room for three solutions. If students discover more, you can make extra copies of this page, or simply give them a sheet of grid paper on which to record extra solutions.

the DIABOLICAL CUBE

Glue your cubes together to make the six shapes shown below. Use these shapes to make a 3 x 3 x 3 cube.

the DIABOLICAL CUBE

Make a solution key by coloring or numbering each of the puzzle pieces below. Give each piece a different color or number so that they are easily distinguished from one another.

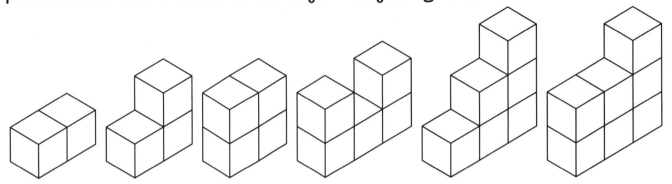

Record each solution you discover in the spaces below by showing which pieces are in each layer of the cube. Use the colors or numbers from above to help you do this.

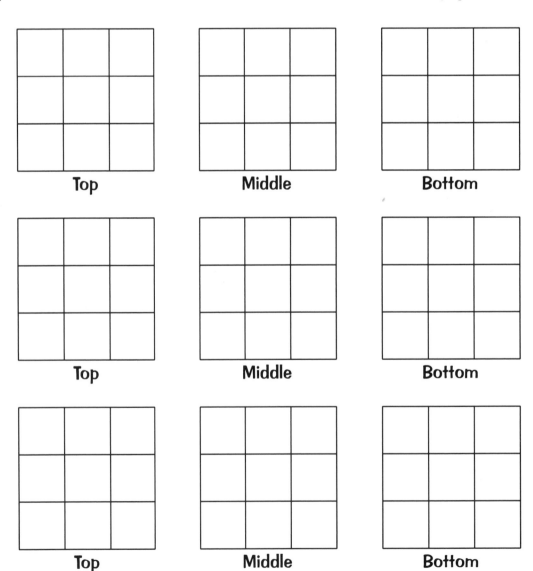

Top	Middle	Bottom
Top	Middle	Bottom
Top	Middle	Bottom

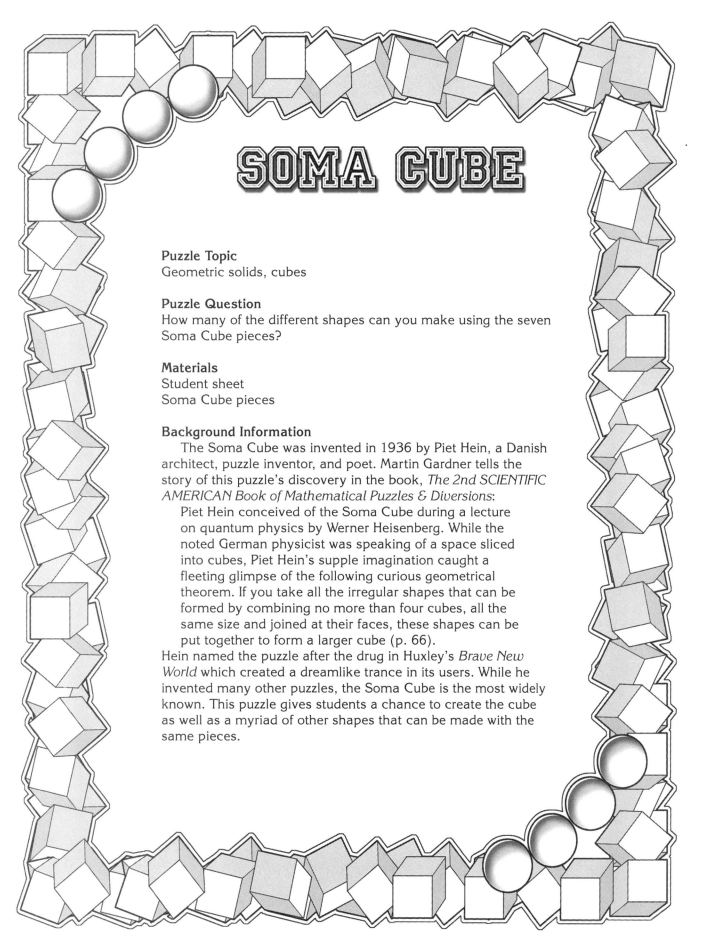

SOMA CUBE

Puzzle Topic
Geometric solids, cubes

Puzzle Question
How many of the different shapes can you make using the seven Soma Cube pieces?

Materials
Student sheet
Soma Cube pieces

Background Information
The Soma Cube was invented in 1936 by Piet Hein, a Danish architect, puzzle inventor, and poet. Martin Gardner tells the story of this puzzle's discovery in the book, *The 2nd SCIENTIFIC AMERICAN Book of Mathematical Puzzles & Diversions*:

Piet Hein conceived of the Soma Cube during a lecture on quantum physics by Werner Heisenberg. While the noted German physicist was speaking of a space sliced into cubes, Piet Hein's supple imagination caught a fleeting glimpse of the following curious geometrical theorem. If you take all the irregular shapes that can be formed by combining no more than four cubes, all the same size and joined at their faces, these shapes can be put together to form a larger cube (p. 66).

Hein named the puzzle after the drug in Huxley's *Brave New World* which created a dreamlike trance in its users. While he invented many other puzzles, the Soma Cube is the most widely known. This puzzle gives students a chance to create the cube as well as a myriad of other shapes that can be made with the same pieces.

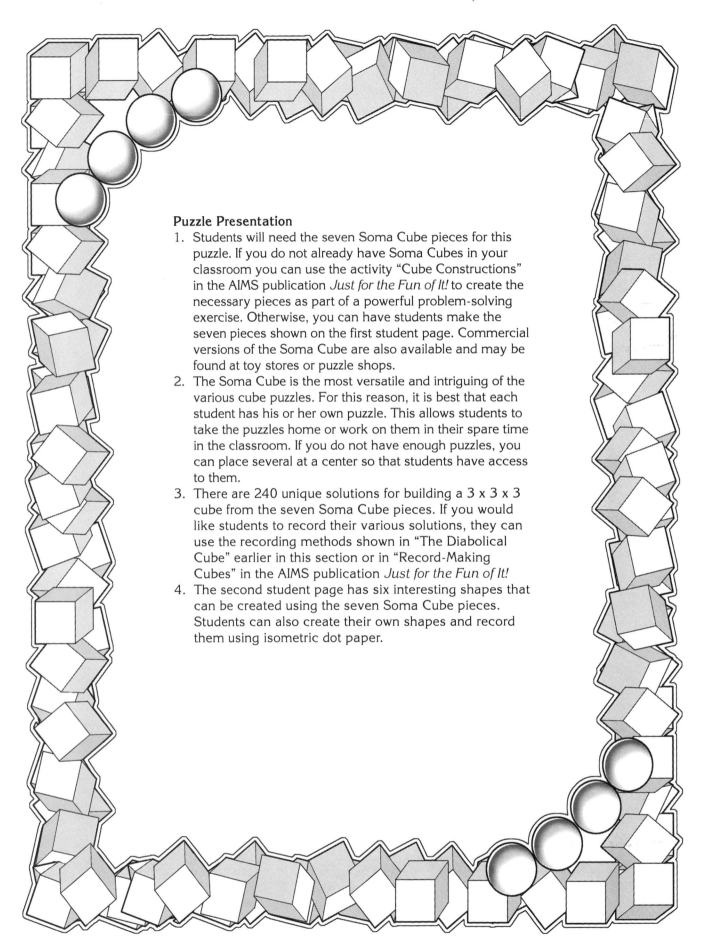

Puzzle Presentation

1. Students will need the seven Soma Cube pieces for this puzzle. If you do not already have Soma Cubes in your classroom you can use the activity "Cube Constructions" in the AIMS publication *Just for the Fun of It!* to create the necessary pieces as part of a powerful problem-solving exercise. Otherwise, you can have students make the seven pieces shown on the first student page. Commercial versions of the Soma Cube are also available and may be found at toy stores or puzzle shops.

2. The Soma Cube is the most versatile and intriguing of the various cube puzzles. For this reason, it is best that each student has his or her own puzzle. This allows students to take the puzzles home or work on them in their spare time in the classroom. If you do not have enough puzzles, you can place several at a center so that students have access to them.

3. There are 240 unique solutions for building a 3 x 3 x 3 cube from the seven Soma Cube pieces. If you would like students to record their various solutions, they can use the recording methods shown in "The Diabolical Cube" earlier in this section or in "Record-Making Cubes" in the AIMS publication *Just for the Fun of It!*

4. The second student page has six interesting shapes that can be created using the seven Soma Cube pieces. Students can also create their own shapes and record them using isometric dot paper.

SOMA CUBE

Use the seven pieces shown below to make a *3 x 3 x 3* cube.

SOMA CUBE

When you have created the 3 x 3 x 3 cube, try to make each of these shapes using your Soma Cube pieces.

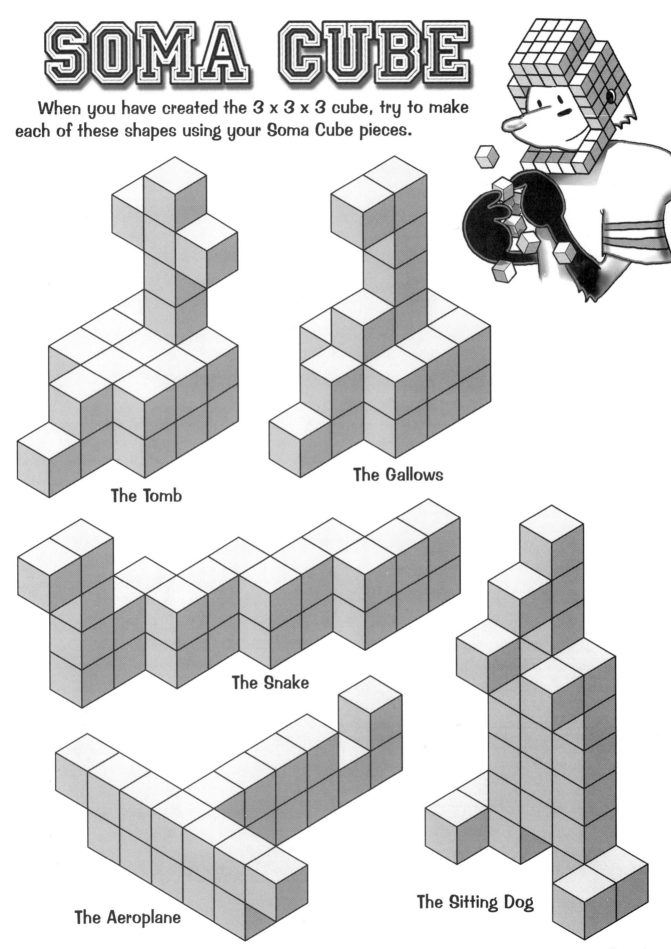

The Tomb

The Gallows

The Snake

The Aeroplane

The Sitting Dog

The TROUBLESOME TETRAHEDRON

Puzzle Topic
Geometric solids, tetrahedrons

Puzzle Question
How can you use the six pieces given to make a tetrahedron, or triangular-based pyramid?

Materials
Student sheet
Puzzle pieces
Triangular base, optional

Puzzle Background
   The Troublesome Tetrahedron is a homemade version of a commercial puzzle which requires you to make a triangular-based pyramid, or tetrahedron, from the six puzzle pieces. In this homemade version of the puzzle, the pieces are constructed by gluing plastic golf balls together. While *The Troublesome Tetrahedron* is similar to the *Perplexing Pyramid I & II* puzzles, it is *much* more difficult. It should not be attempted until your class has done the easier puzzles and has developed the perseverance necessary to solve this more complicated puzzle.

Puzzle Presentation
1. See the *Introduction* for construction instructions.
2. This puzzle, as mentioned previously, is very difficult and will take persistence to solve. Because of this, it may not be appropriate for all students, especially those who have not developed some confidence in their puzzle-solving abilities.
3. The plastic golf balls used for the puzzle pieces may be too slippery to assemble on smooth surfaces. To solve this problem, make a triangular base for each puzzle using three pieces of cardboard (1" x 8.5") taped together like a pool-ball rack.
4. You may want to challenge students who come up with the solution to this puzzle to devise a way to record their solution.

Solution Hint
   The placement of the three pieces that are not straight is critical.

The TROUBLESOME TETRAHEDRON

Assemble the six pieces shown below to form a tetrahedron. Top and side views of how the tetrahedron should look are shown below.

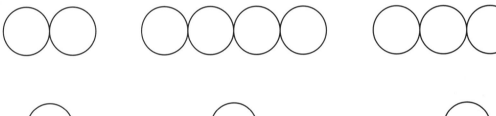

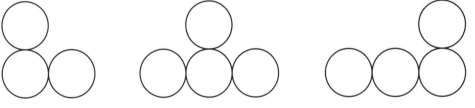

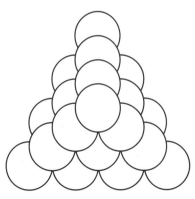

Top view

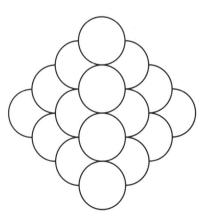

Side view

Three-Dimensional Puzzle Solutions

The Kinder Cube

One of the 13 possible solutions for the Kinder Cube is shown below. The pieces are numbered to indicate which go where.

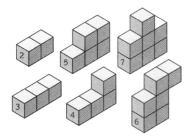

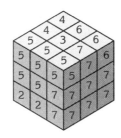

The solutions for the extensions are not limited to those shown here—several of these shapes have multiple solutions.

View One   View Two

2 x 3 x 3 cuboid

View One   View Two

3 x 3 x 3 cube with hole

4 x 4 x 1 cuboid   **4 x 4 x 1 cuboid**

5 x 5 x 1 cuboid with hole   **5 x 5 x 1 cuboid**

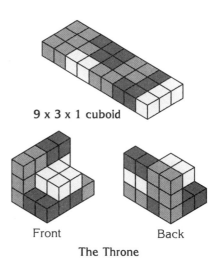

9 x 3 x 1 cuboid

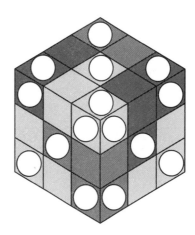

Front   Back

The Throne

Tricube Teaser

This solution shows one possible tricube solution with the dots from the third extension included.

Conway's Cube

Perplexing Pyramids

In the diagrams of the solutions, the different pieces have been printed with different patterns so that a distinction can be made between them.

Perplexing Pyramid I

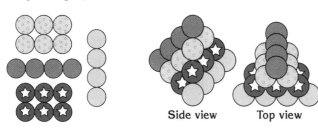

Side view   Top view

Perplexing Pyramid II

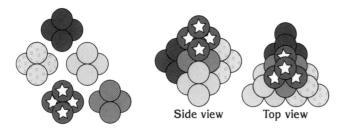

Side view   Top view

Diabolical Cube

One possible solution is given below with the pieces numbered as shown. There are 13 unique solutions to this puzzle.

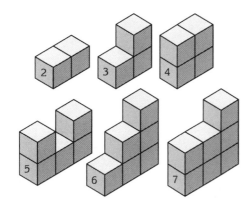

6	2	2
6	4	4
6	4	4

Top

6	7	7
6	7	7
7	7	7

Middle

6	5	5
3	3	5
3	5	5

Bottom

Soma Cube

One of the 240 solutions to the Soma Cube is shown below. The same cube is shown from two different perspectives so that each face can be seen.

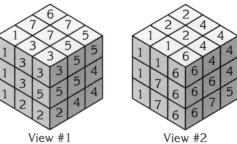

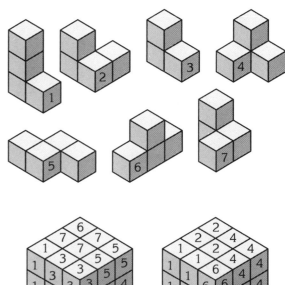

View #1   View #2

The Troublesome Tetrahedron

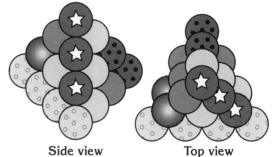

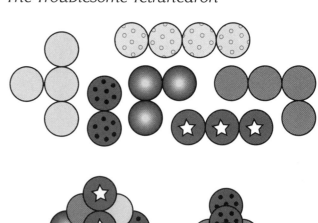

Side view   Top view

Problem Solving and Divergent Thinking Puzzles
Introduction

In order to introduce this section of puzzles, a warm-up challenge has been provided for you. On a piece of paper, draw nine dots as shown below. Then, try to connect each of the dots with four straight lines by following these guidelines. Each dot must be crossed once, but not more than once, and you cannot lift your pencil up from the paper once you have started. Please attempt to solve this puzzle before reading the rest of this introduction.

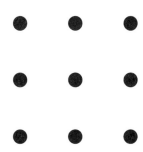

The type of thinking required to solve this problem is very similar to that which students will have to use to solve many of the problems in this section. There are several solutions to the above puzzle, but each requires that you extend the lines beyond the arrangement of dots. In fact, some believe that this puzzle is a possible origin of the phrase "thinking out of the box," which has come to be synonymous with creative and divergent thinking. Although the directions say nothing of the kind, we tend to approach this problem, and others like it, with a notion that you should not be allowed to go beyond the arrangement of dots to solve the puzzle. This kind of thinking boxes us in and contributes to making a fairly simple solution difficult for many to discover.

Like the example above, the puzzles in this section will challenge students to problem solve and think in ways that defy the assumptions which are so often made when approaching puzzles. Recognizing these assumptions and abandoning them can often be the first step to finding a correct solution. As you and your students attempt the puzzles in this section, remember to think beyond the box, and persist until you discover some of the solutions.

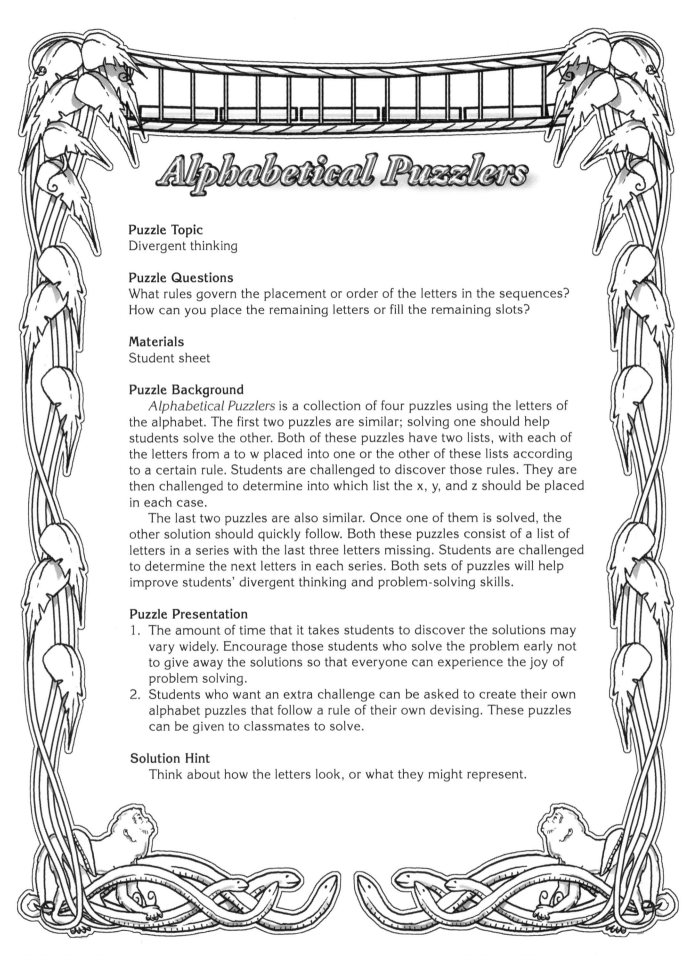

Alphabetical Puzzlers

Puzzle Topic
Divergent thinking

Puzzle Questions
What rules govern the placement or order of the letters in the sequences?
How can you place the remaining letters or fill the remaining slots?

Materials
Student sheet

Puzzle Background
Alphabetical Puzzlers is a collection of four puzzles using the letters of the alphabet. The first two puzzles are similar; solving one should help students solve the other. Both of these puzzles have two lists, with each of the letters from a to w placed into one or the other of these lists according to a certain rule. Students are challenged to discover those rules. They are then challenged to determine into which list the x, y, and z should be placed in each case.

The last two puzzles are also similar. Once one of them is solved, the other solution should quickly follow. Both these puzzles consist of a list of letters in a series with the last three letters missing. Students are challenged to determine the next letters in each series. Both sets of puzzles will help improve students' divergent thinking and problem-solving skills.

Puzzle Presentation
1. The amount of time that it takes students to discover the solutions may vary widely. Encourage those students who solve the problem early not to give away the solutions so that everyone can experience the joy of problem solving.
2. Students who want an extra challenge can be asked to create their own alphabet puzzles that follow a rule of their own devising. These puzzles can be given to classmates to solve.

Solution Hint
Think about how the letters look, or what they might represent.

Alphabetical Puzzlers

Puzzle #1: Each of the lists below groups letters according to a certain rule. Your challenge is to find that rule and use it to determine where the X, Y, and Z would go.

List #1: A E F H I K L M N T V W

List #2: B C D G J O P Q R S U

The rule for this set of lists is:

Puzzle #2: Each of the lists below groups letters according to a certain rule. Your challenge is to find that rule and use it to determine where the x, y, and z would go.

List #1: a c e m n o r s u v w

List #2: b d f g h I j k l p q t

The rule for this set of lists is:

Puzzle #3: What letters come next in this sequence?

O, T, T, F, F, S, S, E, ___, ___, ___

The rule for this sequence is:

Puzzle #4:

What letters come next in this sequence?

J, F, M, A, M, J, J, A, S, ___, ___, ___

The rule for this sequence is:

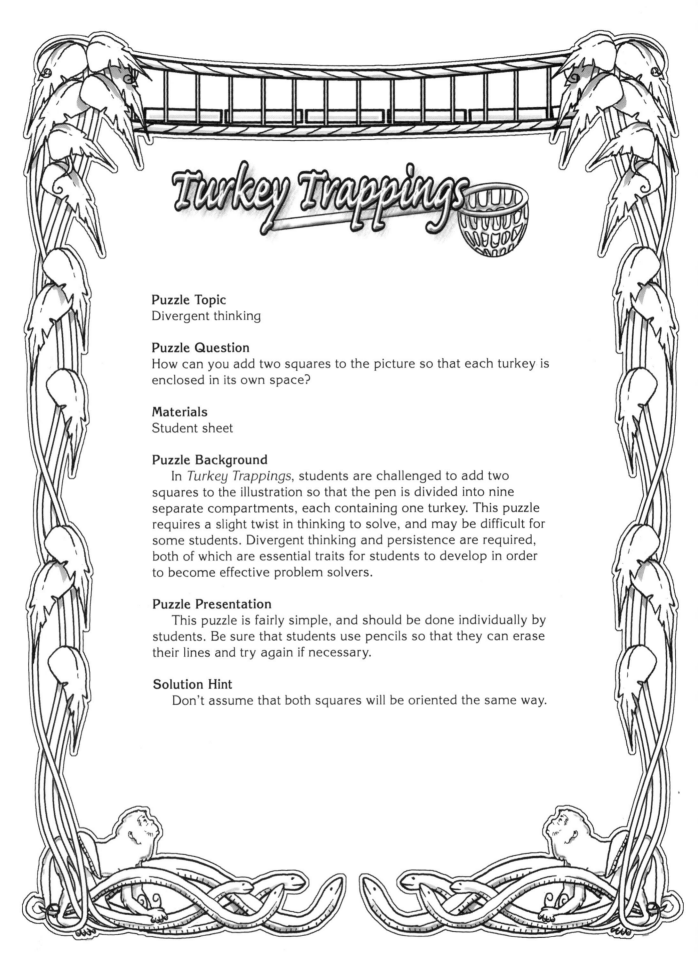

Turkey Trappings

Puzzle Topic
Divergent thinking

Puzzle Question
How can you add two squares to the picture so that each turkey is enclosed in its own space?

Materials
Student sheet

Puzzle Background
In *Turkey Trappings*, students are challenged to add two squares to the illustration so that the pen is divided into nine separate compartments, each containing one turkey. This puzzle requires a slight twist in thinking to solve, and may be difficult for some students. Divergent thinking and persistence are required, both of which are essential traits for students to develop in order to become effective problem solvers.

Puzzle Presentation
This puzzle is fairly simple, and should be done individually by students. Be sure that students use pencils so that they can erase their lines and try again if necessary.

Solution Hint
Don't assume that both squares will be oriented the same way.

Turkey Trappings

Add two squares to the pen below to create nine separate enclosures, each containing one turkey.

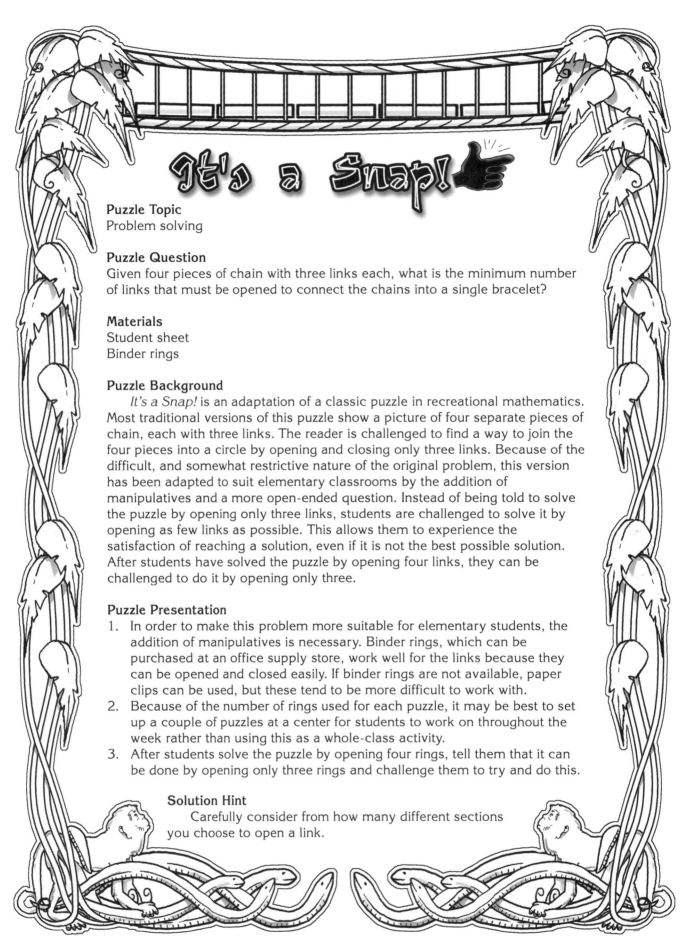

It's a Snap!

Puzzle Topic
Problem solving

Puzzle Question
Given four pieces of chain with three links each, what is the minimum number of links that must be opened to connect the chains into a single bracelet?

Materials
Student sheet
Binder rings

Puzzle Background
It's a Snap! is an adaptation of a classic puzzle in recreational mathematics. Most traditional versions of this puzzle show a picture of four separate pieces of chain, each with three links. The reader is challenged to find a way to join the four pieces into a circle by opening and closing only three links. Because of the difficult, and somewhat restrictive nature of the original problem, this version has been adapted to suit elementary classrooms by the addition of manipulatives and a more open-ended question. Instead of being told to solve the puzzle by opening only three links, students are challenged to solve it by opening as few links as possible. This allows them to experience the satisfaction of reaching a solution, even if it is not the best possible solution. After students have solved the puzzle by opening four links, they can be challenged to do it by opening only three.

Puzzle Presentation
1. In order to make this problem more suitable for elementary students, the addition of manipulatives is necessary. Binder rings, which can be purchased at an office supply store, work well for the links because they can be opened and closed easily. If binder rings are not available, paper clips can be used, but these tend to be more difficult to work with.
2. Because of the number of rings used for each puzzle, it may be best to set up a couple of puzzles at a center for students to work on throughout the week rather than using this as a whole-class activity.
3. After students solve the puzzle by opening four rings, tell them that it can be done by opening only three rings and challenge them to try and do this.

Solution Hint
Carefully consider from how many different sections you choose to open a link.

Your mother has four separate pieces of gold chain, each with three links, that she wants made into a bracelet. The jeweler charges $10 for each link that has to be opened and soldered closed. What is the minimum amount it will cost to have the bracelet made?

Hint: Use 12 snap rings to model the problem.

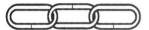 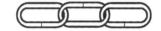 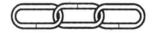 

Show how you solved this problem in the space below.

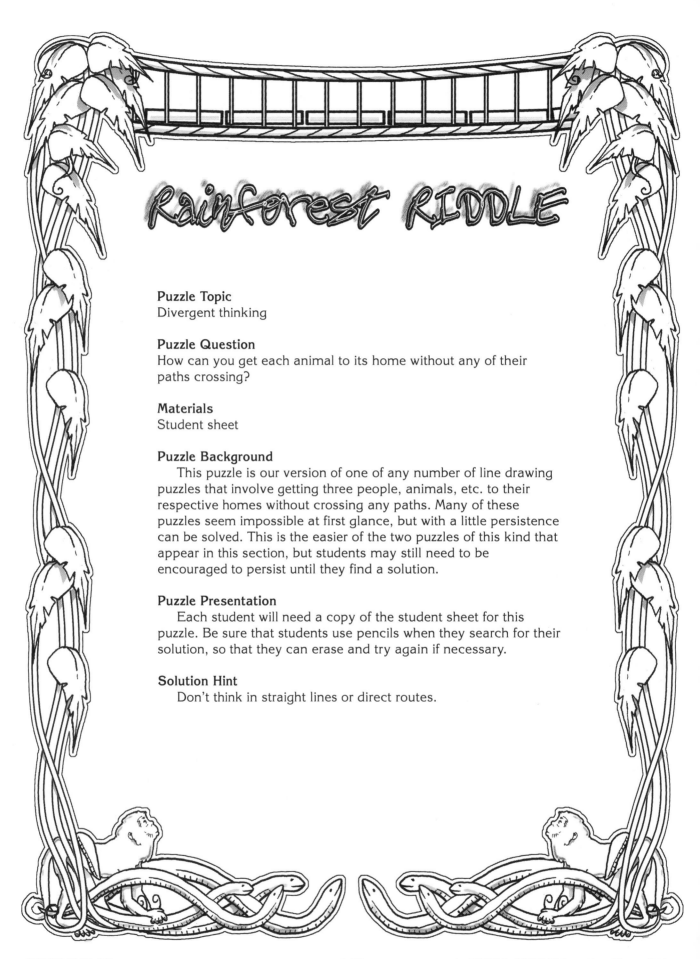

Rainforest Riddle

Puzzle Topic
Divergent thinking

Puzzle Question
How can you get each animal to its home without any of their paths crossing?

Materials
Student sheet

Puzzle Background
    This puzzle is our version of one of any number of line drawing puzzles that involve getting three people, animals, etc. to their respective homes without crossing any paths. Many of these puzzles seem impossible at first glance, but with a little persistence can be solved. This is the easier of the two puzzles of this kind that appear in this section, but students may still need to be encouraged to persist until they find a solution.

Puzzle Presentation
    Each student will need a copy of the student sheet for this puzzle. Be sure that students use pencils when they search for their solution, so that they can erase and try again if necessary.

Solution Hint
    Don't think in straight lines or direct routes.

Rainforest RIDDLE

The anaconda, the jaguar, and the howler monkey all live in the same part of the rainforest. As long as none of them cross paths, everyone stays happy. Show how the anaconda can get to its rock, the jaguar can get to its den, and the monkey can get to its tree without any of the paths crossing.

Den

Tree

Rock

Anaconda

Jaguar

Howler Monkey

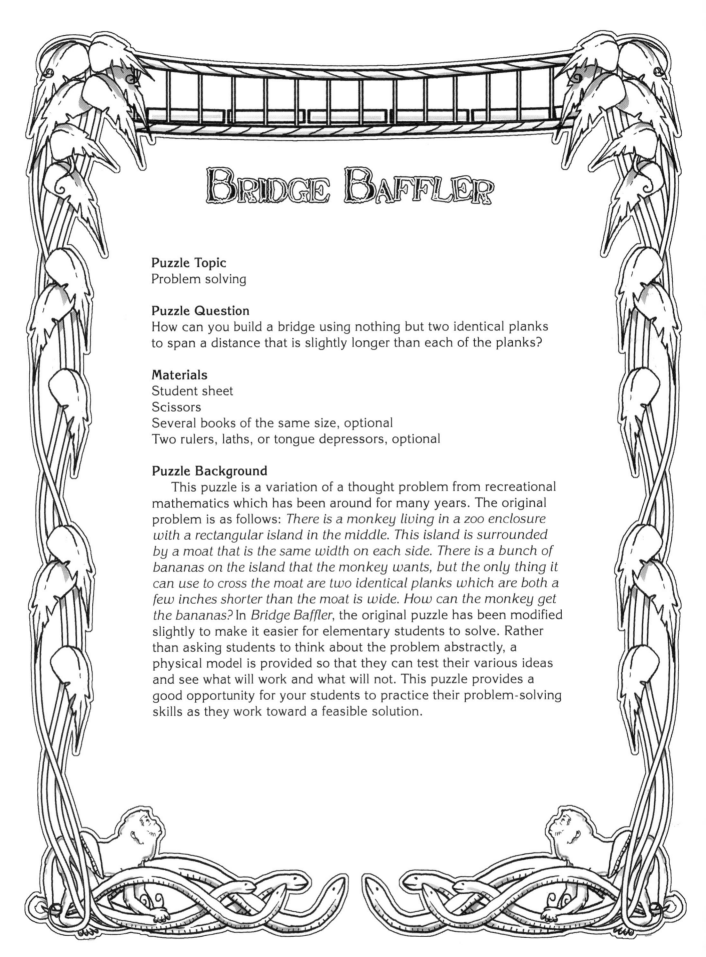

BRIDGE BAFFLER

Puzzle Topic
Problem solving

Puzzle Question
How can you build a bridge using nothing but two identical planks to span a distance that is slightly longer than each of the planks?

Materials
Student sheet
Scissors
Several books of the same size, optional
Two rulers, laths, or tongue depressors, optional

Puzzle Background
   This puzzle is a variation of a thought problem from recreational mathematics which has been around for many years. The original problem is as follows: *There is a monkey living in a zoo enclosure with a rectangular island in the middle. This island is surrounded by a moat that is the same width on each side. There is a bunch of bananas on the island that the monkey wants, but the only thing it can use to cross the moat are two identical planks which are both a few inches shorter than the moat is wide. How can the monkey get the bananas?* In *Bridge Baffler*, the original puzzle has been modified slightly to make it easier for elementary students to solve. Rather than asking students to think about the problem abstractly, a physical model is provided so that they can test their various ideas and see what will work and what will not. This puzzle provides a good opportunity for your students to practice their problem-solving skills as they work toward a feasible solution.

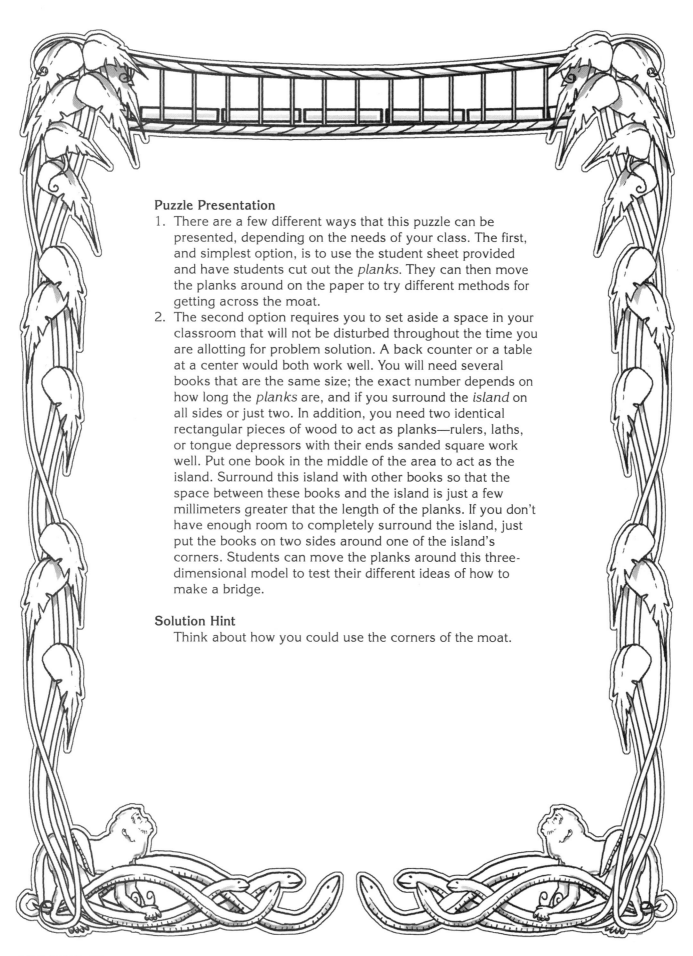

Puzzle Presentation

1. There are a few different ways that this puzzle can be presented, depending on the needs of your class. The first, and simplest option, is to use the student sheet provided and have students cut out the *planks*. They can then move the planks around on the paper to try different methods for getting across the moat.

2. The second option requires you to set aside a space in your classroom that will not be disturbed throughout the time you are allotting for problem solution. A back counter or a table at a center would both work well. You will need several books that are the same size; the exact number depends on how long the *planks* are, and if you surround the *island* on all sides or just two. In addition, you need two identical rectangular pieces of wood to act as planks—rulers, laths, or tongue depressors with their ends sanded square work well. Put one book in the middle of the area to act as the island. Surround this island with other books so that the space between these books and the island is just a few millimeters greater that the length of the planks. If you don't have enough room to completely surround the island, just put the books on two sides around one of the island's corners. Students can move the planks around this three-dimensional model to test their different ideas of how to make a bridge.

Solution Hint

Think about how you could use the corners of the moat.

BRIDGE BAFFLER

Can you build a bridge using ONLY two identical planks to span the gap from a rectangular island to the surrounding land if the gap is just slightly larger than the length of the planks? Cut out the two planks below and use the diagram to show how you would do this.

Surrounding land

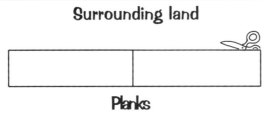

Island

Surrounding land

Surrounding land

Surrounding land

Planks

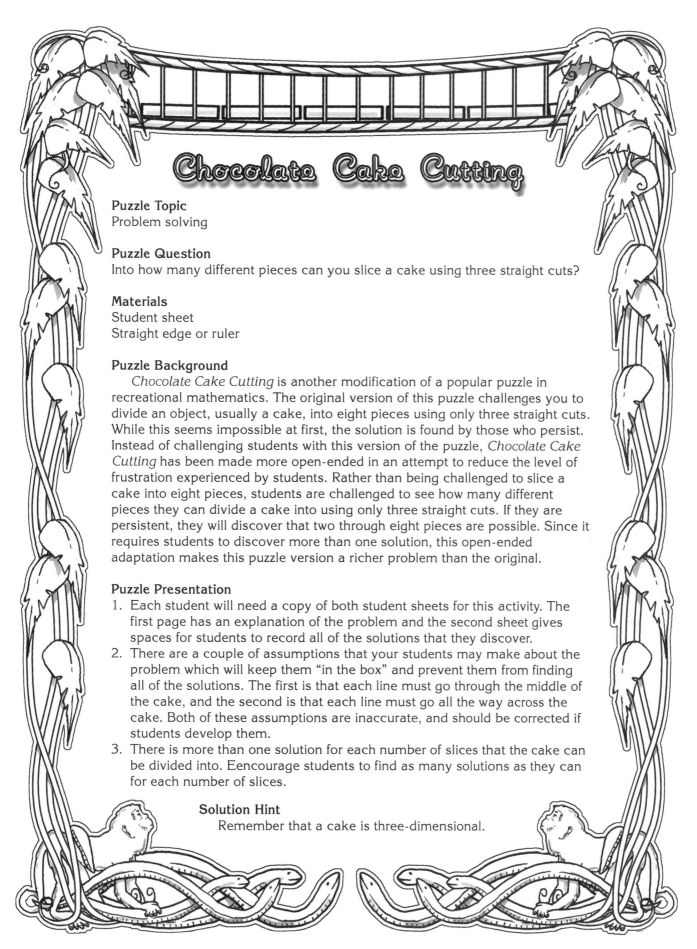

Chocolate Cake Cutting

Puzzle Topic
Problem solving

Puzzle Question
Into how many different pieces can you slice a cake using three straight cuts?

Materials
Student sheet
Straight edge or ruler

Puzzle Background
   Chocolate Cake Cutting is another modification of a popular puzzle in recreational mathematics. The original version of this puzzle challenges you to divide an object, usually a cake, into eight pieces using only three straight cuts. While this seems impossible at first, the solution is found by those who persist. Instead of challenging students with this version of the puzzle, *Chocolate Cake Cutting* has been made more open-ended in an attempt to reduce the level of frustration experienced by students. Rather than being challenged to slice a cake into eight pieces, students are challenged to see how many different pieces they can divide a cake into using only three straight cuts. If they are persistent, they will discover that two through eight pieces are possible. Since it requires students to discover more than one solution, this open-ended adaptation makes this puzzle version a richer problem than the original.

Puzzle Presentation
1. Each student will need a copy of both student sheets for this activity. The first page has an explanation of the problem and the second sheet gives spaces for students to record all of the solutions that they discover.
2. There are a couple of assumptions that your students may make about the problem which will keep them "in the box" and prevent them from finding all of the solutions. The first is that each line must go through the middle of the cake, and the second is that each line must go all the way across the cake. Both of these assumptions are inaccurate, and should be corrected if students develop them.
3. There is more than one solution for each number of slices that the cake can be divided into. Eencourage students to find as many solutions as they can for each number of slices.

   Solution Hint
   Remember that a cake is three-dimensional.

Chocolate Cake Cutting

A cake can be cut into six pieces with three straight cuts as shown below. Your challenge in this problem is to use three straight cuts to make other numbers of pieces. Try to find all of the possible numbers of pieces into which you can cut a cake with exactly three straight cuts. When you discover a solution, record it in one of the spaces on the next sheet.

What is the minimum number of pieces possible? The maximum? Defend your answers.

Chocolate Cake Cutting

Draw each solution you discover in one of the spaces below.

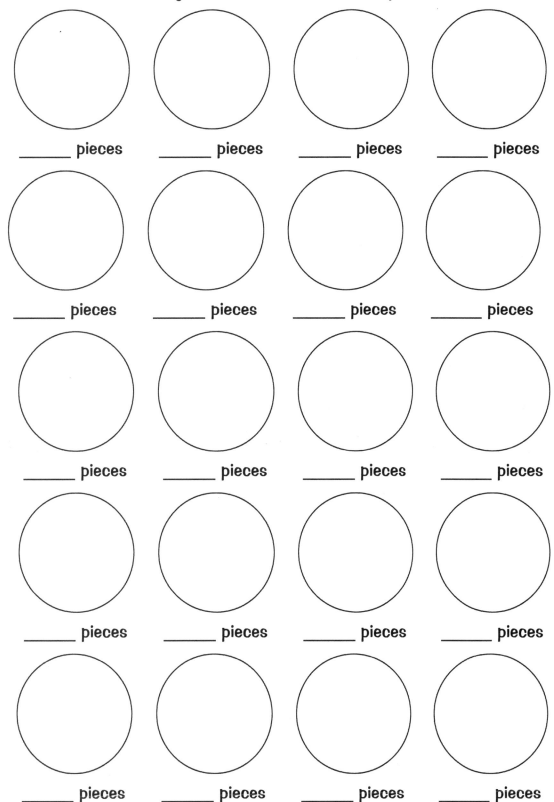

_____ pieces _____ pieces _____ pieces _____ pieces

_____ pieces _____ pieces _____ pieces _____ pieces

_____ pieces _____ pieces _____ pieces _____ pieces

_____ pieces _____ pieces _____ pieces _____ pieces

_____ pieces _____ pieces _____ pieces _____ pieces

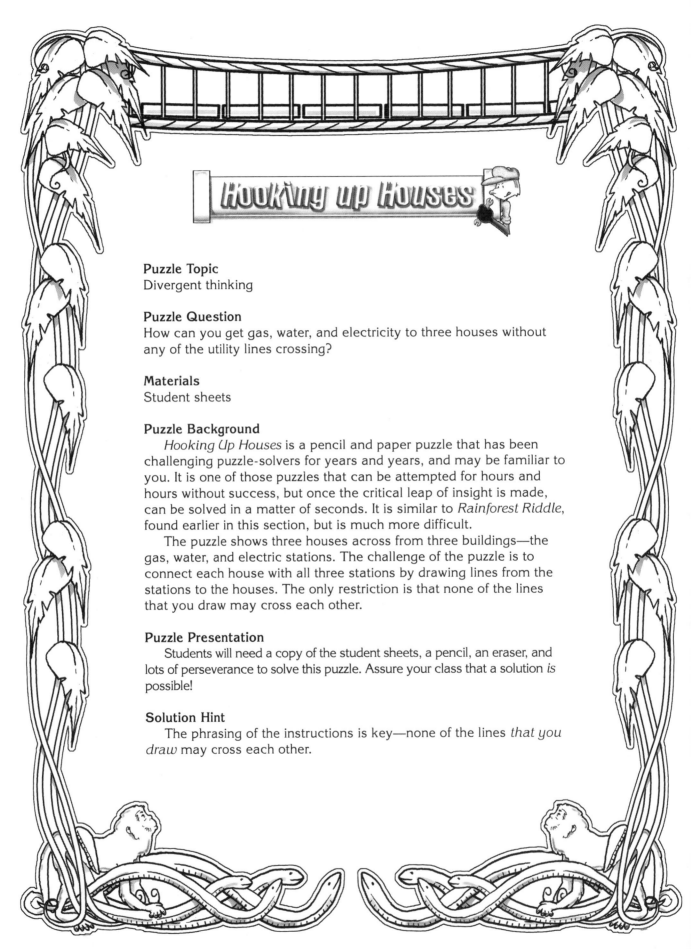

Hooking up Houses

Puzzle Topic
Divergent thinking

Puzzle Question
How can you get gas, water, and electricity to three houses without any of the utility lines crossing?

Materials
Student sheets

Puzzle Background
 Hooking Up Houses is a pencil and paper puzzle that has been challenging puzzle-solvers for years and years, and may be familiar to you. It is one of those puzzles that can be attempted for hours and hours without success, but once the critical leap of insight is made, can be solved in a matter of seconds. It is similar to *Rainforest Riddle*, found earlier in this section, but is much more difficult.
 The puzzle shows three houses across from three buildings—the gas, water, and electric stations. The challenge of the puzzle is to connect each house with all three stations by drawing lines from the stations to the houses. The only restriction is that none of the lines that you draw may cross each other.

Puzzle Presentation
 Students will need a copy of the student sheets, a pencil, an eraser, and lots of perseverance to solve this puzzle. Assure your class that a solution *is* possible!

Solution Hint
 The phrasing of the instructions is key—none of the lines *that you draw* may cross each other.

Hooking up Houses

There is a housing development in town that has just constructed three new houses. Each house needs to be hooked up to the gas company, the water station, and the electric plant. However, safety codes prevent any of the lines running from the utilities to the houses from crossing each other. Your challenge is to help the housing developers figure out a way to get all three services to each house without crossing any of the lines.

Use the model of the neighborhood shown below to record your solution once you have discovered one. All of your work should be done on the smaller models on the next page. Remember that none of the lines you draw may cross each other.

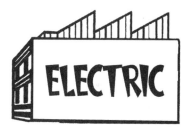

| G | W | E |

| G | W | E |

| G | W | E |

| G | W | E |

| G | W | E |

| G | W | E |

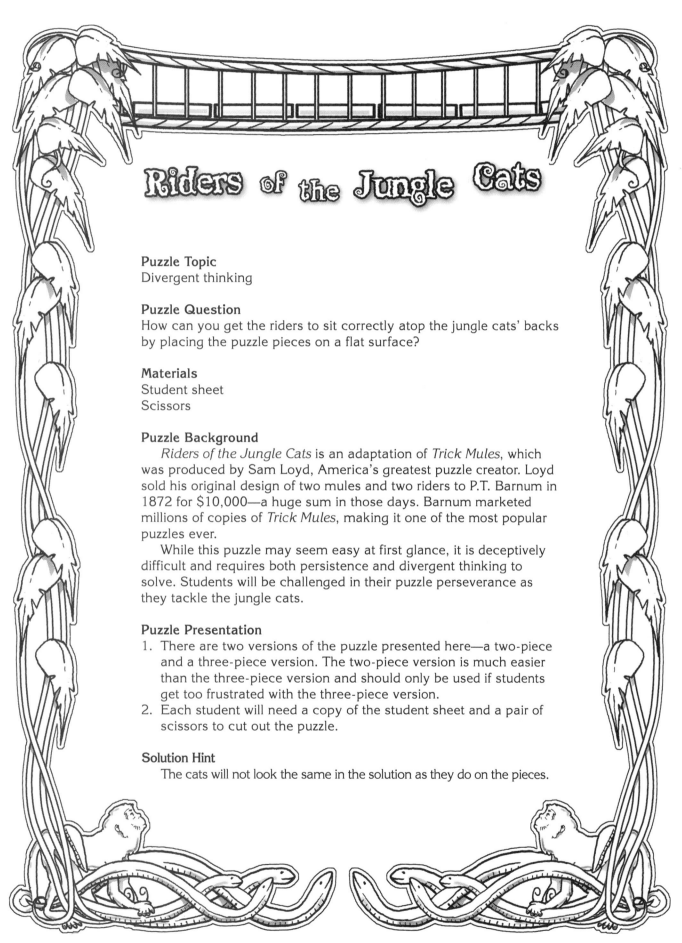

Riders of the Jungle Cats

Puzzle Topic
Divergent thinking

Puzzle Question
How can you get the riders to sit correctly atop the jungle cats' backs by placing the puzzle pieces on a flat surface?

Materials
Student sheet
Scissors

Puzzle Background
Riders of the Jungle Cats is an adaptation of *Trick Mules*, which was produced by Sam Loyd, America's greatest puzzle creator. Loyd sold his original design of two mules and two riders to P.T. Barnum in 1872 for $10,000—a huge sum in those days. Barnum marketed millions of copies of *Trick Mules*, making it one of the most popular puzzles ever.

While this puzzle may seem easy at first glance, it is deceptively difficult and requires both persistence and divergent thinking to solve. Students will be challenged in their puzzle perseverance as they tackle the jungle cats.

Puzzle Presentation
1. There are two versions of the puzzle presented here—a two-piece and a three-piece version. The two-piece version is much easier than the three-piece version and should only be used if students get too frustrated with the three-piece version.
2. Each student will need a copy of the student sheet and a pair of scissors to cut out the puzzle.

Solution Hint
The cats will not look the same in the solution as they do on the pieces.

Riders of the Jungle Cats

Cut out the pieces below and place them flat on your desk in such a way that the two rider are sitting correctly on the two jungle cats' backs. The pieces may overlap, but no folding, cutting, or tearing is allowed.

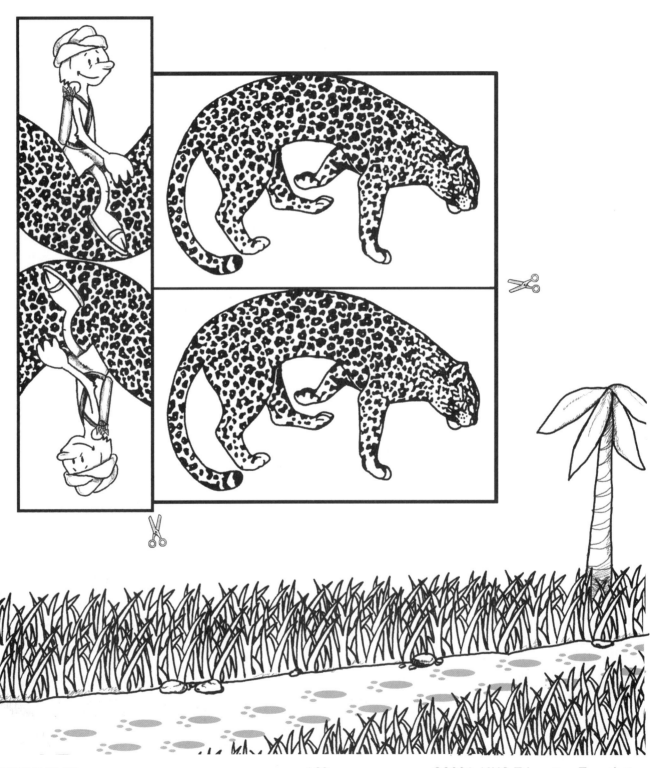

Riders of the Jungle Cats

Cut out the pieces below and place them flat on your desk in such a way that the two rider are sitting correctly on the two jungle cats' backs. The pieces may overlap, but no folding, cutting, or tearing is allowed.

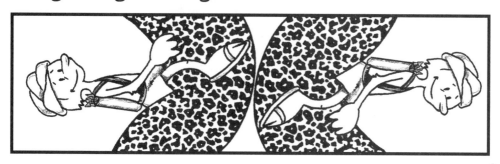

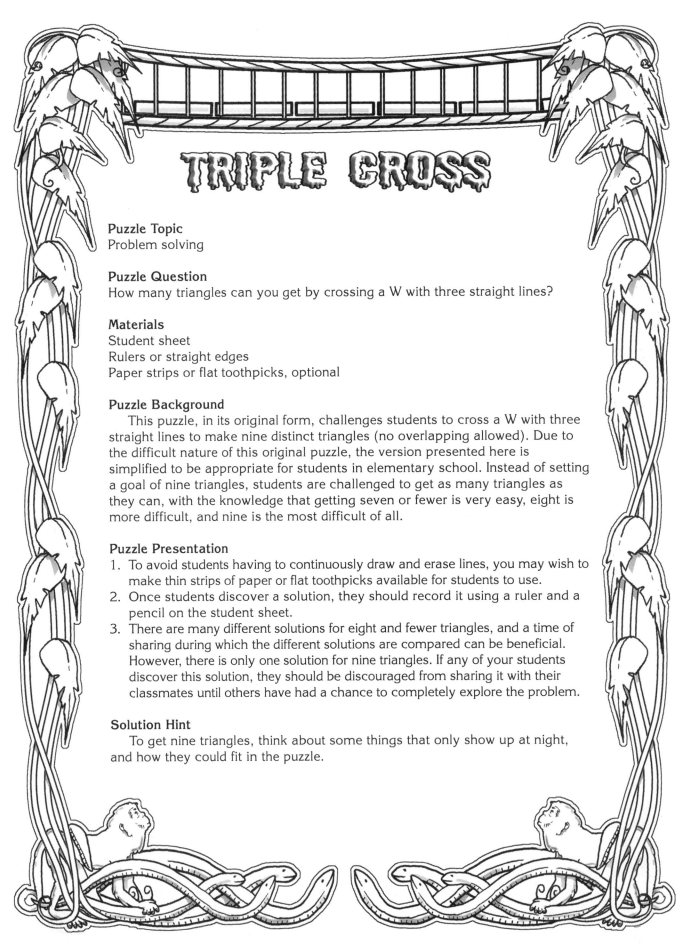

TRIPLE CROSS

Puzzle Topic
Problem solving

Puzzle Question
How many triangles can you get by crossing a W with three straight lines?

Materials
Student sheet
Rulers or straight edges
Paper strips or flat toothpicks, optional

Puzzle Background
   This puzzle, in its original form, challenges students to cross a W with three straight lines to make nine distinct triangles (no overlapping allowed). Due to the difficult nature of this original puzzle, the version presented here is simplified to be appropriate for students in elementary school. Instead of setting a goal of nine triangles, students are challenged to get as many triangles as they can, with the knowledge that getting seven or fewer is very easy, eight is more difficult, and nine is the most difficult of all.

Puzzle Presentation
1. To avoid students having to continuously draw and erase lines, you may wish to make thin strips of paper or flat toothpicks available for students to use.
2. Once students discover a solution, they should record it using a ruler and a pencil on the student sheet.
3. There are many different solutions for eight and fewer triangles, and a time of sharing during which the different solutions are compared can be beneficial. However, there is only one solution for nine triangles. If any of your students discover this solution, they should be discouraged from sharing it with their classmates until others have had a chance to completely explore the problem.

Solution Hint
   To get nine triangles, think about some things that only show up at night, and how they could fit in the puzzle.

TRIPLE CROSS

Cross each W below with three straight lines. See how many distinct triangles you can produce. The triangles cannot overlap each other. It's fairly easy to get seven or fewer triangles, eight is difficult, and nine is the ultimate challenge!

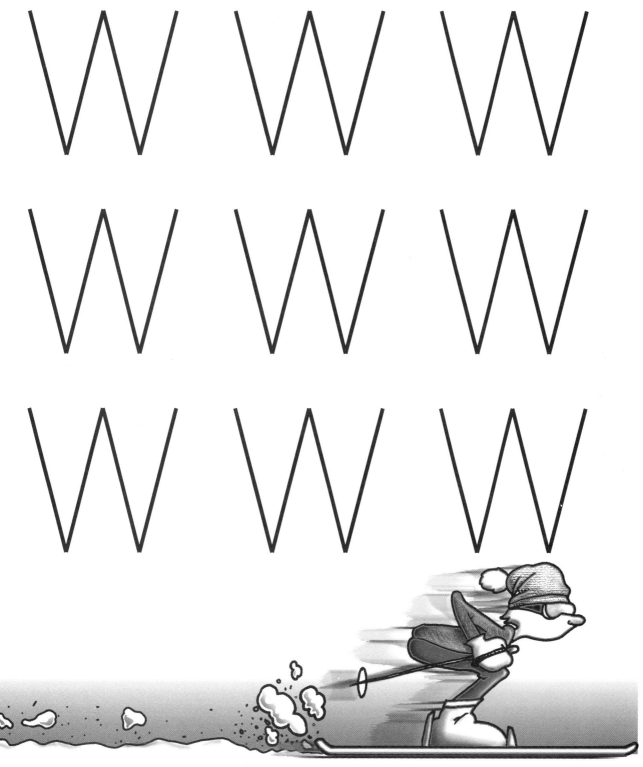

Alphabetical Puzzles

Puzzle #1

The letters in this puzzle are grouped according to their shape. Those letters having only straight lines are in List #1, and those having a curve somewhere are in List #2. Therefore, the letters X, Y, and Z would all go in List #1.

Puzzle #2

The letters in this puzzle are grouped according to their size. Letters which do not go above or below the line (i.e. no stems, tails or dots) are in List #1. Letters which are longer and extend either above or below the line are in List #2. Therefore the letters x and z would go in List #1, while y would go in List #2.

Puzzle #3

The letters in this puzzle are the first letters of the counting numbers, beginning with one. Therefore the next three letters are N, T, E (**N**ine, **T**en, **E**leven).

Puzzle #4

The letters in this puzzle are the first letters of the months of the year. Therefore the next three letters are O, N, D (**O**ctober, **N**ovember, **D**ecember).

Turkey Trappings

It's a Snap!

It is possible to make the bracelet for $30 by opening only three links. To do this, open three links which are all in the same initial piece of chain. This leaves three chains that are three links long, and three open links to use as connecting pieces. Using this method, it is possible to connect the links into a circle and create the bracelet in the most inexpensive way. In the first step, open the three links. In the second step, place the open links between the chains. In the third step, join the chains together to make a complete circle.

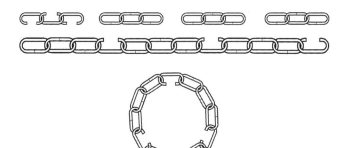

Rainforest Riddle

This is one possible solution. Your students may discover others.

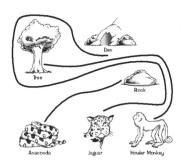

Bridge Baffler

One solution to the problem is shown below. While your students may discover other solutions, this one is the "most correct."

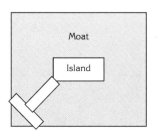

Chocolate Cake Slicing

The diagrams below show one possible solution for each number of slices from two to eight. The third cut in the cake with eight slices is a horizontal cut through the thickness of the cake between its top and bottom.

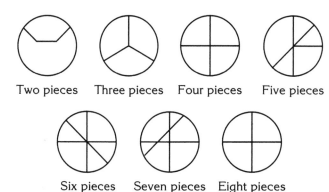

Two pieces   Three pieces   Four pieces   Five pieces

Six pieces   Seven pieces   Eight pieces

Hooking Up Houses

One solution is shown below, but there are many others. Each valid solution requires the lines for some of the utilities to go through some of the houses.

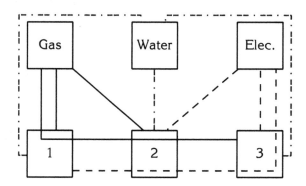

Riders of the Jungle Cats

The solutions for the two-piece and three-piece puzzle are the same. You merely have to arrange the pieces in the same way.

Triple Cross

The solution for nine triangles, as well as sample solutions with both seven and eight triangles are shown below.

Seven Triangles   Eight Triangles   Nine Triangles

Visual Illusions
Introduction

Visual illusions hold a special fascination for most people. There is something strangely appealing when the brain is tricked into *seeing* things that just cannot be. The paradoxes created by these illusions are quite powerful and are usually difficult to explain. Visual illusions, paradoxes, and puzzles have a rich history. In modern times these visual paradoxes are often associated with artists like Salvador Dali and M. C. Escher. However, a study of art history will show they go back hundreds of years to artists like Leonardo da Vinci and Hans Holbein.

In the 20th century, psychologists tried to understand how the brain interprets various visual illusions. Also in the 20th century, mathematicians like Roger Penrose created visual illusions *just for the fun of it*. (See *Up and Down the Staircase* for more on this.) We hope that in the 21st century these puzzles can be used to capture your students' imaginations and show them that puzzles (and the mathematics behind these puzzles) are enjoyable.

Unlike the other puzzles in this book, most of the visual puzzles do not have a solution, per se. The goal in these puzzles is merely to explain why the paradox or illusion works. For some of the puzzles the explanation is fairly complex and beyond the reach of elementary students. However, they can still benefit from the experience of studying the puzzles and developing simple, if incomplete, explanations.

The puzzles in this section are especially conducive to sharing with students' families, since most adults are also fascinated, and stumped, by visual puzzles. As they do this section, encourage students to be both creative in their thinking and observant. They should come to realize—after spending time with these puzzles—that you cannot always believe everything you see, and that sometimes what you observe to be true can change unexpectedly.

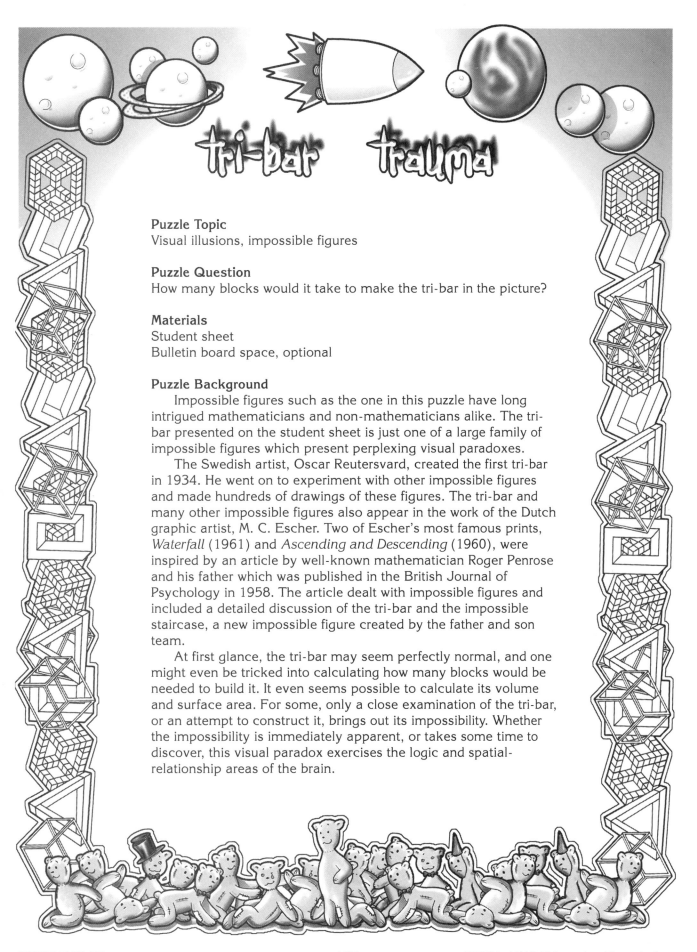

Puzzle Topic
Visual illusions, impossible figures

Puzzle Question
How many blocks would it take to make the tri-bar in the picture?

Materials
Student sheet
Bulletin board space, optional

Puzzle Background
Impossible figures such as the one in this puzzle have long intrigued mathematicians and non-mathematicians alike. The tri-bar presented on the student sheet is just one of a large family of impossible figures which present perplexing visual paradoxes.

The Swedish artist, Oscar Reutersvard, created the first tri-bar in 1934. He went on to experiment with other impossible figures and made hundreds of drawings of these figures. The tri-bar and many other impossible figures also appear in the work of the Dutch graphic artist, M. C. Escher. Two of Escher's most famous prints, *Waterfall* (1961) and *Ascending and Descending* (1960), were inspired by an article by well-known mathematician Roger Penrose and his father which was published in the British Journal of Psychology in 1958. The article dealt with impossible figures and included a detailed discussion of the tri-bar and the impossible staircase, a new impossible figure created by the father and son team.

At first glance, the tri-bar may seem perfectly normal, and one might even be tricked into calculating how many blocks would be needed to build it. It even seems possible to calculate its volume and surface area. For some, only a close examination of the tri-bar, or an attempt to construct it, brings out its impossibility. Whether the impossibility is immediately apparent, or takes some time to discover, this visual paradox exercises the logic and spatial-relationship areas of the brain.

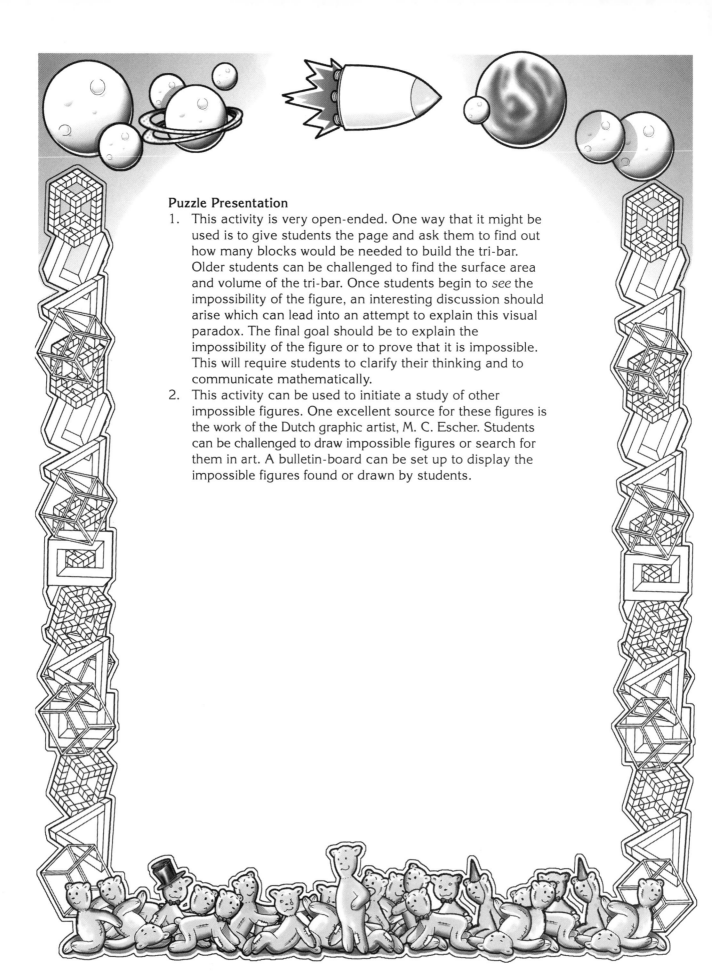

Puzzle Presentation

1. This activity is very open-ended. One way that it might be used is to give students the page and ask them to find out how many blocks would be needed to build the tri-bar. Older students can be challenged to find the surface area and volume of the tri-bar. Once students begin to *see* the impossibility of the figure, an interesting discussion should arise which can lead into an attempt to explain this visual paradox. The final goal should be to explain the impossibility of the figure or to prove that it is impossible. This will require students to clarify their thinking and to communicate mathematically.

2. This activity can be used to initiate a study of other impossible figures. One excellent source for these figures is the work of the Dutch graphic artist, M. C. Escher. Students can be challenged to draw impossible figures or search for them in art. A bulletin-board can be set up to display the impossible figures found or drawn by students.

tri-bar trauma

Study the figure below.

How many blocks would it take to make the tri-bar pictured above?

What do you notice about the tri-bar?

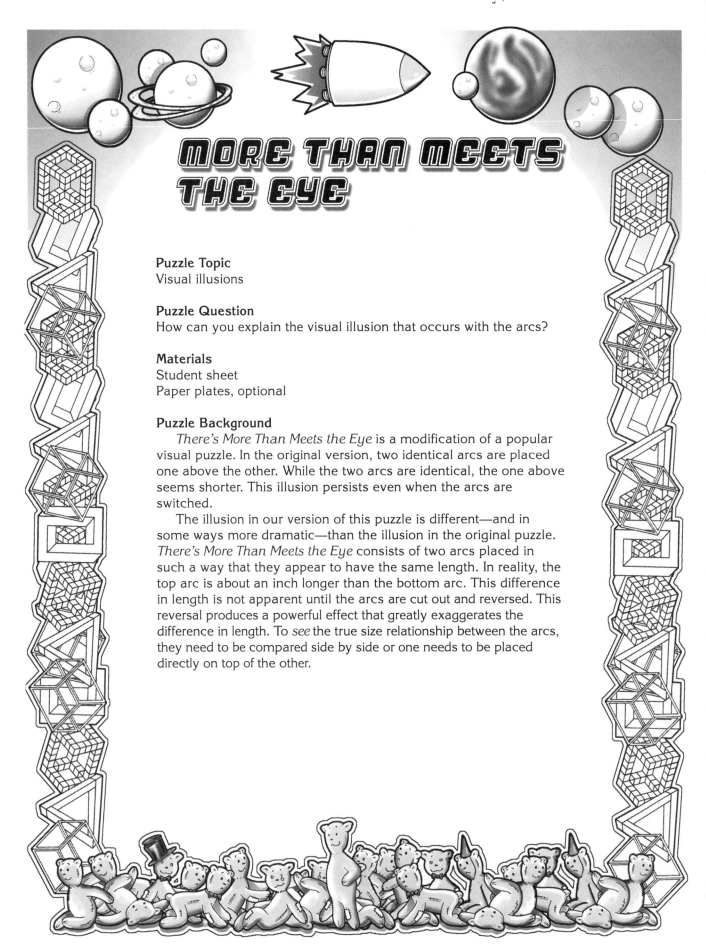

MORE THAN MEETS THE EYE

Puzzle Topic
Visual illusions

Puzzle Question
How can you explain the visual illusion that occurs with the arcs?

Materials
Student sheet
Paper plates, optional

Puzzle Background
There's More Than Meets the Eye is a modification of a popular visual puzzle. In the original version, two identical arcs are placed one above the other. While the two arcs are identical, the one above seems shorter. This illusion persists even when the arcs are switched.

The illusion in our version of this puzzle is different—and in some ways more dramatic—than the illusion in the original puzzle. *There's More Than Meets the Eye* consists of two arcs placed in such a way that they appear to have the same length. In reality, the top arc is about an inch longer than the bottom arc. This difference in length is not apparent until the arcs are cut out and reversed. This reversal produces a powerful effect that greatly exaggerates the difference in length. To *see* the true size relationship between the arcs, they need to be compared side by side or one needs to be placed directly on top of the other.

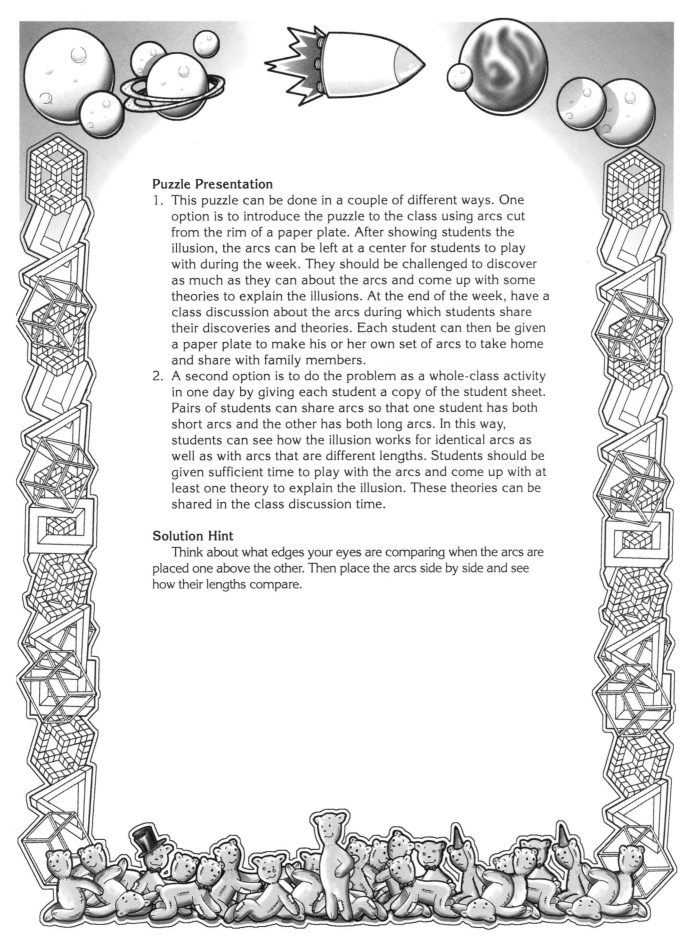

Puzzle Presentation

1. This puzzle can be done in a couple of different ways. One option is to introduce the puzzle to the class using arcs cut from the rim of a paper plate. After showing students the illusion, the arcs can be left at a center for students to play with during the week. They should be challenged to discover as much as they can about the arcs and come up with some theories to explain the illusions. At the end of the week, have a class discussion about the arcs during which students share their discoveries and theories. Each student can then be given a paper plate to make his or her own set of arcs to take home and share with family members.

2. A second option is to do the problem as a whole-class activity in one day by giving each student a copy of the student sheet. Pairs of students can share arcs so that one student has both short arcs and the other has both long arcs. In this way, students can see how the illusion works for identical arcs as well as with arcs that are different lengths. Students should be given sufficient time to play with the arcs and come up with at least one theory to explain the illusion. These theories can be shared in the class discussion time.

Solution Hint

Think about what edges your eyes are comparing when the arcs are placed one above the other. Then place the arcs side by side and see how their lengths compare.

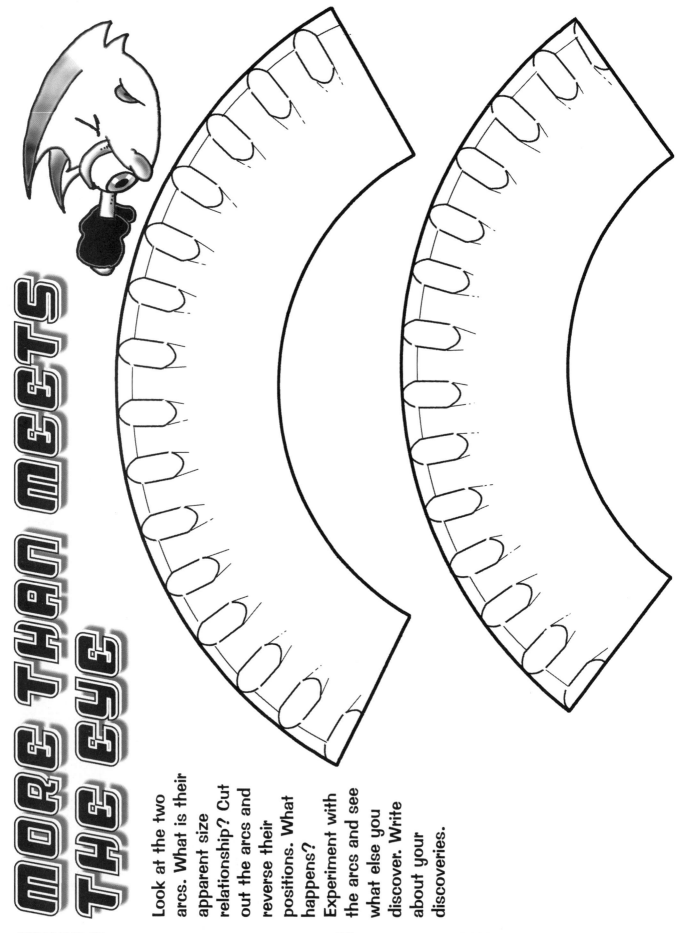

MORE THAN MEETS THE EYE

Look at the two arcs. What is their apparent size relationship? Cut out the arcs and reverse their positions. What happens? Experiment with the arcs and see what else you discover. Write about your discoveries.

172

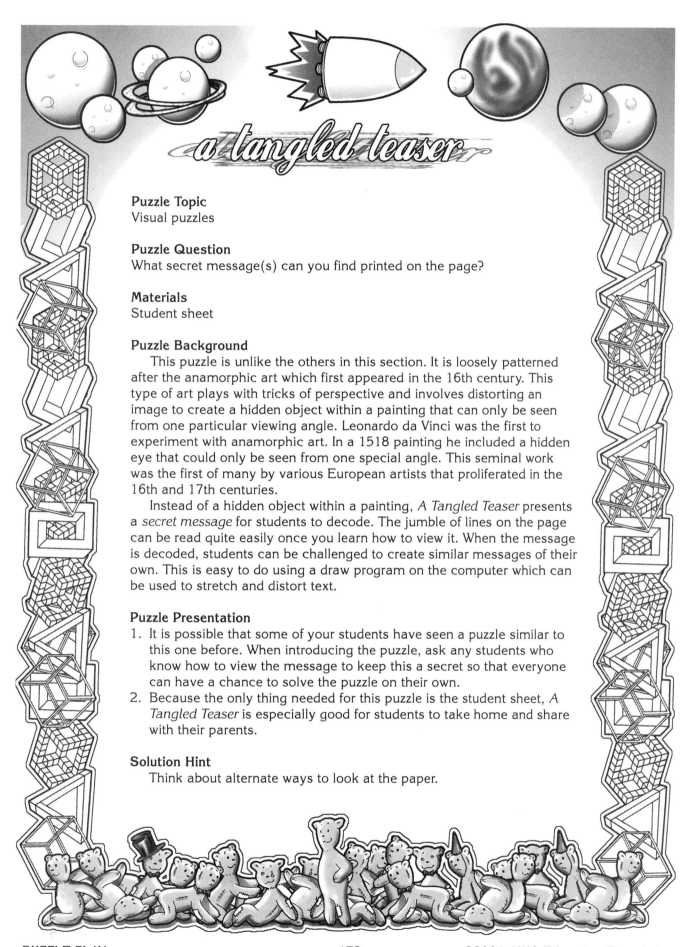

a tangled teaser

Puzzle Topic
Visual puzzles

Puzzle Question
What secret message(s) can you find printed on the page?

Materials
Student sheet

Puzzle Background
This puzzle is unlike the others in this section. It is loosely patterned after the anamorphic art which first appeared in the 16th century. This type of art plays with tricks of perspective and involves distorting an image to create a hidden object within a painting that can only be seen from one particular viewing angle. Leonardo da Vinci was the first to experiment with anamorphic art. In a 1518 painting he included a hidden eye that could only be seen from one special angle. This seminal work was the first of many by various European artists that proliferated in the 16th and 17th centuries.

Instead of a hidden object within a painting, *A Tangled Teaser* presents a *secret message* for students to decode. The jumble of lines on the page can be read quite easily once you learn how to view it. When the message is decoded, students can be challenged to create similar messages of their own. This is easy to do using a draw program on the computer which can be used to stretch and distort text.

Puzzle Presentation
1. It is possible that some of your students have seen a puzzle similar to this one before. When introducing the puzzle, ask any students who know how to view the message to keep this a secret so that everyone can have a chance to solve the puzzle on their own.
2. Because the only thing needed for this puzzle is the student sheet, *A Tangled Teaser* is especially good for students to take home and share with their parents.

Solution Hint
Think about alternate ways to look at the paper.

a tangled teaser

The task in this puzzle is to read the secret message printed below. It may take a while, but careful observation and creative thinking should untangle the mystery.

174

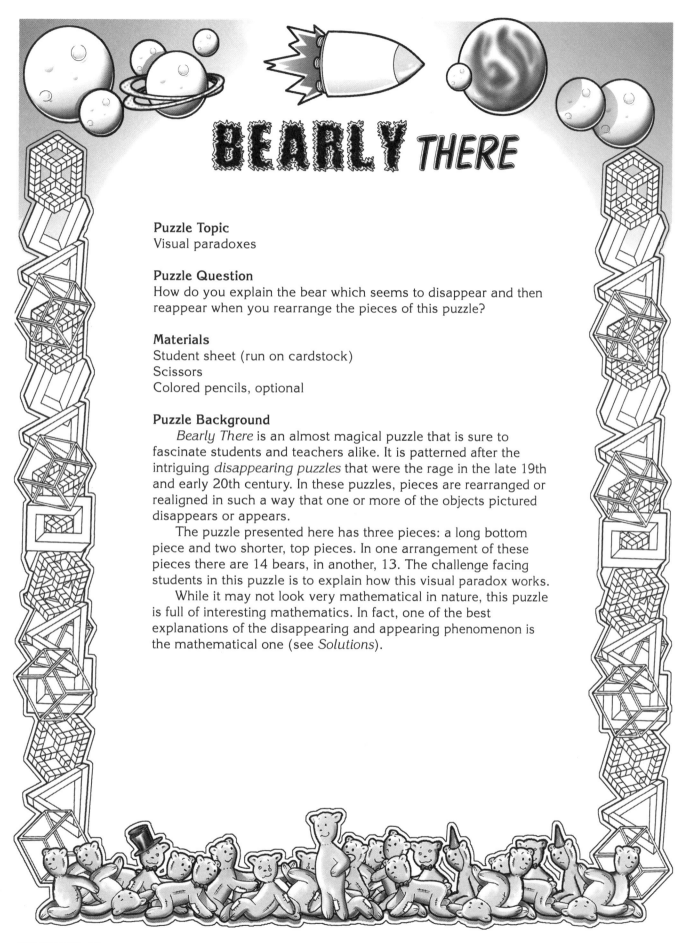

BEARLY THERE

Puzzle Topic
Visual paradoxes

Puzzle Question
How do you explain the bear which seems to disappear and then reappear when you rearrange the pieces of this puzzle?

Materials
Student sheet (run on cardstock)
Scissors
Colored pencils, optional

Puzzle Background
Bearly There is an almost magical puzzle that is sure to fascinate students and teachers alike. It is patterned after the intriguing *disappearing puzzles* that were the rage in the late 19th and early 20th century. In these puzzles, pieces are rearranged or realigned in such a way that one or more of the objects pictured disappears or appears.

The puzzle presented here has three pieces: a long bottom piece and two shorter, top pieces. In one arrangement of these pieces there are 14 bears, in another, 13. The challenge facing students in this puzzle is to explain how this visual paradox works.

While it may not look very mathematical in nature, this puzzle is full of interesting mathematics. In fact, one of the best explanations of the disappearing and appearing phenomenon is the mathematical one (see *Solutions*).

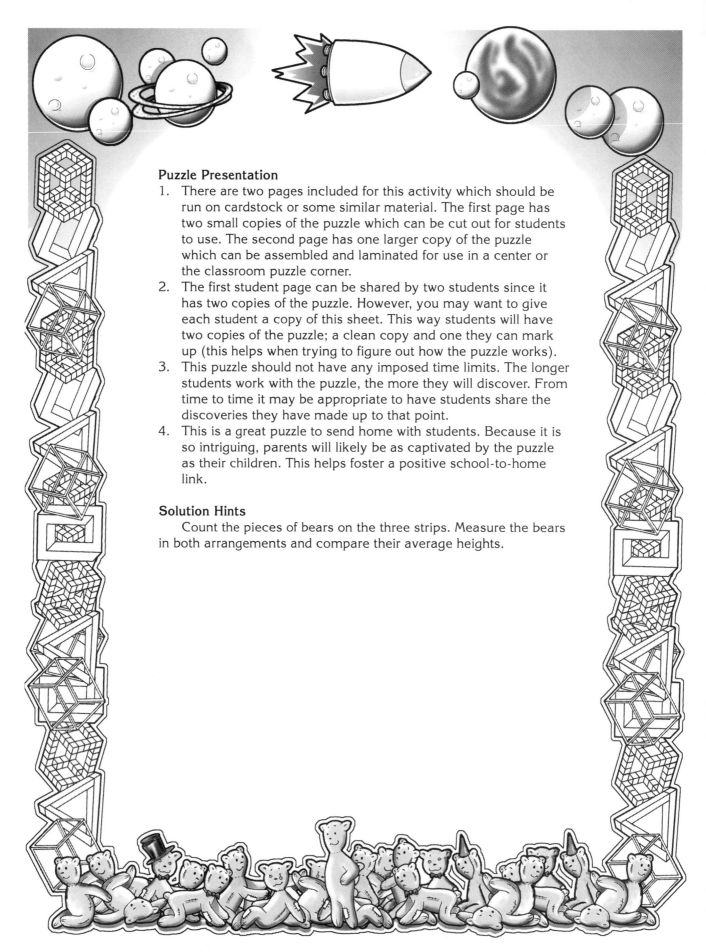

Puzzle Presentation

1. There are two pages included for this activity which should be run on cardstock or some similar material. The first page has two small copies of the puzzle which can be cut out for students to use. The second page has one larger copy of the puzzle which can be assembled and laminated for use in a center or the classroom puzzle corner.

2. The first student page can be shared by two students since it has two copies of the puzzle. However, you may want to give each student a copy of this sheet. This way students will have two copies of the puzzle; a clean copy and one they can mark up (this helps when trying to figure out how the puzzle works).

3. This puzzle should not have any imposed time limits. The longer students work with the puzzle, the more they will discover. From time to time it may be appropriate to have students share the discoveries they have made up to that point.

4. This is a great puzzle to send home with students. Because it is so intriguing, parents will likely be as captivated by the puzzle as their children. This helps foster a positive school-to-home link.

Solution Hints

Count the pieces of bears on the three strips. Measure the bears in both arrangements and compare their average heights.

BEARLY THERE

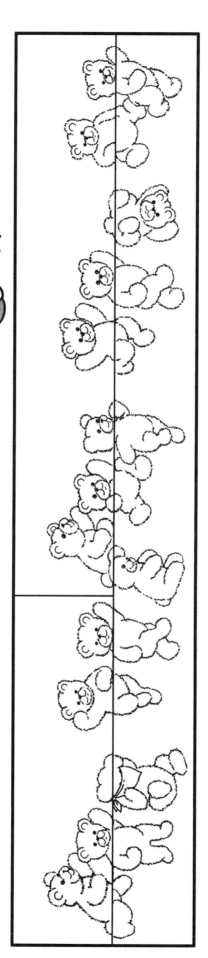

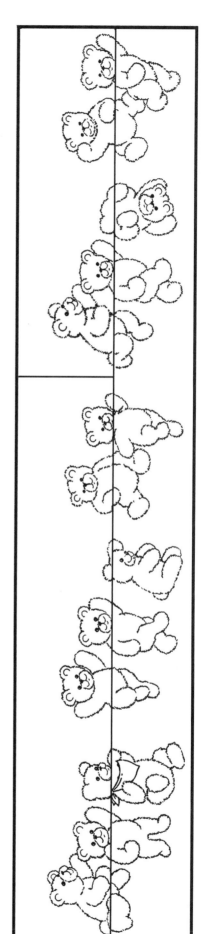

How many bears are on each strip below? Carefully cut one of the strips apart along the lines. Switch the top two pieces and count the bears again. What do you notice? How does this happen?

BEARLY THERE

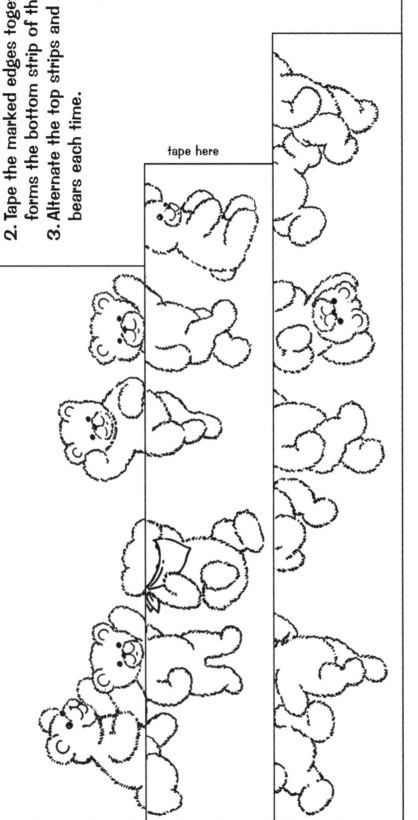

tape here

tape here

PUZZLE PLAY   178   ©2001 AIMS Education Foundation

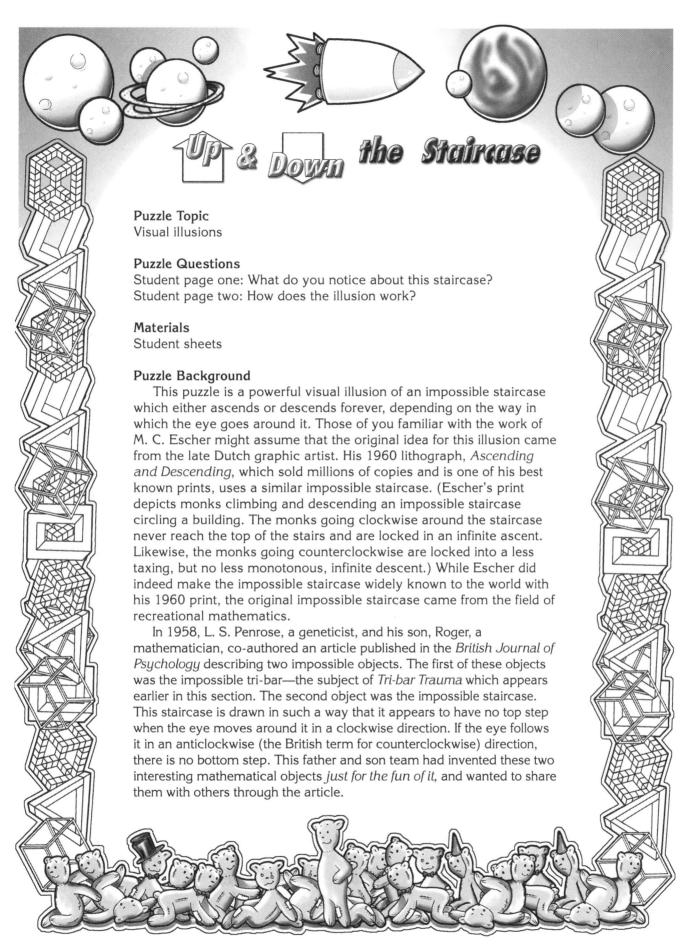

Up & Down the Staircase

Puzzle Topic
Visual illusions

Puzzle Questions
Student page one: What do you notice about this staircase?
Student page two: How does the illusion work?

Materials
Student sheets

Puzzle Background
This puzzle is a powerful visual illusion of an impossible staircase which either ascends or descends forever, depending on the way in which the eye goes around it. Those of you familiar with the work of M. C. Escher might assume that the original idea for this illusion came from the late Dutch graphic artist. His 1960 lithograph, *Ascending and Descending*, which sold millions of copies and is one of his best known prints, uses a similar impossible staircase. (Escher's print depicts monks climbing and descending an impossible staircase circling a building. The monks going clockwise around the staircase never reach the top of the stairs and are locked in an infinite ascent. Likewise, the monks going counterclockwise are locked into a less taxing, but no less monotonous, infinite descent.) While Escher did indeed make the impossible staircase widely known to the world with his 1960 print, the original impossible staircase came from the field of recreational mathematics.

In 1958, L. S. Penrose, a geneticist, and his son, Roger, a mathematician, co-authored an article published in the *British Journal of Psychology* describing two impossible objects. The first of these objects was the impossible tri-bar—the subject of *Tri-bar Trauma* which appears earlier in this section. The second object was the impossible staircase. This staircase is drawn in such a way that it appears to have no top step when the eye moves around it in a clockwise direction. If the eye follows it in an anticlockwise (the British term for counterclockwise) direction, there is no bottom step. This father and son team had invented these two interesting mathematical objects *just for the fun of it,* and wanted to share them with others through the article.

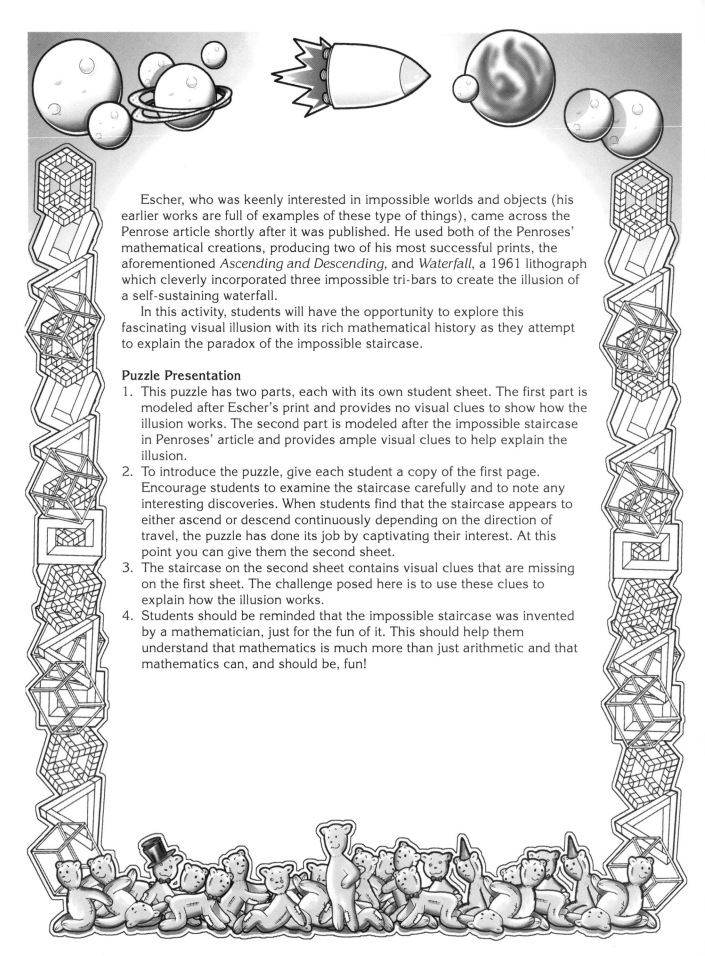

Escher, who was keenly interested in impossible worlds and objects (his earlier works are full of examples of these type of things), came across the Penrose article shortly after it was published. He used both of the Penroses' mathematical creations, producing two of his most successful prints, the aforementioned *Ascending and Descending*, and *Waterfall*, a 1961 lithograph which cleverly incorporated three impossible tri-bars to create the illusion of a self-sustaining waterfall.

In this activity, students will have the opportunity to explore this fascinating visual illusion with its rich mathematical history as they attempt to explain the paradox of the impossible staircase.

Puzzle Presentation
1. This puzzle has two parts, each with its own student sheet. The first part is modeled after Escher's print and provides no visual clues to show how the illusion works. The second part is modeled after the impossible staircase in Penroses' article and provides ample visual clues to help explain the illusion.
2. To introduce the puzzle, give each student a copy of the first page. Encourage students to examine the staircase carefully and to note any interesting discoveries. When students find that the staircase appears to either ascend or descend continuously depending on the direction of travel, the puzzle has done its job by captivating their interest. At this point you can give them the second sheet.
3. The staircase on the second sheet contains visual clues that are missing on the first sheet. The challenge posed here is to use these clues to explain how the illusion works.
4. Students should be reminded that the impossible staircase was invented by a mathematician, just for the fun of it. This should help them understand that mathematics is much more than just arithmetic and that mathematics can, and should be, fun!

Up & Down the Staircase

Carefully examine this staircase. Do you notice anything interesting about it?

181

Up & Down the Staircase

The impossible staircase below is similar to the one invented by the mathematician, Sir Roger Penrose, and his geneticist father, Lionel. This staircase includes some visual clues that should help you discover how this illusion works.

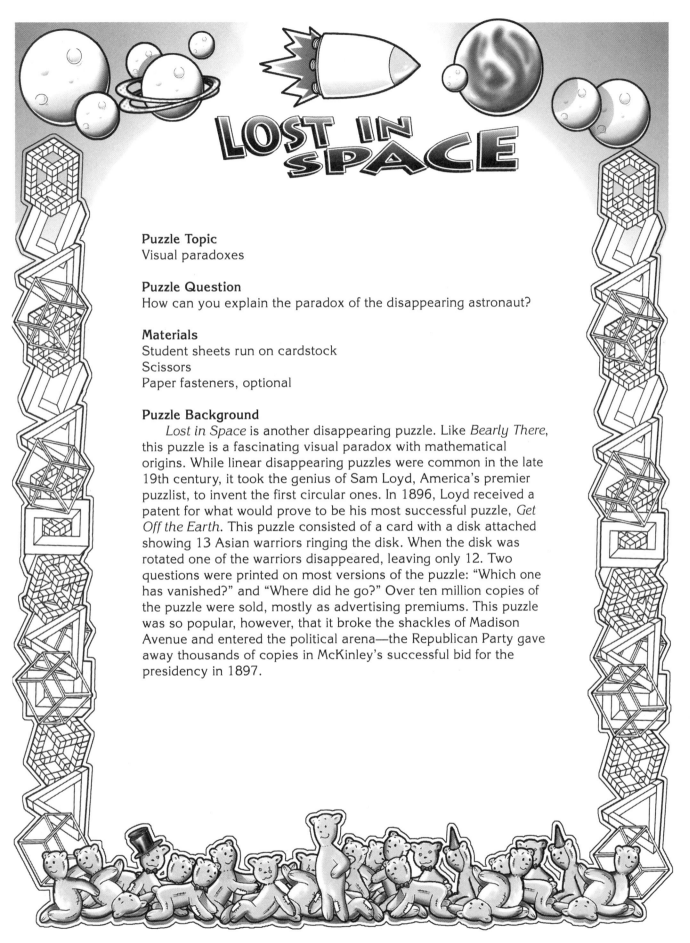

Puzzle Topic
Visual paradoxes

Puzzle Question
How can you explain the paradox of the disappearing astronaut?

Materials
Student sheets run on cardstock
Scissors
Paper fasteners, optional

Puzzle Background
   Lost in Space is another disappearing puzzle. Like *Bearly There*, this puzzle is a fascinating visual paradox with mathematical origins. While linear disappearing puzzles were common in the late 19th century, it took the genius of Sam Loyd, America's premier puzzlist, to invent the first circular ones. In 1896, Loyd received a patent for what would prove to be his most successful puzzle, *Get Off the Earth*. This puzzle consisted of a card with a disk attached showing 13 Asian warriors ringing the disk. When the disk was rotated one of the warriors disappeared, leaving only 12. Two questions were printed on most versions of the puzzle: "Which one has vanished?" and "Where did he go?" Over ten million copies of the puzzle were sold, mostly as advertising premiums. This puzzle was so popular, however, that it broke the shackles of Madison Avenue and entered the political arena—the Republican Party gave away thousands of copies in McKinley's successful bid for the presidency in 1897.

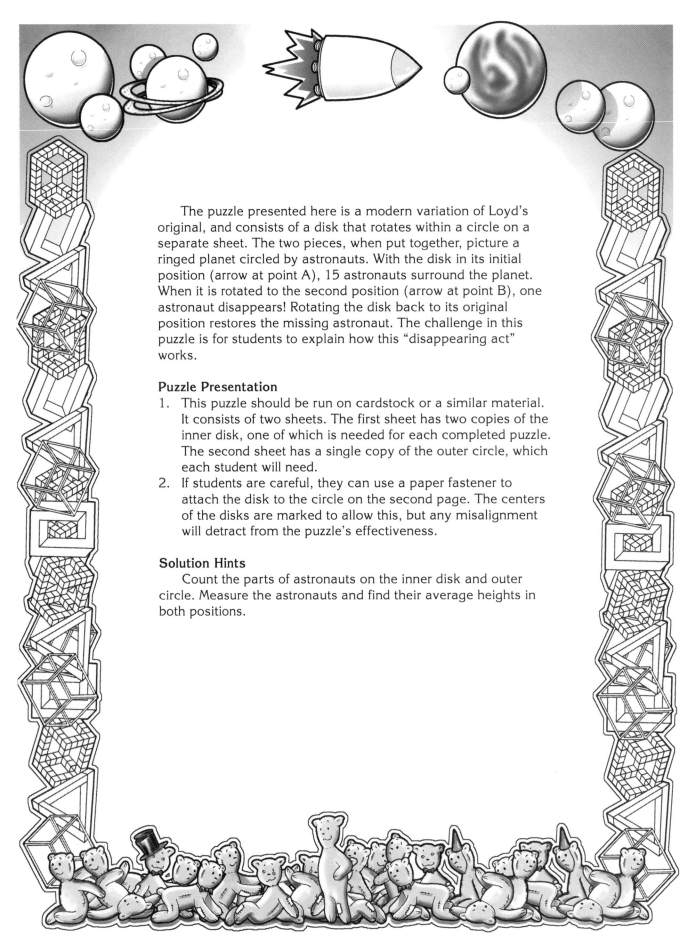

The puzzle presented here is a modern variation of Loyd's original, and consists of a disk that rotates within a circle on a separate sheet. The two pieces, when put together, picture a ringed planet circled by astronauts. With the disk in its initial position (arrow at point A), 15 astronauts surround the planet. When it is rotated to the second position (arrow at point B), one astronaut disappears! Rotating the disk back to its original position restores the missing astronaut. The challenge in this puzzle is for students to explain how this "disappearing act" works.

Puzzle Presentation
1. This puzzle should be run on cardstock or a similar material. It consists of two sheets. The first sheet has two copies of the inner disk, one of which is needed for each completed puzzle. The second sheet has a single copy of the outer circle, which each student will need.
2. If students are careful, they can use a paper fastener to attach the disk to the circle on the second page. The centers of the disks are marked to allow this, but any misalignment will detract from the puzzle's effectiveness.

Solution Hints
Count the parts of astronauts on the inner disk and outer circle. Measure the astronauts and find their average heights in both positions.

184

Each puzzle will need only one disk. Cut one out and share the other with a classmate. To complete the puzzle, follow the directions on the second page.

LOST IN SPACE

Center the disk from the first page within the circle below. Line up the arrow on the disk with the A on the circle. Count the astronauts. Rotate the disk so the arrow points to the B. Count the astronauts again. What happens? How do you explain this?

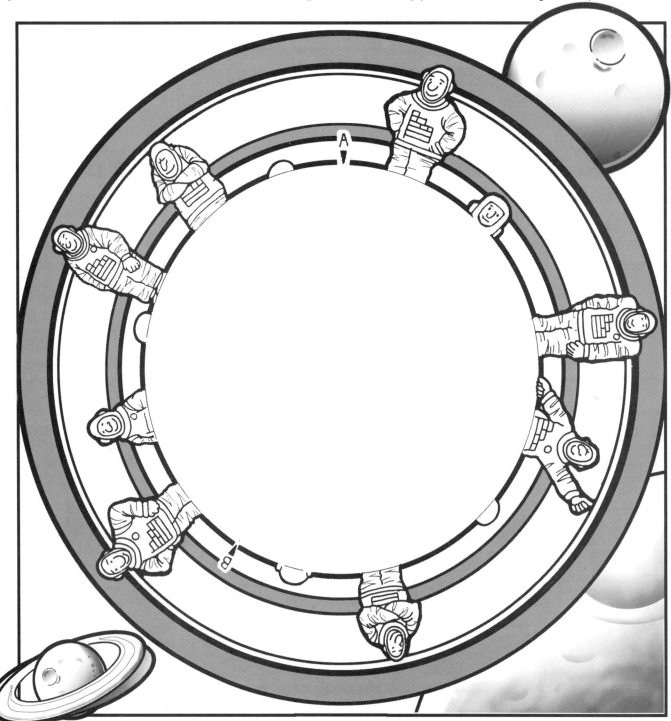

VISUAL ILLUSIONS PUZZLE SOLUTIONS

Tri-Bar Trauma

The paradox in this impossible figure is created by our mind's desire to interpret a two-dimensional drawing as a three-dimensional object. It is not the drawing that is impossible, but our mind's interpretation of it. Each corner of the tri-bar, when viewed alone, is consistent with spatial perspective despite the fact that each corner appears to face a different direction. It is when all three corners are viewed together that the spatial paradox is produced. Further discussion of impossible figures and spatial paradoxes can be found in many places. Bruno Ernst's *Adventures with Impossible Figures*, and *The Paradoxigon* by Nicholas Falletta are both excellent sources. A wealth of information can also be found on the internet by searching for the topic *impossible figures*.

There's More Than Meets the Eye

The illusion in this puzzle is a result of the fact that your eye automatically compares the two edges that are closest to each other—the bottom edge of the top arc (A) and the top edge of the bottom arc (B). In the first arrangement below, the shorter of the two arcs is placed on top. Since in this position, edge A is much shorter than edge B, the difference in length between the two arcs appears even greater than it actually is—to see how much of a difference this makes, look at the second figure where the arcs are placed side by side.

When the two arcs are placed so that the shorter one is below the longer one, as in the third diagram, they seem to be the same length. This happens because the edges that are nearest each other (A and B) are much closer in length. Again, the brain automatically compares the two arcs by looking at the edges closest to each other.

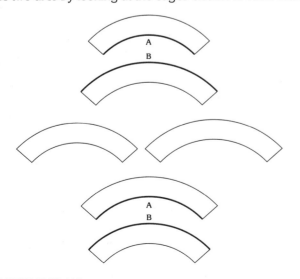

A Tangled Teaser

The trick to seeing the secret messages is to hold the paper at an angle. When the paper is held so that the instructions are pointed towards the floor and you are looking down on it, the message is "When viewed from the right angle." When the paper is held so that the top is pointed towards the floor, the message is "Mathematics is fun!"

Bearly There

The best way to analyze this puzzle is to apply simple mathematics. If you count the parts of bears on each of the three strips, you will find 13 parts on the bottom strip, five parts on the shorter of the top strips, and eight parts on the longer top strip. When the strips are arranged with the longer top strip on the left, each of the bear parts on the bottom is matched up in a one-to-one-correspondence with the bear parts on the top strips. This one-to-one matching produces 13 complete bears with no missing parts. When the top strips are reversed and the shorter strip is placed on the left, there appear to be 14 bears. A careful examination will show that the bears in this position are not all complete. For example, one is missing a face—a trick that is cleverly hidden by the artist's creative use of a bandanna. Also, in this position, there is not a one-to-one match between parts of bears on the bottom and top strips. The sixth bear from the left (which is wholly on the bottom strip) no longer has a separate matching part on the top strip and the seventh bear from the left (which is wholly on the top strip) no longer has a separate matching part on the bottom—again, a fact cleverly disguised by the artist. In this arrangement, there are 12 parts of bears on the bottom strip in one-to-one correspondence with 12 parts of bears on the top strips. The sixth part of a bear from the left—on both the bottom and top strips—has no match on the other strip. Thus, in this position there are 12 bears that have matching parts on the top and bottom strips, one bear that appears only on the bottom strip, and one that appears only on the top strip. Although these 14 bears look complete (other than the missing face), they are not as complete as the 13 bears in the other arrangement. Another way to show this is to measure the bears in both positions. The average height of the 13 bears is much greater than the average height of the 14 bears showing that the 14 bears are not as complete as the 13 bears.

Lost in Space

Like *Bearly There*, this puzzle is best understood in mathematical terms. When the arrow on the inner disk is aligned with the A on the outer circle, 15 astronauts can be counted. When aligned with the B, there are only 14 astronauts. This discrepancy can be explained by counting parts of astronauts on the outer circle and inner disk and seeing how many of them are in one-to-one correspondence in the two positions.

There are 13 *parts* of astronauts on the outer circle and 13 *parts* of astronauts on the inner disk. In addition, there is one *whole* astronaut completely within the inner disk. When the puzzle is aligned in position A, 15 astronauts can be counted. This number includes the one astronaut completely within the inner disk, 12 of the astronauts on the outer circle and inner disk which are in a one-to-one match, one *almost complete* astronaut on the outer circle (at the 10:00 position) and one *almost complete* astronaut on the inner disk (at the 2:30 position). These last two astronauts have no matches—the one on the outer circle is missing boot bottoms, and the one on the inner disk is missing the top of the helmet. In addition, the astronaut in the 7:00 position has no face. Thus, in this position there are 12 matching astronauts, one complete astronaut (on the inner disk), and two partial astronauts (one on the outer circle, and one on the inner disk) for a total of 15 astronauts.

When the disk is aligned in position B, all 13 parts of astronauts on the outer and inner disk are in one-to-one correspondence. These 13 astronauts are added to the one complete astronaut on the inner disk to produce a total of 14 astronauts.

This puzzle can also be explained in purely visual terms. All but one of the 15 astronauts in position A are not visually complete. For example, the astronaut at 1:00 is missing part of the legs, the one at 2:00 is missing part of the shoulders, the one at 2:30 the top of the helmet, and so on. None of the astronauts in this alignment, except for one completely within the inner disk, is whole. When the puzzle is realigned in position B, each of the astronauts is now complete—there are no missing faces, shoulders, legs, etc. It is the artist's skill at making incomplete astronauts look complete that makes this visual paradox work.

Yet another way to understand how this puzzle works is to make a copy of the diagram below and cut it out. By sliding the top part to the right along the diagonal one of the lines disappears. The same principle is used in *Lost in Space*, the difference is that the diagonal line has been curved around into a circle.

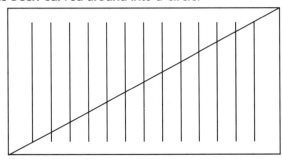

Up and Down the Staircase

The second student sheet in this activity is similar to the original impossible staircase invented by L. S. and Roger Penrose. It includes lines which purport to show the layers of the staircase. These extra lines help uncover the secret of the illusion. To see how, look at the diagram below. The (supposed) lowest layer, which begins at the far left corner, is highlighted. As this layer is continued around the staircase as illustrated, it emerges far above its starting point! This shows that the layers are not in the same plane, but that they actually spiral upward. In fact, only the steps themselves remain in the same plane. It is the carefully chosen angles and differing lengths of sides which mask this spiraling.

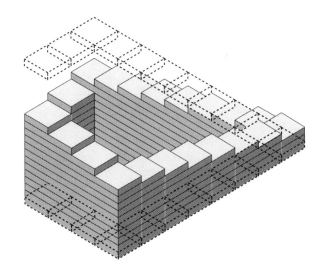

Miscellaneous Puzzles

Introduction

The final section of the book contains the miscellaneous puzzles which do not fit neatly into any category. They cover a wide range of topics, and vary in their level of difficulty. Because there is no specific topic covered, the puzzles can be done in any order. An attempt has still been made, however, to organize the section from least to most difficult.

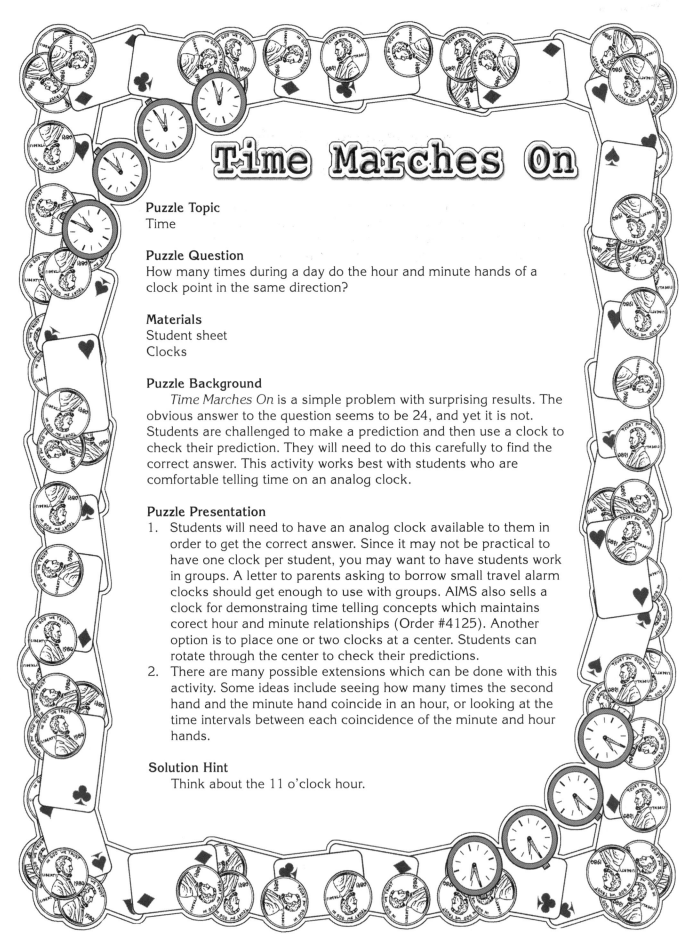

Time Marches On

Puzzle Topic
Time

Puzzle Question
How many times during a day do the hour and minute hands of a clock point in the same direction?

Materials
Student sheet
Clocks

Puzzle Background
   Time Marches On is a simple problem with surprising results. The obvious answer to the question seems to be 24, and yet it is not. Students are challenged to make a prediction and then use a clock to check their prediction. They will need to do this carefully to find the correct answer. This activity works best with students who are comfortable telling time on an analog clock.

Puzzle Presentation
1. Students will need to have an analog clock available to them in order to get the correct answer. Since it may not be practical to have one clock per student, you may want to have students work in groups. A letter to parents asking to borrow small travel alarm clocks should get enough to use with groups. AIMS also sells a clock for demonstraing time telling concepts which maintains corect hour and minute relationships (Order #4125). Another option is to place one or two clocks at a center. Students can rotate through the center to check their predictions.
2. There are many possible extensions which can be done with this activity. Some ideas include seeing how many times the second hand and the minute hand coincide in an hour, or looking at the time intervals between each coincidence of the minute and hour hands.

Solution Hint
   Think about the 11 o'clock hour.

Time Marches On

How many times during the day do the hour and minute hands of a clock point in the same direction?

Make a prediction and write it here.

Now, get a clock and check your prediction. What did you find out?

©2001 AIMS Education Foundation

How Many Squares?

Puzzle Topic
Observation, counting

Puzzle Question
How many squares are there in the figure presented?

Materials
Student sheet

Puzzle Background
This puzzle is not a difficult one, but it does require careful observation in order to arrive at the correct solution. The figure for the puzzle is constructed in such a way that it "hides" some of the squares. Most students quickly count 12-15 squares and think that they have found them all. If this is the case, they need to be told that there are more squares in the figure than they have yet been able to find. This activity will force students to think about the process they are going through as they count and encourages the development of a counting system so that they can justify their solution.

Puzzle Presentation
1. You will have to decide if you want to leave this problem open-ended, or make it a bit more structured for your students. If you wish to leave it open-ended, do not tell students the total number of squares in the picture. Allow them to discover as many as they can and then justify their answers. If your students need more structure, tell them the total number of squares in the problem and merely challenge them to find all of them.
2. A sharing time to close this activity can be very valuable for students as they verbalize the methods that they developed for discovering all of the squares.

Solution Hint
Try to develop a systematic approach to counting the squares. Be sure to count squares of *all* sizes.

How Many Squares?

How many squares, of any size, are in the figure below?

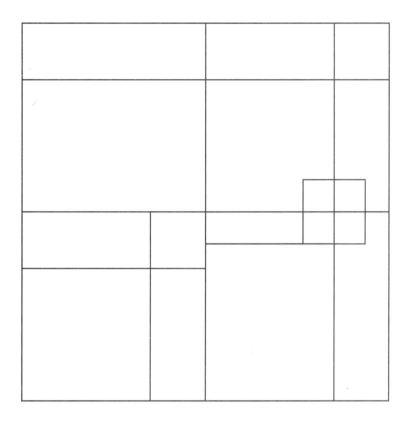

Describe the process you used to find your answer.

193

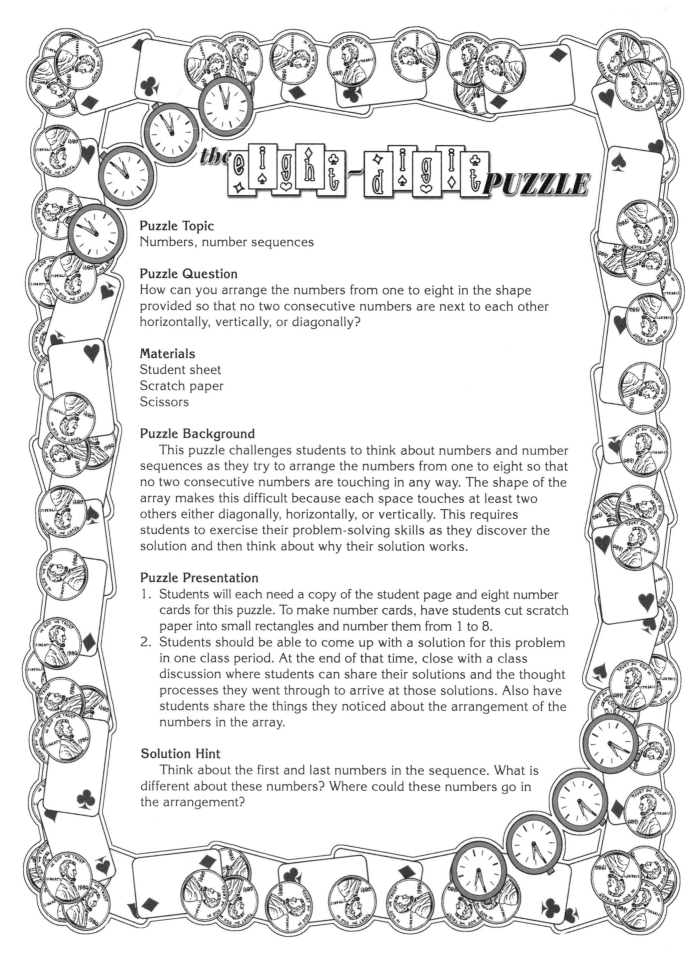

the eight-digit PUZZLE

Puzzle Topic
Numbers, number sequences

Puzzle Question
How can you arrange the numbers from one to eight in the shape provided so that no two consecutive numbers are next to each other horizontally, vertically, or diagonally?

Materials
Student sheet
Scratch paper
Scissors

Puzzle Background
This puzzle challenges students to think about numbers and number sequences as they try to arrange the numbers from one to eight so that no two consecutive numbers are touching in any way. The shape of the array makes this difficult because each space touches at least two others either diagonally, horizontally, or vertically. This requires students to exercise their problem-solving skills as they discover the solution and then think about why their solution works.

Puzzle Presentation
1. Students will each need a copy of the student page and eight number cards for this puzzle. To make number cards, have students cut scratch paper into small rectangles and number them from 1 to 8.
2. Students should be able to come up with a solution for this problem in one class period. At the end of that time, close with a class discussion where students can share their solutions and the thought processes they went through to arrive at those solutions. Also have students share the things they noticed about the arrangement of the numbers in the array.

Solution Hint
Think about the first and last numbers in the sequence. What is different about these numbers? Where could these numbers go in the arrangement?

the eight-digit PUZZLE

Using a piece of scratch paper, cut eight rectangular cards that will fit in the spaces below. Write a 1 on the first card, a 2 on the second card, and so on, until you have the cards numbered from one to eight.

The challenge in this puzzle is to place the number cards in the rectangles so that no two consecutive numbers are next to each other horizontally, vertically, or diagonally. For example, if the five is placed in the far left box, then neither the four nor the six can be placed in the box directly to the right of the five or in the two boxes that are diagonally above and below the five.

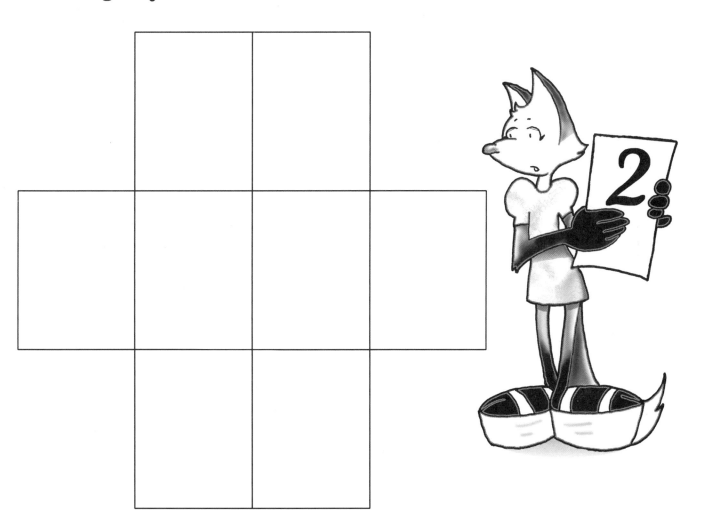

When you discover a solution using your number cards, write the numbers in the correct boxes. Look at the way the numbers are arranged. Write down any interesting things you notice on the back of this paper and prepare to share your thoughts with the rest of the class.

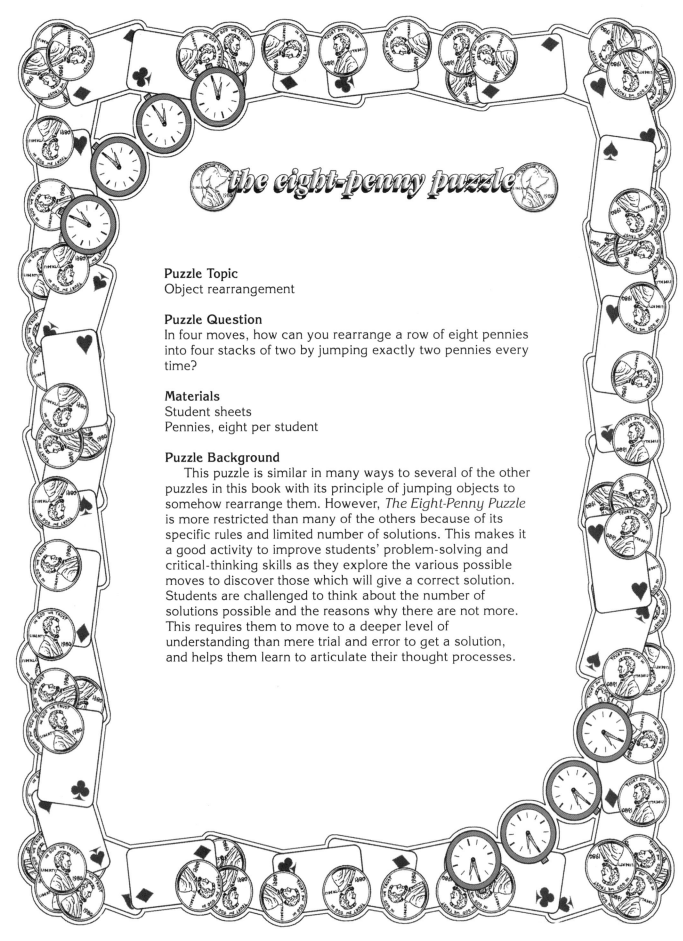

the eight-penny puzzle

Puzzle Topic
Object rearrangement

Puzzle Question
In four moves, how can you rearrange a row of eight pennies into four stacks of two by jumping exactly two pennies every time?

Materials
Student sheets
Pennies, eight per student

Puzzle Background
   This puzzle is similar in many ways to several of the other puzzles in this book with its principle of jumping objects to somehow rearrange them. However, *The Eight-Penny Puzzle* is more restricted than many of the others because of its specific rules and limited number of solutions. This makes it a good activity to improve students' problem-solving and critical-thinking skills as they explore the various possible moves to discover those which will give a correct solution. Students are challenged to think about the number of solutions possible and the reasons why there are not more. This requires them to move to a deeper level of understanding than mere trial and error to get a solution, and helps them learn to articulate their thought processes.

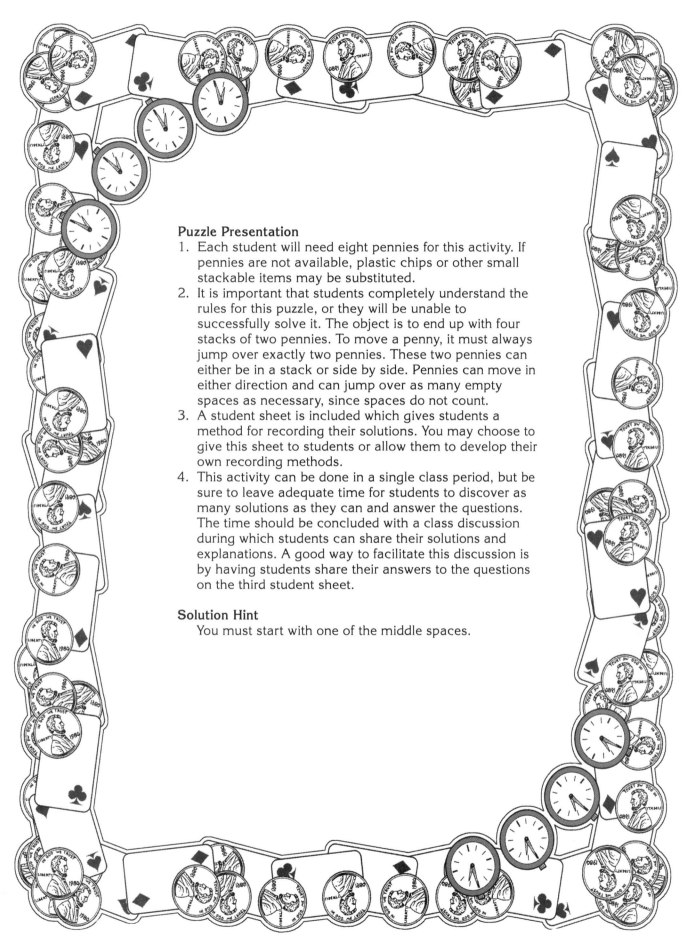

Puzzle Presentation

1. Each student will need eight pennies for this activity. If pennies are not available, plastic chips or other small stackable items may be substituted.

2. It is important that students completely understand the rules for this puzzle, or they will be unable to successfully solve it. The object is to end up with four stacks of two pennies. To move a penny, it must always jump over exactly two pennies. These two pennies can either be in a stack or side by side. Pennies can move in either direction and can jump over as many empty spaces as necessary, since spaces do not count.

3. A student sheet is included which gives students a method for recording their solutions. You may choose to give this sheet to students or allow them to develop their own recording methods.

4. This activity can be done in a single class period, but be sure to leave adequate time for students to discover as many solutions as they can and answer the questions. The time should be concluded with a class discussion during which students can share their solutions and explanations. A good way to facilitate this discussion is by having students share their answers to the questions on the third student sheet.

Solution Hint

You must start with one of the middle spaces.

Place one penny in each of the eight spaces below.

The challenge in this puzzle is to move the eight pennies into four stacks of two in exactly four moves.

To move a penny, it must jump over exactly two other pennies and land on top of a single penny.

You may jump either a two-penny stack or two single pennies.

You may jump as many empty spaces as you need to—spaces do not count.

Pennies can move in either direction, but can never land in an empty space.

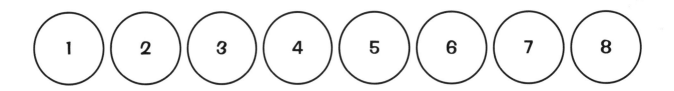

Record each solution you discover in the tables below by writing the space where the penny started in the first column, and the space it jumped to in the second. If you find more solutions than you have spaces for, use the back of this paper to record them.

Move #	Space # →	Space #
1		
2		
3		
4		

Stacks in spaces:

_____ _____ _____ _____

Move #	Space # →	Space #
1		
2		
3		
4		

Stacks in spaces:

_____ _____ _____ _____

Move #	Space # →	Space #
1		
2		
3		
4		

Stacks in spaces:

_____ _____ _____ _____

Move #	Space # →	Space #
1		
2		
3		
4		

Stacks in spaces:

_____ _____ _____ _____

Move #	Space # →	Space #
1		
2		
3		
4		

Stacks in spaces:

_____ _____ _____ _____

Move #	Space # →	Space #
1		
2		
3		
4		

Stacks in spaces:

_____ _____ _____ _____

When you have found as many solutions as possible, answer the following questions. Be prepared to share your answers with the class.

1. How many different solutions did you find? (Solutions are different if the stacks end in different spaces.)

2. How many variations did you find of each different solution? (In a variation the moves are in a different order, but the stacks end in the same place.)

3. How many different solutions do you think are possible? Justify your answer.

4. How many different variations do you think are possible? Justify your answer.

5. Describe any other interesting discoveries you made while doing this puzzle.

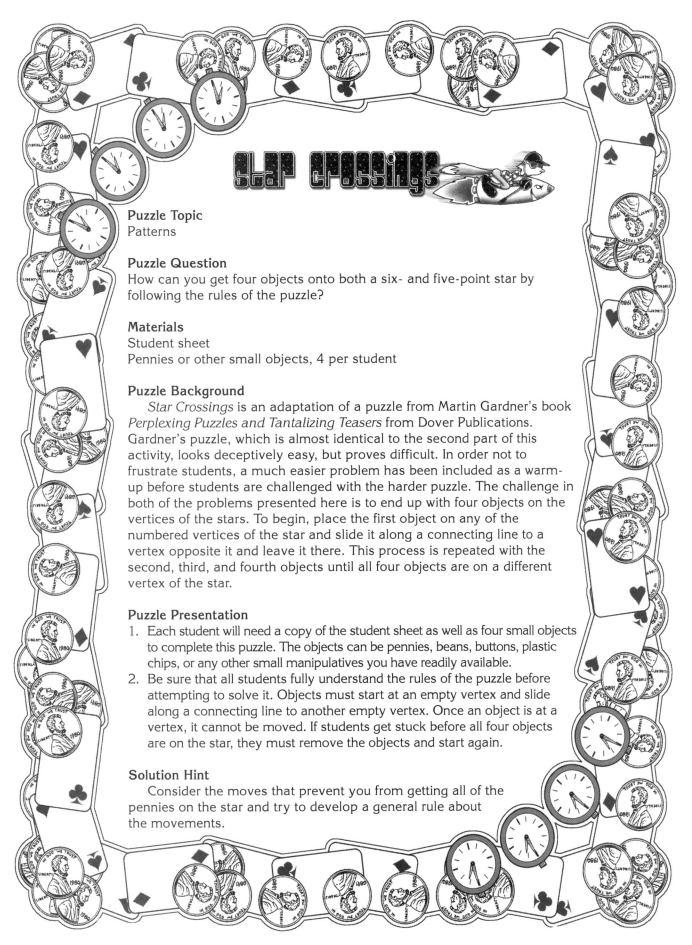

Star Crossings

Puzzle Topic
Patterns

Puzzle Question
How can you get four objects onto both a six- and five-point star by following the rules of the puzzle?

Materials
Student sheet
Pennies or other small objects, 4 per student

Puzzle Background
   Star Crossings is an adaptation of a puzzle from Martin Gardner's book *Perplexing Puzzles and Tantalizing Teasers* from Dover Publications. Gardner's puzzle, which is almost identical to the second part of this activity, looks deceptively easy, but proves difficult. In order not to frustrate students, a much easier problem has been included as a warm-up before students are challenged with the harder puzzle. The challenge in both of the problems presented here is to end up with four objects on the vertices of the stars. To begin, place the first object on any of the numbered vertices of the star and slide it along a connecting line to a vertex opposite it and leave it there. This process is repeated with the second, third, and fourth objects until all four objects are on a different vertex of the star.

Puzzle Presentation
1. Each student will need a copy of the student sheet as well as four small objects to complete this puzzle. The objects can be pennies, beans, buttons, plastic chips, or any other small manipulatives you have readily available.
2. Be sure that all students fully understand the rules of the puzzle before attempting to solve it. Objects must start at an empty vertex and slide along a connecting line to another empty vertex. Once an object is at a vertex, it cannot be moved. If students get stuck before all four objects are on the star, they must remove the objects and start again.

Solution Hint
   Consider the moves that prevent you from getting all of the pennies on the star and try to develop a general rule about the movements.

To do these puzzles you will need four small objects. The rules for both puzzles are the same. Place the first object at any numbered point on the star. Slide the object along one of the connecting lines to an opposite point and leave it there. Repeat this process with the next three objects, one at a time. If you get stuck, take all of the objects off the star and begin again. When you have successfully placed all four objects, make a record of your solution. Do this by recording the starting and ending positions for each of the four moves. For example, if your first move starts at point three and slides to point one, record that move as 3-1. Try the six-point star first. Once you have gotten several solutions for that, move on to the five point star. Try to find at least four different solutions for each star.

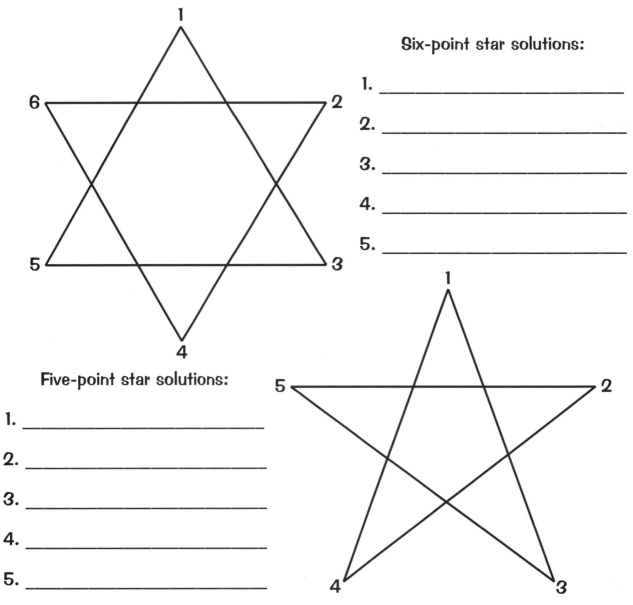

Six-point star solutions:

1. _____

2. _____

3. _____

4. _____

5. _____

Five-point star solutions:

1. _____

2. _____

3. _____

4. _____

5. _____

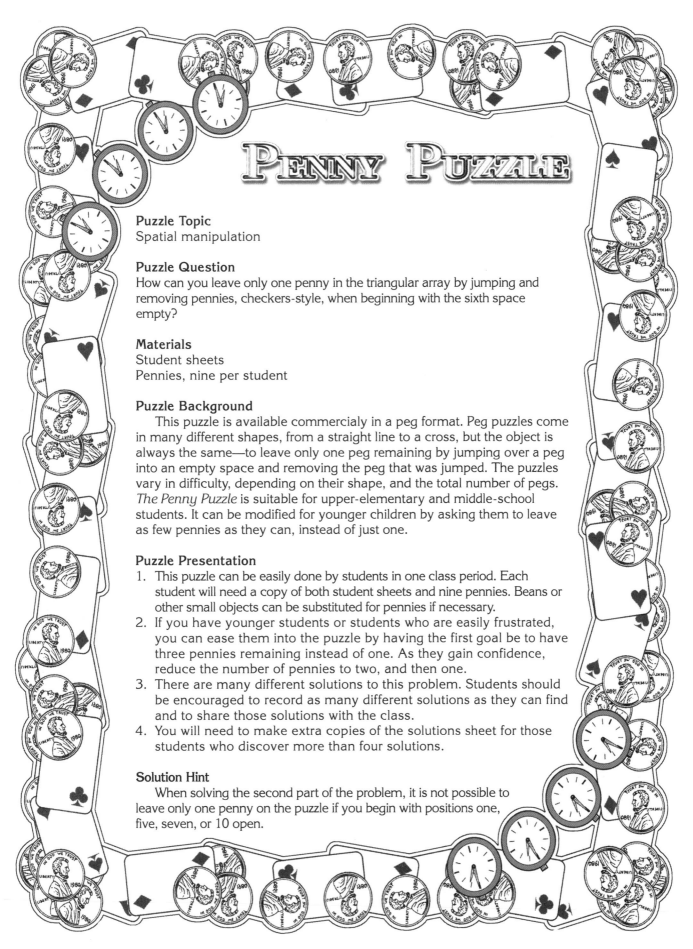

PENNY PUZZLE

Puzzle Topic
Spatial manipulation

Puzzle Question
How can you leave only one penny in the triangular array by jumping and removing pennies, checkers-style, when beginning with the sixth space empty?

Materials
Student sheets
Pennies, nine per student

Puzzle Background
This puzzle is available commercialy in a peg format. Peg puzzles come in many different shapes, from a straight line to a cross, but the object is always the same—to leave only one peg remaining by jumping over a peg into an empty space and removing the peg that was jumped. The puzzles vary in difficulty, depending on their shape, and the total number of pegs. *The Penny Puzzle* is suitable for upper-elementary and middle-school students. It can be modified for younger children by asking them to leave as few pennies as they can, instead of just one.

Puzzle Presentation
1. This puzzle can be easily done by students in one class period. Each student will need a copy of both student sheets and nine pennies. Beans or other small objects can be substituted for pennies if necessary.
2. If you have younger students or students who are easily frustrated, you can ease them into the puzzle by having the first goal be to have three pennies remaining instead of one. As they gain confidence, reduce the number of pennies to two, and then one.
3. There are many different solutions to this problem. Students should be encouraged to record as many different solutions as they can find and to share those solutions with the class.
4. You will need to make extra copies of the solutions sheet for those students who discover more than four solutions.

Solution Hint
When solving the second part of the problem, it is not possible to leave only one penny on the puzzle if you begin with positions one, five, seven, or 10 open.

PENNY PUZZLE

Place nine pennies in the triangle below leaving space six empty. Jump the coins as you would in a game of checkers—over one coin into an empty space directly beyond, removing the coin jumped. The challenge of the puzzle is to continue jumping and removing coins until there is only one penny left on the board. The spaces are numbered so that you can record your solutions in the tables on the next page.

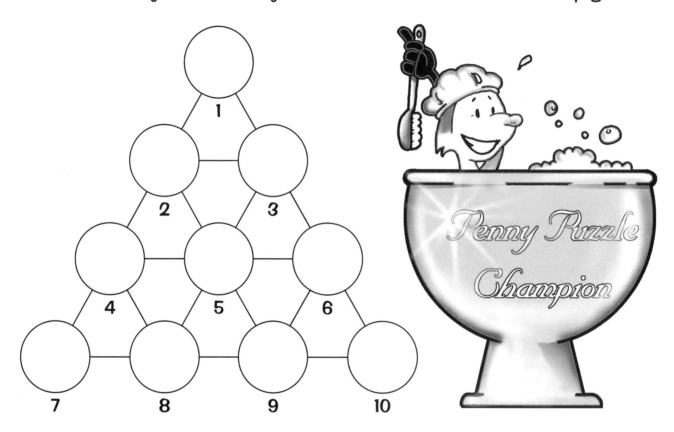

Once you have gotten at least two different solutions for the puzzle, try solving it again when a different space is left open at the start. Record any solutions you find on the next page.

Answer these questions on the back of the paper.

1. What do you notice about the different solutions you found which started with space six empty?
2. Which spaces were you able to leave blank at the beginning and reach a solution?
3. How do you explain this?

Record each different solution you discover in the tables below. If you run out of room, ask your teacher for a second sheet.

Space # ____ empty at start

Move #	Starting space #	Ending space #
1		
2		
3		
Last penny in space #		

Space # ____ empty at start

Move #	Starting space #	Ending space #
1		
2		
3		
Last penny in space #		

Space # ____ empty at start

Move #	Starting space #	Ending space #
1		
2		
3		
Last penny in space #		

Space # ____ empty at start

Move #	Starting space #	Ending space #
1		
2		
3		
Last penny in space #		

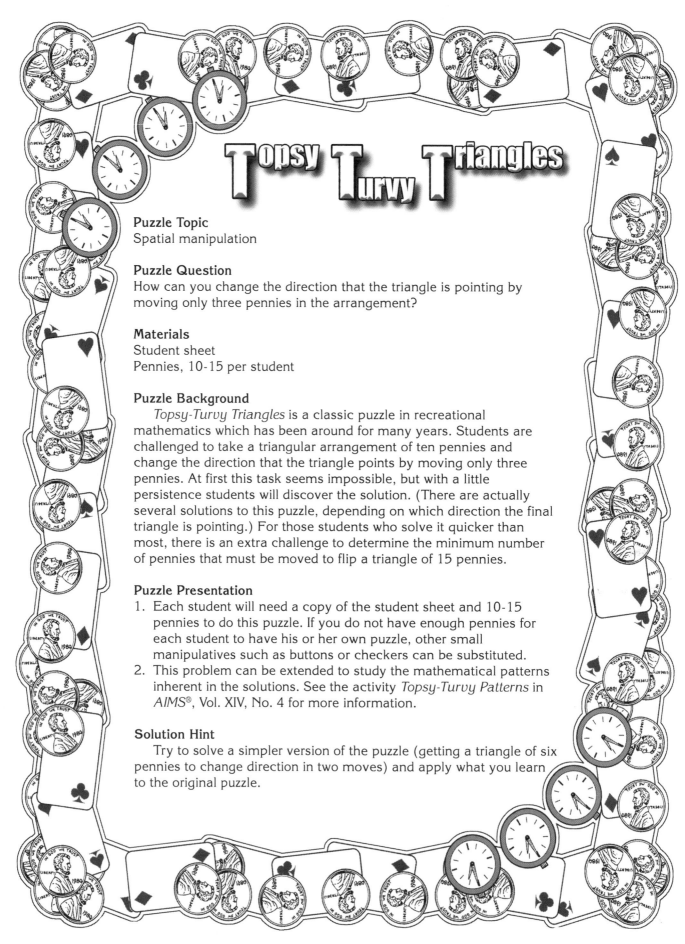

Topsy Turvy Triangles

Puzzle Topic
Spatial manipulation

Puzzle Question
How can you change the direction that the triangle is pointing by moving only three pennies in the arrangement?

Materials
Student sheet
Pennies, 10-15 per student

Puzzle Background
   Topsy-Turvy Triangles is a classic puzzle in recreational mathematics which has been around for many years. Students are challenged to take a triangular arrangement of ten pennies and change the direction that the triangle points by moving only three pennies. At first this task seems impossible, but with a little persistence students will discover the solution. (There are actually several solutions to this puzzle, depending on which direction the final triangle is pointing.) For those students who solve it quicker than most, there is an extra challenge to determine the minimum number of pennies that must be moved to flip a triangle of 15 pennies.

Puzzle Presentation
1. Each student will need a copy of the student sheet and 10-15 pennies to do this puzzle. If you do not have enough pennies for each student to have his or her own puzzle, other small manipulatives such as buttons or checkers can be substituted.
2. This problem can be extended to study the mathematical patterns inherent in the solutions. See the activity *Topsy-Turvy Patterns* in *AIMS®*, Vol. XIV, No. 4 for more information.

Solution Hint
   Try to solve a simpler version of the puzzle (getting a triangle of six pennies to change direction in two moves) and apply what you learn to the original puzzle.

Topsy Turvy Triangles

Arrange 10 pennies on your desk as shown in the diagram below. The challenge in this puzzle is to change the direction that the triangle is pointing by moving only three pennies.

Once you get a solution, draw it below, showing which three pennies you moved and where you moved them to.

My Solution:

Extra Challenge: Add one more row of pennies to the triangle above (15 pennies total) and determine the minimum number of pennies you have to move in order to change the direction the triangle faces.

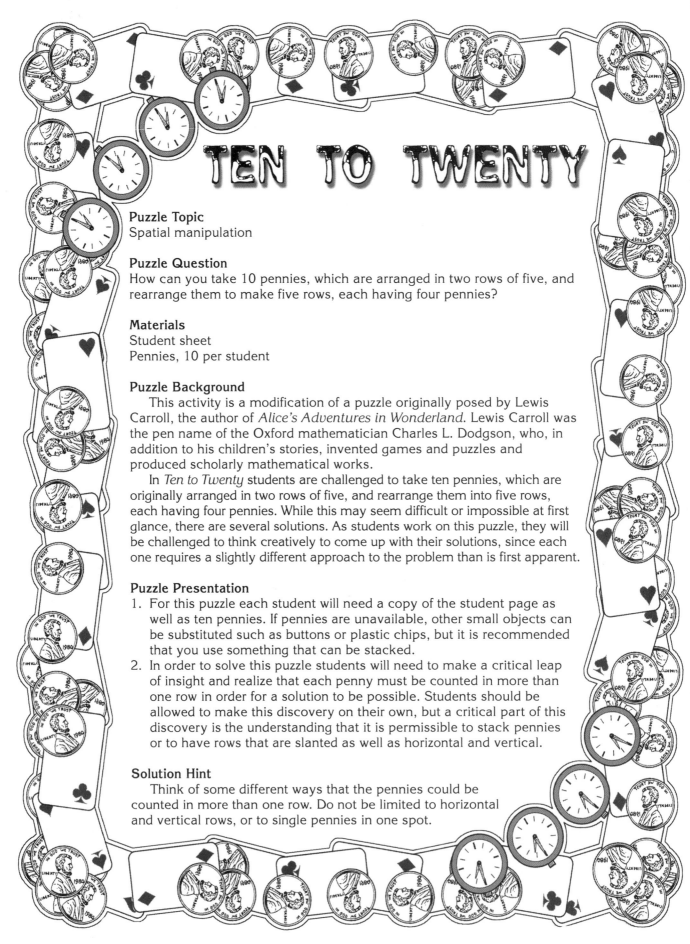

TEN TO TWENTY

Puzzle Topic
Spatial manipulation

Puzzle Question
How can you take 10 pennies, which are arranged in two rows of five, and rearrange them to make five rows, each having four pennies?

Materials
Student sheet
Pennies, 10 per student

Puzzle Background
    This activity is a modification of a puzzle originally posed by Lewis Carroll, the author of *Alice's Adventures in Wonderland*. Lewis Carroll was the pen name of the Oxford mathematician Charles L. Dodgson, who, in addition to his children's stories, invented games and puzzles and produced scholarly mathematical works.

    In *Ten to Twenty* students are challenged to take ten pennies, which are originally arranged in two rows of five, and rearrange them into five rows, each having four pennies. While this may seem difficult or impossible at first glance, there are several solutions. As students work on this puzzle, they will be challenged to think creatively to come up with their solutions, since each one requires a slightly different approach to the problem than is first apparent.

Puzzle Presentation
1. For this puzzle each student will need a copy of the student page as well as ten pennies. If pennies are unavailable, other small objects can be substituted such as buttons or plastic chips, but it is recommended that you use something that can be stacked.
2. In order to solve this puzzle students will need to make a critical leap of insight and realize that each penny must be counted in more than one row in order for a solution to be possible. Students should be allowed to make this discovery on their own, but a critical part of this discovery is the understanding that it is permissible to stack pennies or to have rows that are slanted as well as horizontal and vertical.

Solution Hint
    Think of some different ways that the pennies could be counted in more than one row. Do not be limited to horizontal and vertical rows, or to single pennies in one spot.

TEN TO TWENTY

Place ten pennies in two rows of five as shown below. Now, rearrange the pennies to make five rows, each with four pennies. While this might seem impossible, there are several solutions. Sketch your solutions below.

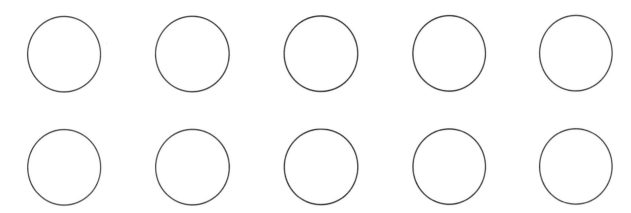

Miscellaneous Puzzle Solutions

Time Marches On

There are 22 times during a 24-hour day when the hour and minute hands of a clock point in the same direction.

12:00	1:05	2:10	3:16	4:21	5:26
6:32	7:37	8:43	9:48	10:54	12:00
1:05	2:10	3:16	4:21	5:26	6:32
7:37	8:43	9:48	10:54		

Notice that there is no time in the 11 o'clock hour (morning or evening) when both hands point the same direction. This is because by the time the hands would actually be pointing in the same direction, it is 12:00. This one deviation from the pattern of one coincidence each hour accounts for the total of 22 instead of 24 times when a clock's hands point in the same direction.

How Many Squares?

The total number of squares in the figure is the square root of 289.

Eight-Digit Puzzle

The solution shown has several flips and rotations, but the numbers will always be in the same relative positions with the 1 and 8 in the center boxes and the 2 and 7 in the side boxes. Do you see why? The center boxes touch every box except the side boxes opposite them. Therefore, only the 1 and the 8 can go in these boxes since they each have only one number (2 and 7) as neighbors. Once these center numbers are placed, the others go in quite easily.

	5	3	
2	8	1	7
	6	4	

Eight Penny Puzzle

There are a number of different solutions for this problem when a solution is defined by the spaces in which the stacks of pennies end up. Each of these solutions have several variations depending on the order in which you jump the pennies, but the end result is the same. A few solutions are listed below. It is important to note that the first move must be from either space 4 or space 5, the middle two positions. A little experimenting will show why this is the case.

Move #	Space # →	Space #
1	4	7
2	6	2
3	1	3
4	8	5

Stacks in spaces:
2 3 5 7

Move #	Space # →	Space #
1	5	2
2	3	7
3	8	6
4	1	4

Stacks in spaces:
2 4 6 7

Move #	Space # →	Space #
1	5	2
2	3	7
3	6	8
4	1	4

Stacks in spaces:
2 4 7 8

Move #	Space # →	Space #
1	4	7
2	6	2
3	3	1
4	5	8

Stacks in spaces:
1 2 7 8

Star Crossings

There are many different solutions for both the six-point and the five-point star. A few for each are listed below.

Six-point star
1. 1-5, 6-2, 1-3, 4-6
2. 6-4, 3-1, 2-4, 5-1
3. 2-6, 5-3, 4-2, 1-5
4. 3-1, 3-5, 6-4, 6-2
5. 1-3, 2-4, 5-1, 2-6

Five-point star
1. 1-3, 2-5, 4-2, 4-1
2. 5-3, 4-1, 2-4, 5-2
3. 1-4, 3-1, 5-3, 2-5
4. 4-2, 3-5, 1-4, 1-3
5. 2-5, 1-3, 4-1, 2-4

Observations

To correctly solve the five-point star every time, there is one simple rule that must be followed: A penny can never be slid onto a vertex that is adjacent to the one where the previous penny was placed.

For example, if the first penny is placed on vertex five, the second penny cannot go on vertex one or vertex four. If the second penny is then placed on vertex two, the third penny cannot go on vertex one or vertex three. The only exception to this rule is the placement of the last penny, which may go adjacent to the one placed before it.

The diagram below shows the necessary progression when two pennies are placed on adjacent vertices one after another. After the third penny is placed, the puzzle becomes unsolvable because the two remaining vertices are adjacent, and therefore not connected by a straight line.

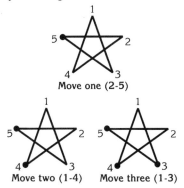

Move one (2-5)

Move two (1-4) Move three (1-3)

Topsy-Turvy Triangles

In order to change the direction of the triangle, the pennies at each corner must be moved as illustrated below.

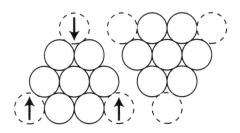

To solve the 15 penny triangle, five pennies must be moved, as illustrated below.

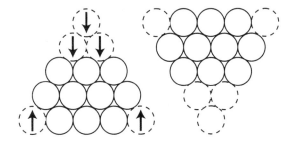

Penny Puzzle

It is possible to solve the puzzle (have only one penny remaining) when you leave spaces two, three, four, six, eight, or nine empty at the beginning. Because the triangle is equilateral, the solutions arrived at by leaving the space six blank (as called for in the instructions) are the same as the ones you would get if you left space two, three, four, eight, or nine blank. They are merely flips and/or rotations of those solutions. It is not possible to solve the puzzle if the fifth spot is left open at the start, because this does not allow you to make any moves. It is also impossible to leave only one penny remaining when you leave space one, seven, or 10 (the corners) open.

Two different solutions are recorded below. For all solutions starting with the same empty space, the last penny will always be left in the same place. For example, in each solution which starts with space six empty, the last penny left will be in space nine, regardless of the order of the moves in between.

Space # 6 empty at start		
Move #	Starting space #	Ending space #
1	1	6
2	10	3
3	4	1
4	1	6
5	8	3
6	3	10
7	10	8
8	7	9
Last penny in space #	9	

Space # 6 empty at start		
Move #	Starting space #	Ending space #
1	1	6
2	8	3
3	10	8
4	3	10
5	7	9
6	10	8
7	2	7
8	7	9
Last penny in space #	9	

Ten to Twenty

There are several different solutions possible, some which involve stacking the pennies, and some which do not. Three examples are shown below.

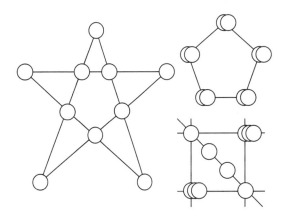

The AIMS Program

AIMS is the acronym for "Activities Integrating Mathematics and Science." Such integration enriches learning and makes it meaningful and holistic. AIMS began as a project of Fresno Pacific University to integrate the study of mathematics and science in grades K-9, but has since expanded to include language arts, social studies, and other disciplines.

AIMS is a continuing program of the non-profit AIMS Education Foundation. It had its inception in a National Science Foundation funded program whose purpose was to explore the effectiveness of integrating mathematics and science. The project directors in cooperation with 80 elementary classroom teachers devoted two years to a thorough field-testing of the results and implications of integration.

The approach met with such positive results that the decision was made to launch a program to create instructional materials incorporating this concept. Despite the fact that thoughtful educators have long recommended an integrative approach, very little appropriate material was available in 1981 when the project began. A series of writing projects have ensued and today the AIMS Education Foundation is committed to continue the creation of new integrated activities on a permanent basis.

The AIMS program is funded through the sale of this developing series of books and proceeds from the Foundation's endowment. All net income from program and products flows into a trust fund administered by the AIMS Education Foundation. Use of these funds is restricted to support of research, development, and publication of new materials. Writers donate all their rights to the Foundation to support its on-going program. No royalties are paid to the writers.

The rationale for integration lies in the fact that science, mathematics, language arts, social studies, etc., are integrally interwoven in the real world from which it follows that they should be similarly treated in the classroom where we are preparing students to live in that world. Teachers who use the AIMS program give enthusiastic endorsement to the effectiveness of this approach.

Science encompasses the art of questioning, investigating, hypothesizing, discovering, and communicating. Mathematics is a language that provides clarity, objectivity, and understanding. The language arts provide us powerful tools of communication. Many of the major contemporary societal issues stem from advancements in science and must be studied in the context of the social sciences. Therefore, it is timely that all of us take seriously a more holistic mode of educating our students. This goal motivates all who are associated with the AIMS Program. We invite you to join us in this effort.

Meaningful integration of knowledge is a major recommendation coming from the nation's professional science and mathematics associations. The American Association for the Advancement of Science in *Science for All Americans* strongly recommends the integration of mathematics, science, and technology. The National Council of Teachers of Mathematics places strong emphasis on applications of mathematics such as are found in science investigations. AIMS is fully aligned with these recommendations.

Extensive field testing of AIMS investigations confirms these beneficial results.

1. Mathematics becomes more meaningful, hence more useful, when it is applied to situations that interest students.
2. The extent to which science is studied and understood is increased, with a significant economy of time, when mathematics and science are integrated.
3. There is improved quality of learning and retention, supporting the thesis that learning which is meaningful and relevant is more effective.
4. Motivation and involvement are increased dramatically as students investigate real-world situations and participate actively in the process.
   We invite you to become part of this classroom teacher movement by using an integrated approach to learning and sharing any suggestions you may have. The AIMS Program welcomes you!

AIMS Education Foundation Programs

A Day with AIMS®

Intensive one-day workshops are offered to introduce educators to the philosophy and rationale of AIMS. Participants will discuss the methodology of AIMS and the strategies by which AIMS principles may be incorporated into curriculum. Each participant will take part in a variety of hands-on AIMS investigations to gain an understanding of such aspects as the scientific/mathematical content, classroom management, and connections with other curricular areas. *A Day with AIMS®* workshops may be offered anywhere in the United States. Necessary supplies and take-home materials are usually included in the enrollment fee.

A Week with AIMS®

Throughout the nation, AIMS offers many one-week workshops each year, usually in the summer. Each workshop lasts five days and includes at least 30 hours of AIMS hands-on instruction. Participants are grouped according to the grade level(s) in which they are interested. Instructors are members of the AIMS Instructional Leadership Network. Supplies for the activities and a generous supply of take-home materials are included in the enrollment fee. Sites are selected on the basis of applications submitted by educational organizations. If chosen to host a workshop, the host agency agrees to provide specified facilities and cooperate in the promotion of the workshop. The AIMS Education Foundation supplies workshop materials as well as the travel, housing, and meals for instructors.

AIMS One-Week Perspectives Workshops

Each summer, Fresno Pacific University offers AIMS one-week workshops on its campus in Fresno, California. AIMS Program Directors and highly qualified members of the AIMS National Leadership Network serve as instructors.

The AIMS Instructional Leadership Program

This is an AIMS staff-development program seeking to prepare facilitators for leadership roles in science/math education in their home districts or regions. Upon successful completion of the program, trained facilitators may become members of the AIMS Instructional Leadership Network, qualified to conduct AIMS workshops, teach AIMS in-service courses for college credit, and serve as AIMS consultants. Intensive training is provided in mathematics, science, process and thinking skills, workshop management, and other relevant topics.

College Credit and Grants

Those who participate in workshops may often qualify for college credit. If the workshop takes place on the campus of Fresno Pacific University, that institution may grant appropriate credit. If the workshop takes place off-campus, arrangements can sometimes be made for credit to be granted by another institution. In addition, the applicant's home school district is often willing to grant in-service or professional-development credit. Many educators who participate in AIMS workshops are recipients of various types of educational grants, either local or national. Nationally known foundations and funding agencies have long recognized the value of AIMS mathematics and science workshops to educators. The AIMS Education Foundation encourages educators interested in attending or hosting workshops to explore the possibilities suggested above. Although the Foundation strongly supports such interest, it reminds applicants that they have the primary responsibility for fulfilling *current* requirements.

For current information regarding the programs described above, please complete the following:

Information Request

Please send current information on the items checked:

___ *Basic Information Packet* on AIMS materials
___ *AIMS Instructional Leadership Program*
___ *AIMS One-Week Perspectives* workshops

___ *A Week with AIMS®* workshops
___ Hosting information for *A Day with AIMS®* workshops
___ Hosting information for *A Week with AIMS®* workshops

Name _____ Phone _____

Address _____

     Street   City   State   Zip

We invite you to subscribe to *AIMS*®!

Each issue of *AIMS*® contains a variety of material useful to educators at all grade levels. Feature articles of lasting value deal with topics such as mathematical or science concepts, curriculum, assessment, the teaching of process skills, and historical background. Several of the latest AIMS math/science investigations are always included, along with their reproducible activity sheets. As needs direct and space allows, various issues contain news of current developments, such as workshop schedules, activities of the AIMS Instructional Leadership Network, and announcements of upcoming publications.

AIMS® is published monthly, August through May. Subscriptions are on an annual basis only. A subscription entered at any time will begin with the next issue, but will also include the previous issues of that volume. Readers have preferred this arrangement because articles and activities within an annual volume are often interrelated.

Please note that an *AIMS*® subscription automatically includes duplication rights for one school site for all issues included in the subscription. Many schools build cost-effective library resources with their subscriptions.

YES! I am interested in subscribing to *AIMS*®.

Name _____   Home Phone _____

Address _____   City, State, Zip _____

Please send the following volumes (subject to availability):

_____ Volume VII (1992-93) $15.00	_____ Volume XII (1997-98) $30.00
_____ Volume VIII (1993-94) $15.00	_____ Volume XIII (1998-99) $30.00
_____ Volume IX (1994-95) $15.00	_____ Volume XIV (1999-00) $30.00
_____ Volume X (1995-96) $15.00	_____ Volume XV (2000-01) $30.00
_____ Volume XI (1996-97) $30.00	_____ Volume XVI (2001-02) $30.00

_____ **Limited offer: Volumes XVI & XVII (2001-2003) $55.00**
(Note: Prices may change without notice)

Check your method of payment:

❏ Check enclosed in the amount of $ _____

❏ Purchase order attached (Please include the P.O.#, the authorizing signature, and position of the authorizing person.)

❏ Credit Card   ❏ Visa   ❏ MasterCard   Amount $ _____

Card # _____   Expiration Date _____

Signature _____   Today's Date _____

Make checks payable to **AIMS Education Foundation.**
Mail to *AIMS*® Magazine, P.O. Box 8120, Fresno, CA 93747-8120.
Phone (559) 255-4094 or (888) 733-2467 FAX (559) 255-6396
AIMS Homepage: http://www.AIMSedu.org/

AIMS Program Publications

GRADES K-4 SERIES

Bats Incredible!
Brinca de Alegria Hacia la Primavera con las Matemáticas y Ciencias
Cáete de Gusto Hacia el Otoño con la Matemáticas y Ciencias
Cycles of Knowing and Growing
Fall Into Math and Science
Field Detectives
Glide Into Winter With Math and Science
Hardhatting in a Geo-World (Revised Edition, 1996)
Jaw Breakers and Heart Thumpers (Revised Edition, 1995)
Los Cincos Sentidos
Overhead and Underfoot (Revised Edition, 1994)
Patine al Invierno con Matemáticas y Ciencias
Popping With Power (Revised Edition, 1996)
Primariamente Física (Revised Edition, 1994)
Primarily Earth
Primariamente Plantas
Primarily Physics (Revised Edition, 1994)
Primarily Plants
Sense-able Science
Spring Into Math and Science
Under Construction

GRADES K-6 SERIES

Budding Botanist
Critters
El Botanista Principiante
Exploring Environments
Fabulous Fractions
Mostly Magnets
Ositos Nada Más
Primarily Bears
Principalmente Imanes
Water Precious Water

GRADES 5-9 SERIES

Actions with Fractions
Brick Layers
Brick Layers II
Conexiones Eléctricas
Down to Earth
Electrical Connections
Finding Your Bearings (Revised Edition, 1996)
Floaters and Sinkers (Revised Edition, 1995)
From Head to Toe
Fun With Foods
Gravity Rules!
Historical Connections in Mathematics, Volume I
Historical Connections in Mathematics, Volume II
Historical Connections in Mathematics, Volume III
Just for the Fun of It!
Looking at Lines
Machine Shop
Magnificent Microworld Adventures
Math + Science, A Solution
Mutiplication the Algebra Way
Off the Wall Science: A Poster Series Revisited
Our Wonderful World
Out of This World (Revised Edition, 1994)
Paper Square Geometry: The Mathematics of Origami
Pieces and Patterns, A Patchwork in Math and Science
Piezas y Diseños, un Mosaic de Matemáticas y Ciencias
Proportional Reasoning
Puzzle Play
Ray's Reflections
Soap Films and Bubbles
Spatial Visualization
The Sky's the Limit (Revised Edition, 1994)
The Amazing Circle, Volume 1
Through the Eyes of the Explorers:
   Minds-on Math & Mapping
What's Next, Volume 1
What's Next, Volume 2
What's Next, Volume 3

For further information write to:

AIMS Education Foundation • P.O. Box 8120 • Fresno, California 93747-8120
www.AIMSedu.org/ • Fax 559•255•6396

AIMS Duplication Rights Program

AIMS has received many requests from school districts for the purchase of unlimited duplication rights to AIMS materials. In response, the AIMS Education Foundation has formulated the program outlined below. There is a built-in flexibility which, we trust, will provide for those who use AIMS materials extensively to purchase such rights for either individual activities or entire books.

It is the goal of the AIMS Education Foundation to make its materials and programs available at reasonable cost. All income from the sale of publications and duplication rights is used to support AIMS programs; hence, strict adherence to regulations governing duplication is essential. Duplication of AIMS materials beyond limits set by copyright laws and those specified below is strictly forbidden.

Limited Duplication Rights

Any purchaser of an AIMS book may make up to *200 copies* of any activity in that book for use at *one school site*. Beyond that, rights must be purchased according to the appropriate category.

Unlimited Duplication Rights for Single Activities

An individual or school may purchase the right to make an unlimited number of copies of a single activity. The royalty is $5.00 per activity per school site.

Examples: 3 activities x 1 site x $5.00 = $15.00
9 activities x 3 sites x $5.00 = $135.00

Unlimited Duplication Rights for Entire Books

A school or district may purchase the right to make an unlimited number of copies of a single, *specified* book. The royalty is $20.00 per book per school site. This is in addition to the cost of the book.

Examples: 5 books x 1 site   x $20.00 = $100.00
12 books x 10 sites x $20.00 = $2400.00

Magazine/Newsletter Duplication Rights

Those who purchase *AIMS*® (magazine)/*Newsletter* are hereby granted permission to make up to 200 copies of any portion of it, provided these copies will be used for educational purposes.

Workshop Instructors' Duplication Rights

Workshop instructors may distribute to registered workshop participants a maximum of 100 copies of any article and/or 100 copies of no more than eight activities, provided these six conditions are met:

1. Since all AIMS activities are based upon the *AIMS Model of Mathematics* and the *AIMS Model of Learning*, leaders must include in their presentations an explanation of these two models.
2. Workshop instructors must relate the AIMS activities presented to these basic explanations of the AIMS philosophy of education.
3. The copyright notice must appear on all materials distributed.
4. Instructors must provide information enabling participants to order books and magazines from the Foundation.
5. Instructors must inform participants of their limited duplication rights as outlined below.
6. Only student pages may be duplicated.

Written permission must be obtained for duplication beyond the limits listed above. Additional royalty payments may be required.

Workshop Participants' Rights

Those enrolled in workshops in which AIMS student activity sheets are distributed may duplicate a maximum of 35 copies or enough to use the lessons one time with one class, whichever is less. Beyond that, rights must be purchased according to the appropriate category.

Application for Duplication Rights

The purchasing agency or individual must clearly specify the following:
1. Name, address, and telephone number
2. Titles of the books for Unlimited Duplication Rights contracts
3. Titles of activities for Unlimited Duplication Rights contracts
4. Names and addresses of school sites for which duplication rights are being purchased.

NOTE: Books to be duplicated must be purchased separately and are not included in the contract for Unlimited Duplication Rights.

The requested duplication rights are automatically authorized when proper payment is received, although a *Certificate of Duplication Rights* will be issued when the application is processed.

Address all correspondence to: **Contract Division**
AIMS Education Foundation   **www.AIMSedu.org/**
P.O. Box 8120   **Fax 559•255•6396**
Fresno, CA 93747-8120